WHEN WE THRIVE, OUR WORLD THRIVES

Stories of Young People Growing Up with Adversity

Connie K. Chung, EdD

with Vishal Talreja and Dream a Dream Staff and Programme Participants

For Young People and Their Supporters
Who Are Dreaming, Learning, and Thriving Together

Contents

Praise for *When We Thrive, Our World Thrives*: Stories of Young People Growing Up with Adversity

There are millions of young people who face difficult circumstances while they are growing up. This book is a testament to the fact that if young people are provided the right kind of care and support, they grow up to become happy, resilient, and responsible human beings. This, in essence, should be the purpose of education. Dream a Dream has done great work with young people. I wish to see that every single child gets the opportunity to thrive, so that collectively we become a happier and better society.

— Shri Manish Sisodia,
Deputy Chief Minister and Education Minister,
Delhi Government

Adverse childhood experiences shape and weigh on lives perhaps more than anything. Yet research shows that some people break this downward spiral with remarkable resilience. Such research carries real meaning only where we can relate to individual life stories. This is where *When We Thrive, Our World Thrives* makes an amazing contribution, showing the strengths of human capabilities that makes for the well-being of humanity.

— Andreas Schleicher,
Director for Education and Skills,
and Special Advisor on Education Policy to the Secretary-
General at the Organisation for Economic
Co-operation and Development (OECD)

Nothing could be more critical than working towards a world where all of us, and our children, thrive. [This] beautiful and important book elevates stories of children's truth and hope, building on years of hands-on experiments creating environments where all children can thrive. It is my hope that readers leave this book surer of the role they play in creating a life for themselves and others where all of us thrive.

— Shaheen Mistri,
CEO and Founder Trustee,
Teach for India

What could be more important — to society or to you — than ensuring that every young person has the power to be a giver, i.e., to have a life? This beautifully clear book shows how you, indeed all of us, can make this happen. It explains the research simply, points to policy, and — most of all — welcomes you along as Vishal and team gently, lovingly help challenged young people onto rich, confident life journeys.

— Bill Drayton,
CEO, Ashoka: *"Everyone a Changemaker"*

Hearing voices of the young [people] and listening to stories of their journey through challenges and opportunities can be very inspirational, not only for young people but also for all those who seek to create a better future for all. I congratulate the entire team at Dream a Dream for their impressive efforts over the last two decades and for sharing through these stories and illustrating how it is possible to overcome adversity, grow, and thrive.

— Rukmini Banerji,
CEO, Pratham Education Foundation

When We Thrive, Our World Thrives: Stories of Young People from India is incredibly thoughtful and unique — a must-read for anyone who cares deeply about child and youth development. The authors have put together a riveting account of intimate and heartfelt stories of young people, who, despite the cards they were dealt with, overcame their childhood adversities and are thriving. The stories are balanced beautifully with empirical evidence research and best practices. This book moves the heart while grounding us in thought. As we read about and celebrate those who made it, what can we do about those who have not?

— Professor Tan Oon Seng,
Director, Centre for Research in Child Development,
National Institute of Education, Singapore

Informed by Dream a Dream's own inspiring journey of empowering young people from vulnerable backgrounds to flourish in a fast-changing world, this book is packed with eye-opening and compelling insights. A must-read for anyone interested in understanding how our sense of self-worth, value, and dignity come to be, and how these can be developed in young people.

— Roopa Kudva,
Managing Partner,
OmIdyar Network India

The growing awareness of the negative impact of adverse childhood experiences (ACEs) on children can leave us feeling hopeless. *When We Thrive, Our World Thrives* provides a much-needed map for nurturing children in ways that overcome the effects of ACEs. This book elegantly weaves research about the psychosocial needs of children with the inspiring stories of young people that are thriving thanks to Dream a Dream's sensitive, strength-based approach. This book is an important contribution to the literature on child development, providing a beacon of hope for all who are working to change the prospects of young people in this world.

— Peggy Taylor, MEd,
Co-founder, Partners for Youth Empowerment

I had the honour to read ... the book, *When We Thrive, Our World Thrives: Stories of Young People from India.* Today, India is one of the youngest countries globally, with more than 54% of the population below 25 years of age. Yet the book shares accounts of adversities that many young people have been through, sometimes from their early years. These multi-layered adversities often lead to scars that can be multi-faceted and continue to manifest over time. But this book also shares stories of connections, care, empathy, persistence, endurance, hope, and kindness as nurturing adults around continue to be available to hold space for them. The book promises to give you goosebumps and hope simultaneously, and it will fundamentally touch you to the core.

— Nita Aggarwal,
Programme Manager, Porticus

This is a beautiful, illuminating book that points the way to providing all children, including those who've experienced trauma and adversity, with the care and support to develop as adults who both thrive and change the patterns of the world so that future generations of children grow up with the care and support necessary to live up to their potential. *When We Thrive, Our World Thrives* makes incredibly accessible the stories of young people and the latest research that will help all of us shape a better world.

— Wendy Kopp,
CEO and Co-founder, Teach for All

If one is architecting approaches to change the life trajectories of children in the global south, this book is foundational learning to develop critical understanding of the oppression and trauma many children undergo in their growing up years. This book unleashes the authentic voices of young people of the south and is an essential read for all leaders in the field! The narrative style of this book clearly outlines the multiple levels of challenges and the intersectional nature of issues for children in India. This style, coupled with the patterns carried through multiple generations of "power-over" systems such as colonialism, gender, caste, ableism, and on-going poverty, allows us to see through these authentic personal narratives and how critical it is for all of us to take more holistic approaches to solution-making for true transformation. Only by putting power back into the hands of children and young people will we create a more equitable system where every child finds their power to express and take action with safety and a sense of belonging and dignity.

— Sumitra Pasupathy,
Co-founder, Playeum, and Staff,
Ashoka: Innovators for the Public

The stories in *When We Thrive, Our World Thrives* are so powerful because Dream a Dream's work is so personal and powerful. Dream a Dream's focus on building life skills in the youth gets at the heart of what the youth need today. Skills like resiliency, problem solving, critical thinking, collaboration, and so on are all skills that help the youth thrive in the difficult and complex environments in India they are living in. These skills can help the youth with academic performance, persistence in school, mental health and well-being, and they are especially important for girls due to the extra barriers they face.

— Erin Ganju,
Managing Director, Echidna Giving

Dream a Dream has been at the forefront of the movement to bring the human dimensions of learning in from the margins to the core of education. It has pioneered curriculum development and pedagogy that promote thriving in its profoundest sense, and most significantly, in the most challenging contexts of adversity. This book gives a sense of the lived reality of what that means and its value. Every educator should read it.

— Valerie Hannon,
Author, Co-founder,
Innovation Unit and Global Education Leaders Partnership

I am delighted to read these trailblazing stories of young changemakers, transforming their communities and our society at large. Amplifying the voices of the Asian youth is a core pillar at AVPN; shedding light on their journeys and how they overcame hurdles in life through sheer talent and resilience resonates deeply. The book emphasises the need for influential mentors, and I congratulate the Dream a Dream team for their years of consistent efforts in changing the lives of the youth. Indeed, shaping future leaders is the need of the hour as we stride towards achieving sustainable development goals.

— Naina Subberwal Batra,
CEO, AVPN

Dream a Dream's uplifting mission and continuing legacy of empowering young people in India are beautifully illustrated in *When We Thrive, Our World Thrives*. [This is] a book which … will empower adults to form positive, caring connections with young people so that everyone, irrespective of age and background, thrives and contributes to the world in their way.

— Joanne McEachen,
CEO and Founder, The Learner First

This book presents an important milestone for the world. It demonstrates with scientific approach and practical examples that despite the most difficult childhood circumstances, children can thrive if timely support, characterised by empathy and long-term commitment, is in place.

The book also tells a story of how the personal transformation of Vishal Talreja as a young Indian student spending a summer in Finland led to a work that has transformed the lives of many children of India. I am proud and grateful for being able to follow the work of Dream a Dream for the past ten years. And the story continues.

— Pilvi Torsti,
Adjunct Professor,
State Secretary, and Founder,
HEI Schools and UWC Mostar, Finland

This book is a strong reminder that life is not a sprint but a journey. It is easy to write off a student based on behaviour or performance, without understanding the root causes of such behaviour. These write-offs by parents, teachers, or other adults act as daily reminders of the false sense of worthlessness or frustration that some children feel and exacerbate over the course of their life. Imagine the damage this can cause to an individual, a society, and the world at large. We can stem the damage. Each chapter in the book highlights true stories of children from vulnerable backgrounds, and how with the right support, they can deal with their adversities and solve day-to-day real-life problems and relationship issues.

— Geeta Goel,
Managing Director,
Michael & Susan Dell Foundation India

How can a child who has been beaten up, chased, and hit; a child who has run away from school, fallen into gambling, and grown up in poverty become a compassionate caring adult who helps others and gets a college degree? Read this book to understand that it is in the micro moments when we respond with empathy and curiosity rather than judgement and punishment that miracles of human transformation happen.

— **Deepa Narayan, PhD,**
Author of CHUP, and Host,
What's A Man Podcast

Mr. Vishal Talreja is one of the most important educators in today's world. His stories from Dream a Dream are beyond inspirational. The methodology [Dream a Dream has] developed on how young people in adversity can overcome and thrive are very important today as we witness ever-increasing inequality on a global scale, especially after COVID-19. It is fascinating to see Dr. Connie Chung, a world-leading future education expert, joining him to understand the necessary life skills for these young people backed by research. I hope this book will give a solid basis to scale up their insights and experiences for young people around the world.

— **Yuhyun Park, PhD,**
Founder and CEO, DQ Institute

I have always been amazed to see how Dream a Dream has been able to make changes in the lives of so many youngsters. This book presents a realistic insight into how youths from disadvantaged backgrounds have a huge potential to explore themselves if nurtured with love, care, and an understanding that their needs have a place too. I highly recommend this book to everyone because somewhere we have all felt misunderstood by those who as parents, educators, and acquaintances could not understand the issues experienced by a generation of youngsters.

— **Anshu Gupta,**
Founder Director, Goonj, and
Winner of Ramon Magsaysay Award

Ananya Trust has been very fortunate to have partnered with Dream a Dream since its inception. Over the years, Dream a Dream has provided the space and resources where young adults are encouraged, enabled, and empowered to dream, not 'a' dream but numerous dreams. Children, especially from backgrounds where they have no right to dream, are given plenty of opportunities to dream and make them come true. No visions of a better future nor dreams, however fantastic or unrealistic, are ever ridiculed. The stories in this book say it all. We wish Dream a Dream all the best in their future endeavours and wish the book great success.

— Dr. Shashi Rao,
Founder Trustee, Ananya Trust

The story of Dream a Dream is an incredible one that started from humble beginnings in Bengaluru back in 1999, and then forged forward with purpose, perseverance, and passion to positively impact the lives of over five million children over the last two decades. And this story would not have been possible if it was not for the selflessness and commitment of each member of the Dream a Dream team. Their tireless work, grounded in deep care and empathy for every child, has changed the trajectory of millions of lives and has shone the light on an inspiring path for achieving similar outcomes anywhere in the world. The book, *When We Thrive, Our World Thrives* gives us a glimpse of this remarkable journey through the lens of some of the young people whose lives have been impacted.

— Arjun Dugal,
Co-founder, Dream a Dream,
CTO, Financial Services at Capital One

I am so happy to endorse *When We Thrive, Our World Thrives*, a book that documents the wonderful work Dream a Dream has been doing, using the arts for healing and well-being. When we work with the arts, we work with the whole individual, including the parts of us that are unseen…. It is clear, now more than ever, there is need for a paradigm shift to heal the fragmented and polarised world we live in. With this book, Dream a Dream shows us a way forward towards integration and wholeness, by working with the individual, to effect transformation in the collective.

— Brinda Jacob-Janvrin,
Co-founder, Dream a Dream, and
Founder and Managing Trustee, Studio for Movement Arts and Therapies

This is a beautiful book full of hope and possibility! Dream a Dream has proven over and over again that if you just give the youth from disadvantaged backgrounds an opportunity, they have a tremendous ability to be resilient to adversity and can thrive and fulfil their potential. There is a blueprint for a way to a better future.

— Joann McPike,
Founder, THINK Global School

Foreword

In August 1999, at the age of 21, I got an opportunity to be part of a student exchange programme in Finland. Three months in Finland introduced me to the idea of dignity of labour and respect for all human beings. This was a critical shift as I had grown up in a deeply caste- and class-based environment where it was considered normal to discriminate against another human being. Finland for a young 21-year-old like me was refreshingly different.

The first person I made friends with was a young university student who had just come back from a six-month volunteer work in a remote village in India. She would work at a bar in the evenings to save money for her education. I kept thinking how could a decent girl work at a bar. How could I be friends with a girl who works at a bar? Could she not find a more respectable job? My prejudice was clear. I began to question why I was discriminating against someone because of her choice of work.

On another occasion, I was invited to a Finnish home for an Indian meal. It was a beautiful home. The host was excited to tell me about his profession. He pulled out a beautifully starched uniform and proudly told me that he was a security guard at a five-star hotel. I was shocked that a security guard could have such a beautiful home.

What shocked me, even more, was that he was proud of who he was and the work he did. My biases played out again. These experiences got me thinking about how deep my cultural prejudices and biases run. I wondered how deeply entrenched were the ideas based on class and caste in my upbringing that growing up I had accepted them to be my sole reality.

I wrote a note in my diary that day: "I want to go back to India and change the way we look at dignity in my country. I want to build a country on the foundation of respect and appreciation for each person irrespective of their backgrounds." Soon after my return, I got an opportunity to meet and co-create a new dream with 11-other like-minded people, and Dream a Dream was born. The 11 co-founders of Dream a Dream are Brinda S Jacob, Neha Shah (Arya), Vishal Talreja, Rahul Mathur, Supreeta Sampath, Pramod Ramprasad, Sandeep R Wadhwa, Rashmi Bajaj, Arjun Dugal, Shweta Kothari, and Vishwa Prasad.

My journey with the young people in this book has been a journey of understanding the complex nature of dignity in India. I have had the honour of experiencing the lives of these young people at close quarters and knowing that their stories will inspire a new generation of young people and guide us, adults, to engage with them with care, respect, and dignity. Their stories need to be told not because they are sensational or because they make Dream a Dream look good but because their stories speak truth to power. Their stories are not linear growth stories but stories of rises and falls, ups and downs, failures and successes; each pivot in their life has been an insight for us on how we show up for young people in our work. These are stories of resilience and stories of a call for help. These are stories of thriving as well as stories of the failure of the society.

These stories are as much about them as it is about the society we have created. It is a mirror to the structural barriers and systemic inequities we perpetuate on young people, and it is a call to action to relook at some of our limiting belief systems. Their stories show us what is possible and give us a glimpse of a society we can become with tenets of love, care, respect, dignity, and trust.

I invite you to read these stories not as stories of 'heroes' but as stories that show us a way to help thousands of young people to thrive and shape a new society. In that, the author, Dr. Connie K. Chung has done a brilliant job of weaving moments of transformation in the lives of the young people featured here with evidence of pedagogical approaches that are universal and will work for many children in many contexts.

I met Connie in 2016 when she was a lecturer and researcher at Harvard Graduate School of Education. I was moved by her deep empathy, ability to listen well, and genuineness. Over the years, as we have shared our life experiences — I with young people at Dream a Dream and she with her experiences as a foster parent, educator, researcher, and strategic consultant in the United States — we knew that our frustrations, successes, failures, and moments of clarity were similar, and our friendship and respect for each other strengthened over the years.

In 2019, I invited Connie to Dream a Dream to see our work and find ways to engage her. Our conversations in Bengaluru led to the idea of this book, and it excited us both. I knew I wanted a book grounded in research, yet one that was primarily about young people and their truth. It needed to be a book that was easy to read and yet had the nuanced eye of a researcher. Connie was simply perfect for the job, and she has been absolutely inspiring in the journey of authoring this book.

The stories chronicled in this book are as much about the young people as it is about us learning what young people need from the ecosystem of support that can surround them! It is through the twenty stories in this book that I have as an individual worked through my own biases and continue to be a better human being, and for that I am eternally grateful to the young people who have shared their stories. To the reader, all I ask is to process the stories with empathy and curiosity, to learn as much about yourself as about the young people. A journey of learning awaits you … and I hope we all begin to understand why and how we must show up in the world if we want every child to have a thriving life.

— **Vishal Talreja**
Co-founder and Trustee, Dream a Dream
Bengaluru
April 2022

01

Introduction

The first time I met Vishal, he made me cry. It was January 2016, and I was visiting Delhi as the associate director of the Global Education Innovation Initiative at the Harvard Graduate School of Education. Together with our global partners, we were planning to write a second book in a series about shifting education systems to provide better support to students that addressed their holistic needs for growth, not just in academics.

Our Indian partners had identified Dream a Dream as the organisation in India that was furthest along in terms of providing professional development to teachers that enabled them to address the needs of the whole child. As the co-founder of Dream a Dream, Vishal had come to meet us. During the conference, he gathered about five of us in a circle. He told us what I later came to know as Prasanna's story, which is the first story I tell in this book. As he shared how he and another colleague had followed Prasanna to his village to find him after he disappeared from his school, I teared up. As a researcher, I am trained to be both sensitive and hold boundaries in my listening, but his story struck a chord that was both personal and professional.

By that time, I was in my second year of fostering a then-11-year-old boy, becoming familiar with the placement and relational instability and trauma that shadow youth in care. I was also in my 22nd year of working with and for young people. Prior to earning my doctorate in education, I had taught in one of the materially wealthiest places in the world, yet my students had had the same positive response to simple acts of caring as Dream a Dream's participants that I heard in Vishal's story. During the first year of my teaching, for example, I was pulled aside by one of the assistant principals who told me, "The students say you care about them; that's important. You're doing a good job." I was glad to hear the encouragement, but I also had difficulty receiving it. "Caring?" I thought to myself. "Shouldn't students be saying that I had *taught* them something? Information delivery of some kind?"

I had these thoughts even though I had been intentional about expressing care to my students. Some of it was based on instinct and empathy — for example, flopping onto my belly as a 22-year-old Harvard Overseas Teaching Fellow, working with second graders at a school in Athens, Greece, so I could make eye contact while they were sitting on the floor — but others were deliberate decisions. Education philosopher Nel Nodding's work about the ethics of caring as a means to shape the character of young people; Parker J. Palmer's books about teaching in ways that addressed the whole person; and Vito Perrone's charge that one of the primary duties of an educator in a democracy is to prepare students to think critically and contribute positively to their communities, had all shaped my approach to teaching. But these aspects were not yet the orthodoxy in education in 1999, even in my own head. For an American education system then-focused on standards and accountability narrowly defined by measurable achievements in academics, caring relationships were understood as "nice to have," and not yet the fundamental and foundational elements of working with young people.

Yet, the acts of caring and of making space for their ideas and creativity made an impression on my students. When one of my former students graduated in the top 5% of her engineering major at Stanford University, she had the opportunity to name a high school teacher who influenced her the most. She chose me, her English teacher, whom she had for three years, for world literature, British literature, and AP literature. At the awards ceremony, she named a few of the things she appreciated about me. I was surprised by what made her list; I had brought her and her classmates bagels in the morning, and I had come to her dance recital, she said. When another former student reached out to me, in 2022, 18 years after she was my student as a senior in high school, she wrote, "Thank you … for giving us space to discuss, question, and form ideas." Another student had written at the end of the academic year, "Thank you for teaching us about life as well as literature" and another exclaimed, "I was asked to be more creative in your class than in my art class!" It was when I returned to graduate school as a doctoral student that I learned that offering spaces to reflect, be creative, and learn about topics that are relevant to young peoples' lives are not just the preferences of a few young people but research-recommended practices.

How Dream a Dream's Practices Reflect Findings from Research Literature about Positive Youth Development

As I interviewed the graduates of Dream a Dream for this book, I heard echoes of the voices of my former students and best practices from research literature. Dream a Dream participants commented on the care and the time that Dream a Dream facilitators devoted to them; they, too, appreciated that facilitators talked to them about "life," and supported their interests, whether it was dancing, launching a new business, or singing. They, too, remembered the snacks that Dream a Dream provided and the open, safe space in which they could share their own ideas, question their beliefs, and express themselves in creative ways.

If we look at the literature on human development and on positive youth development, the qualities I practised as a classroom teacher and that Dream a Dream facilitators practised in their Life Skills Programmes and Career Connect Centres, follow the research on effective developmental relationships. The Search Institute, for example, reports that "relationships are developmental when young people 1) discover who they are 2) develop the ability to shape their own lives 3) learn how to engage with and contribute to the world around them."[1] The Search Institute's Developmental Relationships Framework further lists five key elements of developmental relationships: 1) express care 2) challenge growth 3) provide support 4) share power 5) expand possibilities.[2] During the interviews I conducted for this book, young people told me over and over again how Dream a Dream facilitators and programmes included all five elements in their interactions with them. Young people also told me it was the care, support, encouragement to grow, power sharing, and expanded possibilities that they appreciated about Dream a Dream.

Dream a Dream's focus on equity and equipping its staff and participants with changemaking skills also resonated with me. The brutal beating of Rodney King by police officers in 1992 happened

---

[1] Search Institute, (n.d.). Developmental Relationships. https://www.search-institute.org/developmental-relationships/

[2] Search Institute (n.d.). Developmental Relationships Framework. https://www.search-institute.org/developmental-relationships/developmental-relationships-framework/

when I was a high school junior studying Advanced Placement United States History. The subsequent discussion of the event in my class by my teacher raised a whole host of questions for me about whether and how we engage the big questions about equity and justice our young people might have about the world outside our classrooms. It led me to apply to be in one of the first cohorts of the Freedom Schools launched by Children's Defense Fund as a Fellow sponsored by Harvard University's W. E. B. Du Bois Research Institute. The experience of teaching Vietnamese and African American fourth graders in South San Francisco in the summer of 1994 ultimately shaped my decision to become an educator. I wanted to see if I could find a different way to teach than how I had been taught, and to teach people the skills with which they could create positive change in the community around them. This quest led me to collaborate with Facing History and Ourselves as a teacher and to study community organising as a doctoral student; I ended up writing a dissertation about civic education and what it means to educate people how to work with others across differences to identify and solve shared problems together.

Nevertheless, when I conducted the interviews with the 20 young people from Dream a Dream whose stories are chronicled in this book, I did not expect that they would speak about contributing positively to their communities as part of what they appreciated about Dream a Dream. Yet when asked broadly about the impact of their experience with Dream a Dream, they not only shared about how Dream a Dream's approach helped them as individuals, but also about how they were taking what they had learned and sharing them with their families and communities to make positive changes. It is no surprise, given that Vishal has been recognised globally as a changemaker by organisations such as Ashoka and Eisenhower Fellowships and Dream a Dream's work has been recognised by organisations such as Brookings Institution, HundrED.org, Lego Foundation, Global Development Network (GDN), WISE, and the Delhi government among others. Their pioneering, changemaking approach is in the DNA of their programmes; their graduates and staff are working intentionally to create positive change in their communities alongside others. As Dream a Dream graduates thrived, their families and communities often also followed suit.

Others also note that thriving is not just an individual effort but also a collective, system-wide endeavour. More recently, Dr. Bruce Perry wrote the following about what it takes to help young people with trauma backgrounds: *"I believe that if you don't recognize the built-in biases in yourself and the structural biases in your systems — biases regarding race, gender, sexual orientation — you can't truly be trauma-informed. Marginalised peoples — excluded, minimised, shamed — are traumatised peoples, because…, humans are fundamentally relational creatures. To be excluded or dehumanised in an organisation, community, or society you are part of results in prolonged, uncontrollable stress that is sensitising. Marginalisation is a fundamental trauma. This is why I believe that a truly trauma-informed system is an anti-racist system."*[3]

Vishal and Dream a Dream staff came to similar conclusions after their field experience of working day in and out with young people over the years. They had engaged clinical psychologists Dr. Fiona Kennedy and Dr. David Pearson to develop a trauma-sensitive mentoring programme for Dream a Dream. They had also trained Dream a Dream facilitators by engaging the expertise

---

[3] Perry, B. & Winfrey, O. (2021). What happened to you? Conversations on trauma, resilience, and healing. Flatiron Books.

of experienced creative arts facilitators — Charlie Murphy, Peggy Taylor, and Nadia Chaney. As you will read in the Afterward, Dream a Dream is now more deliberately turning to address systemic barriers in India, after reaching the same conclusion that Dr. Perry had — that we cannot address trauma solely at the individual level, particularly for people who have been systematically and historically marginalised by caste, gender, religion, race, sexual orientation, neurodivergence, or other characteristics.

Yet at the same time, we need to recognise that youth with trauma and adversity in their backgrounds are still youth. Those of us who work with them must live in the tension of knowing that while some of the young peoples' needs and strengths are specific to their backgrounds, their needs and strengths are also drawn from common developmental needs that *all* youth and people have. Adversity shapes us, among other factors, but it should not entirely and solely define us, nor our approach to working with young people.

Researchers have known for a while, for example, about what young people need to access their intrinsic motivation. We all have three basic psychological needs, according to researchers Edward Deci and Richard Ryan, who developed Self-Determination Theory[4]: 1) relatedness ("the experience of warmth, bonding, and care...; of connecting to and feeling significant to others") 2) autonomy ("the experience of volition and willingness … when one's actions, thoughts, and feelings are self-endorsed and authentic") and 3) competence ("the experience of effectiveness and mastery")[5].

---

[4] American Psychological Association, n.d. "The intrinsic motivation of Edward Deci and Richard Ryan." https://www.apa.org/members/content/intrinsic-motivation

[5] Vansteenkiste, M. (n.d.). "Basic psychological needs" https://selfdeterminationtheory.org/application-basic-psychological-needs/

Researcher Arlen Moller writes that providing meaningful choices supports autonomy; providing challenges and feedback calibrated to individuals support competence; and giving and receiving warm regard in the context of stable relationships support relatedness[6].

Dream a Dream, through their After School Life Skills Programme using creative arts and sports and through their Career Connect Centre Programmes and their scholarship programme, has developed a model by which they are offering safe, caring, supportive environments (relatedness) in which youth are encouraged to make choices and take creative risks (autonomy), and where youth are learning to become competent in life skills (competence). Educators call the arena that is helpful to target for learning as the "zone of proximal development" where the challenge or "risk" or new experience is just beyond what a youth is currently capable of, so that they can accomplish the task with support from others[7]. If the task is below their ability, they are likely to become bored and lose interest; if the task or activity is too far beyond their ability, they would feel overwhelmed and may feel worse afterwards. Dr. Perry writes, "*Healthy development involves a series of challenges and exposure to new things. And failure is an important part of the process... The key is to have challenges that are achievable — close enough to your current capabilities that you will succeed with some encouragement, practice, and repetition.*"[8]

With their focus on sports and creative arts as the mechanism by which they are developing life skills, and by providing youth

---

[6] Moller, A. (n.d.) "Intrinsic Motivation." https://selfdeterminationtheory.org/application-intrinsic-motivation/

[7] Science Direct (n.d.). Zone of proximal development. https://www.sciencedirect.com/topics/psychology/zone-of-proximal-development

[8] Perry, B. & Winfrey, O. (2021). What happened to you? Conversations on trauma, resilience, and healing. Flatiron Books. p. 195

with opportunities such as travel and outdoor experiential camps, Vishal and the Dream a Dream team also had landed on by their lived-experience expertise, the practices that help youth to heal and thrive. Dr. Perry writes, *"Schools tend to minimise powerful healing and resilience-building activities like sports, music, and art. These are often viewed as elective or enrichment activities, when in fact they can be the very bedrock of academic learning, thanks to their regulatory and relational elements. Patterned, repetitive, rhythmic activity makes the overactive and overly reactive core regulatory networks get back 'in balance.' Music falls into this category — both playing and listening. All sports involve doses of it too. Dance, too. And of course, each of these activities also has very important relational elements. You learn when to pass the ball to your teammate; you learn how to move with your dance partner; you synchronise playing your violin with other members of the orchestra. Finally, there are cognitive elements to sports, music, and other arts; they engage, activate, and synchronise activity throughout the brain, from the bottom up and from the top down. These are whole-brain healthy activities."*[9]

Young people told me in their words, about the impact of these activities that Dr. Perry recommends, and that Dream a Dream had started to implement more than 20 years ago. Young people told me in the interviews how Dream a Dream offered a safe, caring environment and relationships in which they were encouraged to try new activities as they felt ready, and where they built their confidence, step by step.

---

[9] Ibid. p. 277.

How Young People Told Their Stories for the Book

This is one of the first times, if not the very first time, we hear directly from young people thriving, in spite of their backgrounds of adversity in India, talk about what mattered to them in a book. Through these stories, we tell the "how" of Dream a Dream's programmes and how young people understand and appreciate what they experienced.

The young adults included in the book were selected to represent a range of backgrounds, including diverse faith and cultural backgrounds. There are an equal number of males and females, and a balance of those who could speak about the after-school life skills programme and the career connect programme. Young people who were able to converse in English were dominant, but there were several youths for whom translation was necessary.

The initial interviews for most participants were conducted in person; second and third interviews were conducted over the phone. After initial interviews in 2019, there was a follow-up second interview in 2020 to answer any gaps in information that the young people provided in 2019; in 2020, as chapters were drafted, I identified clarifying questions, and Dream a Dream staff reached out to young people to ask for their answers. As I wrote the stories, Dream a Dream participants and staff, including Vishal, reviewed and provided feedback and confirmation of facts and relevant contexts. Where Vishal and staff inserted comments and contexts in the body of the chapter, those comments were attributed to them specifically or more broadly to Dream a Dream staff so readers can know which observations were made by staff, which stemmed from research, and which came from my analysis.

In addition to giving written and oral consent, young people had the opportunity to decline to answer any questions and to retract or revise any answers they gave. Where some stories are shorter and some are longer than the others, the different lengths follow the individual person's willingness to share.

Once the final drafts were completed, young adults were also given another opportunity to read their chapters, provide edits, and give consent to having the stories be published; they were given the opportunity to use pseudonyms or first names only, and to share or not share their photographs. Vishal talked through with them some of the possible positive and negative consequences of sharing their stories, yet young people consented to share, for the benefit of other youth, and so that everyone would know what is possible when young people are supported with care and intentionality.

What We Hope Readers Gain from the Book

I deliberately chose a more clinical, drier tone to tell the stories, rather than a more dramatic one. I wanted to walk the line between sharing enough details so that readers can empathise with the young peoples' backgrounds and recognise the intensity of their experiences but not so much as to take away from the purpose of telling the stories, which is to help readers understand that much of these young peoples' stories remain yet to be written. Their backgrounds, when tempered and met with caring and consistent support, can influence, but do not define their future. I wanted to leave room for the fact that young people are still writing their stories with choices they have yet to make.

When Vishal approached me to write a book about Dream a Dream's graduates, I had already written a few books in collaboration with other researchers, about teaching and learning 21ˢᵗ century skills so that young people and our communities can thrive as whole people. They were academic books, however, and I knew that I wanted to write books for a more general audience. I thought that if we wove research and practical information into young peoples' stories, it might be a way to share with parents, educators, and the public, more broadly, about the positive impact of evidence-based, practical, youth-centred, and youth-empowering ways to support young people. Thus, throughout the chapters, you will find "information boxes" that highlight key ideas, with resources for further reading and learning.

I also knew from having been in the field of working with young people for almost three decades that we needed a better balance between our stories of shortcomings and failures and our stories of brilliance and success. Particularly for our younger and more vulnerable populations, we tend to focus on deficits rather than strengths and on what they need more than what they can contribute and teach us. The social, cultural, historical, and political contexts that influence why we tend to focus on deficits rather than strengths is the topic for a whole another book; but at heart, I wanted to help shift the narrative towards more strength-based storytelling, centred on the voices of young people. I wanted to share these stories with the rest of India and the world because these are inspiring stories told through the voices of young people about what mattered to *them* as they lived through challenging life circumstances, with the support of Dream a Dream and their facilitators.

I also wanted to ground their stories with findings from research, knowing that stories by themselves can easily be dismissed as "anecdotes" by those with power over money, resources, and policies. For example, we have known in research for a while about what helps youth from backgrounds of adversity. Dr. Bruce Perry summarised it thus: *"The summary of research on the most effective treatments to help child trauma victims [says that] 'What works best is anything that increases the quality and number of relationships in the child's life.'"*[10] You will find echoes of that research finding in the stories that young people tell in this book; not surprisingly, many of their recollections about Dream a Dream revolve around what quality relationships can look like, from their perspective.

Thus, we hope these stories help people in the education and child welfare world in a couple of ways. The first is taking a long-term view of the efforts of educators, social workers, and others who work with young people. Often, those of us who work in these systems encounter our young people for a short time. For the most part, we do not necessarily see the positive outcomes of the time and effort and care that we invest in these people. But by interviewing people in their late twenties and asking them about their experiences and what helped them succeed helps us to see that our daily, minute by minute — what I would call — "micro-moments," or "micro-actions," are some of the things that young people remember, well after we have worked with them when they were 10, 12, 14 years old. We find out what they still carry and hold in their memory about what mattered to them as being impactful. With the book, we hope to inspire, encourage, and give hope to those hard-working supporters who are helping our young people.

The second thing we hope to accomplish with this book is to show and reinforce the idea that young people's adverse backgrounds do

---

[10] Jay, M. (2017). *Supernormal: The untold story of adversity and resilience.* Twelve Books.

not define them and their futures, and that they, in fact, can thrive. That with proper care and support, thriving is possible is a mindset that is important for both young people and their supporters to have. As Dr. Perry writes, "*What we're learning is that having access to a number of invested, caring people is actually a better predictor of good outcomes following trauma than having access to a therapist.*"[11] We hope that these stories show that.

Dream a Dream gave me independence to design and execute the project, from beginning until the end, honouring my integrity as a researcher. But the one thing Vishal told me at the beginning of the project was about what he did NOT want the book to be; he did not want me to tell a simple story of victims and heroic rescuers. In fact, what I found as I interviewed young people and Dream a Dream staff was that young people helped shape Dream a Dream, sometimes, by becoming part of the leadership team.

As I listened to the young people, many who had become staff members of Dream a Dream and had helped shape the organisation, the book also became a story about Dream a Dream's growth. Its co-founder, leadership team, and staff worked on themselves by listening to feedback and reflecting deeply on what was and was not working and why. They identified and absorbed the advice and counsel from experienced experts, including researchers and young people. As they listened to young people about what young peoples' needs were, and the kinds of shifts that were needed, Dream a Dream grew along with the youth in their organisational programming content and structure. An example of this shift and growth is the building of the Career Connect Programme, told in

---

[11] Ibid. p.230.

Chapter 11, in Pavithra KL's story. Thus, the stories and chapters are organised so that while reading the chapters in the book, readers can get a glimpse of how Dream a Dream has evolved over its 20+ year journey.

In addition, the stories in this book do not follow a smooth-as-butter, "everything is perfect" kind of storylines. Healing from trauma is a complex endeavour, and so is walking with young people on their journeys. There is satisfaction and reward but also disappointment and frustration experienced by both young people and their supporters in their work together, and both need to practice patience and grace. Young people and their supporters also exercise their agency in their choices to offer, accept, or decline support, particularly in circumstances when they were hurt, taken advantage of, or disappointed. Indeed, one of the things missing from these stories are the stories of those who did not choose to continue to find support from Dream a Dream, why they made that decision, and what happened to them. But I hope what shines through the stories of those who chose to stay is how young people and their supporters persevered and persisted in their efforts towards healing and healthy connections, even through conflicts and challenges. What matters is that we accompany each other in our journeys and hold a steady and safe space for each other, even as our circumstances might wax and wane.

All of us journey on roads that twist and turn, run up and down, and sometimes double back and end abruptly. Journeys are rarely conducted on straight roads. Growth and change happen during this process because we are human: organic, malleable, and susceptible to influences, internal and external. How we change depends on our ability to exercise our will and on our desire to grow; the paths on which we find ourselves and our environment;

and how we are challenged, protected, supported, and nurtured — or not — by those who surround us. We, in turn, also can shape our journeys. We can strike out in new directions, join new travel partners, and create new pathways. As pilgrims, we can share our stories about our journeys, what enabled us to continue walking through the hills and valleys, and who accompanied us along the way. Vishal's Afterward gives an update on where the young people are in 2022, three years after my initial interviews with them in 2019. The varied paths that these young adults have taken through the global pandemic show that the route to "thriving" is full of ups and downs. I would argue that "thriving" is a dynamic process that happens in moments of adversity *and* ease, in green pastures *and* in shadowed valleys.

This continual evolution and internally motivated growth are something I want to highlight as core themes that emerged as the youth told their stories. The youth who chose to stay with Dream a Dream saw changemaking, humility, generosity, inclusion, willingness to listen and change, and other values and attitudes modelled by the staff. Dream a Dream, like the young people they worked with, faced challenges and worked through their mistakes — growing pains that ranged from small to seismic — but they were open and transparent about acknowledging them, grew from them, and drew on their supporters to help them. They grew as they listened to young people and responded to their needs. I hope readers are as inspired by Dream a Dream's journey as they are by the stories of young people.

Writing this book was a patient work of weaving together stories that had been written by the choices that young people, Vishal, Dream a Dream, and their supporters had made over the more than 20 years that Dream a Dream has been in existence, and the work that researchers have been doing over decades to find evidence-based practices that help all of us to thrive. My hope is that the stories give hope about what is possible when we accompany young people in their journeys, with care and consistency. These stories show us that when all young people thrive, our communities thrive.

— Connie K. Chung, EdD,
California,
Easter 2022

02

With Caring Support, Children from Adverse Backgrounds Can Thrive

Prasanna H.

[Prasanna H., Bangalore, 2019]

Defying Expectations

Research about adverse childhood experiences (ACEs) show that those with higher ACEs scores are more likely to suffer from negative health, social, and economic consequences later in life[12]. Based on the circumstances of his childhood, Prasanna

---

[12] In a study conducted in the United States, compared to participants with no ACEs, those with higher ACE scores were more likely to report high school non-completion, unemployment, and living in a household below the federal poverty level (Metzler et al, 2017). Metzler, M., Merrick, M.T., Klevens, J., Ports, K.A., & Ford, D. C. (2017). Adverse childhood experiences and life opportunities: Shifting the narrative. *Children and Youth Services Review, 72*(2017), 141-149. *https://doi.org/10.1016/j.childyouth.2016.10.021.* For more information about ACEs, see the information provided on the United States' Centers for Disease Control and Prevention, for example: https://www.cdc.gov/violenceprevention/aces/index.html

scores a nine out of 10 for his ACE profile. This means that he faced a number of difficult circumstances while growing up.

Researcher B.B. Robbie Rossman writes that challenges may come in an "adversity package"[13], when one misfortune sets off other problems. Clinical psychologist Meg Jay observes that most early adversities are not one-time events ("shock traumas"[14]) but are "strain traumas" where there is an ongoing impact on adulthood[15].

Yet, today, Prasanna is married to his childhood sweetheart, Sukanya, and is the father of a baby girl. Having earned a bachelor of arts in business economics, he works full time as a communications staff member at Dream a Dream. He is currently pursuing a second BA degree in law by taking classes part time. He is financially supporting his brother and his mother. Prasanna has great hopes that his daughter will have a different childhood than his, firmly believing that "what happened to me in my childhood should not happen to my child."

Prasanna's background of adversity, while part of his history, did not lead to the consequences that research predicted and does not define his present. How is his story possible?

---

[13] Rossman, B.B. R. (2000). "Time heals all: How much and for whom?" *Journal of Emotional Abuse 2*(1), 31-50.

[14] Kris, E. (1956). "The recovery of childhood memories in psychoanalysis," *The Psychoanalytic Study of the Child* 11, 54-88.

[15] Jay, M. (2017). *Supernormal: The secret world of the family hero.* Hachette Book Group. p.12.

> ### INFORMATION BOX 2A: ADVERSE CHILDHOOD EXPERIENCES
>
> Adverse childhood experiences (ACEs) are potentially traumatic incidents that children may suffer between the age of 0 to 17. These events can include experiencing or witnessing physical, verbal, or sexual abuse; growing up in a household with divorce, substance abuse, or mental health issues; or growing up with very little emotional or financial support. An ACE score is a tally of multiple experiences of abuse, neglect, violence, and household dysfunction. High ACE scores are associated with chronic illness, mental illness, and substance abuse in adulthood among other adverse impacts (CDC, 2019).
>
> The initial ACE study led by Vincent J. Felitti and colleagues (1998) took place in the late 1990s in the United States and examined eighteen thousand middle-class families, including 70% Caucasian and 70% college-educated individuals. As paediatrician Nadine Burke Harris notes, "the body of research sparked by the ACE study makes it clear that adverse childhood experiences in and of themselves are a risk factor for many of the most common and serious diseases in the United States (and worldwide), regardless of income or race or access to care" (p.39). While studies about ACEs are lacking in India, multiple studies around the world suggest that up to 75% of young people are exposed to at least one ACE event (Jay, p.5).
>
> **Sources:**
>
> Center for Disease Control and Prevention (2019). Preventing Adverse Childhood Experiences.
>
> https://www.cdc.gov/media/releases/2019/p1105-prevent-aces.html
>
> Felitti, V. J. et. al. (1998). "Relationship of childhood abuse and household dysfunction to many of the leading causes of death in adults: The adverse childhood experiences (ACE) study," American Journal of Preventative Medicine 14, no. 4: 245-258.
>
> Harris, N. B. (2018). The deepest well: Healing the long-term effects of childhood adversity. Houghton Mifflin Harcourt Publishing Company: New York.
>
> Jay, M. (2017). Supernormal: The secret world of the family hero. Hachette Book Group.
>
> WHO (n.d.). Violence and injury prevention: Adverse childhood experiences international questionnaire (ACE_IQ). https://www.who.int/publications/m/item/adverse-childhood-experiences-international-questionnaire-(ace-iq)

A Challenging Beginning

Prasanna's story represents millions of children in India and elsewhere who face similar adverse circumstances while growing up. Prasanna's father was an alcoholic who beat his wife and children when he drank too much. Physical punishment was routine both at school and at home for Prasanna. He was even beaten by his mother as punishment, even though she tried her best to care for Prasanna and his brother. When her husband would beat her very badly, she would report him to the police. Prasanna's father would be detained for a week or so and then released. After particularly severe beatings, his mother would leave to go stay with her parents. Growing up, Prasanna would overhear her say to her friends, "If it were not for my children, I would prefer to die," because of her difficult life with an alcoholic and abusive husband. Those comments would leave him feeling sad and hopeless. Research shows that those who grow up in a home with domestic violence are more likely to commit suicide, more likely to abuse drugs or alcohol, and more likely to commit a violent crime[16].

Mirroring his mother's abuse at the hands of his father, Prasanna received beatings from teachers whenever he got into trouble at the government school he attended. He would respond by refusing to go to school or running away from school once there. He would play with his friends instead, seeking fun and happiness where he could. Once, when the result of his school examination arrived at home, his parents saw that he had scored poorly, given how much school he had missed. They responded by beating him. The physical punishment that was meant to goad him into better behaviour and into attending school did not work. Prasanna continued to avoid school, sometimes resorting to stealing guava and other fruits from local farms, for a brief taste of sweet, sticky pleasure somewhere in his life. Once, he and his friends were caught stealing by the owner of a fruit stand and were beaten up.

---

[16] Childhood Domestic Violence Association (n.d.). What is the impact of CDV? https://cdv.org/what-is-cdv/the-impact/

 **INFORMATION BOX 2B: LONG-TERM EFFECTS OF PHYSICAL PUNISHMENT**

While data about the impact of physical punishment in India is scarce, longitudinal studies in New Zealand, the United States, and by the United Nations Children's Fund show that young children who have been subject to forms of corporal punishment are more likely to be aggressive and violent a few years later (Smith, 2006; Sege & Siegel, 2018). Corporal punishment may also legitimise violence in interpersonal relationships; children tend to internalise the social relations they experienced, thus leading to generational cycles of violence (ibid).

Consequences associated with corporal punishment include the following:

1) increased risk of mental health disorders and cognition problems
2) increased likelihood of children being prone to defiance and aggression in the future
3) negative changes in brain architecture that mirror the impact of toxic stress

Additional research has shown that physical punishment is not effective in stopping or changing children's poor behaviour (Sege & Siegel, 2018).

For resources to replace corporal punishment with more effective means, see the Global Initiative to End All Corporal Punishment of Children: https://endcorporalpunishment.org/

Sources:

Global Initiative to End All Corporal Punishment of Children (n.d.). https://endcorporalpunishment.org/

Sege, R. D. & Siegel, B. S. (2018). Effective Discipline to Raise Healthy Children. Pediatrics, 142 (6). Council on Child Abuse and Neglect and Committee on Psychosocial Aspects of Child and Family Health. https://doi.org/10.1542/peds.2018-3112

Smith, A. B. (2006). The State of Research on the Effects of Punishment. Social Policy Journal Of New Zealand Te Puna Whakaaro, (27). Government of New Zealand, Ministry of Social Development.

His mother could not understand why Prasanna had stopped going to school and was spending his time aimlessly. She began to inquire into residential boarding schools. Given the emotional and economic turbulence at home, his mother wanted to provide a place for Prasanna that would give him a more secure environment and more nutritious food than what he could get at home. She wanted him to have a better education than the one offered by their local school, even if it meant that he would live away from his family. Initially, she placed him in a youth hostel, where basic amenities were provided, but where he was continued to be treated horribly by the staff.

But Prasanna was motivated to hear that if his behaviour improved, he might be able to go to another, better boarding school. Prasanna began to work harder at school. When he was about 10 years old, his mother and school authorities agreed to enrol him at Ananya Trust, a boarding school that had just opened for children from backgrounds like his. Ananya Trust was started by Dr. Shashi Rao, an educator with a doctorate in education from the United States. She had a firm belief in providing a caring, nurturing, child-centred environment for children. She was committed to helping children maintain ties to their families. The children at Ananya Trust, including Prasanna, boarded and studied at the school Monday through Friday, and then, went home on the weekends.

In the more nurturing environment at Ananya Trust, Prasanna began to channel more positively the curiosity and the thirst for adventure that had led him to his previous escapades with his friends, such as running away from school and stealing to taste forbidden fruits. He dreamt about travelling to different places, exploring different aspects of himself and his interests, and learning more about the world beyond Bangalore. But his family's economic condition was such that Prasanna had to fight for his family's survival instead. He picked up odd jobs here and there, working from age 10, doing manual labour, such as working at construction sites. He did not want to work, but he needed to work, to earn, for example, to have enough bus fare to get home from Ananya Trust to see his family on the weekends. He could not stop working because of his family, even though he wanted to, many times.

Even as he grew older, the sense of empathy for his family and the economic challenges that they faced, coupled with the heavy sense of responsibility thrust upon him at such an early age, stayed with him. When interviewed for this chapter at age 27, he still spoke about his twin desires to take flight to seek adventure and travel and the sense of responsibility and empathy that have kept him grounded, for now.

INFORMATION BOX 2C: CHILD LABOUR IN INDIA

According to the 2011 census, which is the most recent official data available, there were 10.1 million Indian children aged 5–14 engaged in informal labour (ILO, 2017). This is 3.9% of the entire child population in India (ibid). This amounts to approximately 13% of the Indian workforce, which means that about 1 in every 10 workers in India is a child (Oxfam India, 2018). Between 2001 and 2011 that number decreased by 2.6 million (ILO, 2017). While the numbers decreased in rural areas, they increased in urban areas (ILO, 2017).

In 1986, India introduced the Child Labour Act that allowed children below 14 to be involved in "non-hazardous" work such as working on farms and making handicrafts (ILO, 2016). In 2016, an amendment to the law was proposed to prohibit children below the age of 14 to work in any industry (Goyal, 2017).

According to the report published by International Labour Organisation and UNICEF additional 9 million children are at risk of being pushed towards child labour by the end of 2022 globally during the pandemic. In India, the closure of schools and the financial crisis faced by families, during the pandemic, are likely pushing children into poverty and thus, child labour and unsafe migration.

Sources:

Goyal, S. (2017). Child Labour in India [Abstract]. International Journal of Social Science and Economic Research, 02(12).

International Labour Organisation (2016, June 02). Hazardous Work List: India. https://www.ilo.org/newdelhi/areasofwork/child-labour/legal-framework/WCMS_486746/lang—en/index.htm

International Labour Organisation (2017, June 8). Fact Sheet: Child Labour in India. https://www.ilo.org/newdelhi/whatwedo/publications/WCMS_557089/lang—en/index.htm

International Labour Office and United Nations Children's Fund (2021). Child Labour: Global estimates 2020, trends and the road forward. New York. https://data.unicef.org/resources/child-labour-2020-global-estimates-trends-and-the-road-forward/

Oxfam India (2018, November 20). Child Labour & Child Rights In India: Myth or Reality. https://www.oxfamindia.org/blog/child-labour-india

Nurtured by Dream a Dream

Prasanna's appetite for adventure was both appeased and whetted further in 2002, when Prasanna was 11 years old. That year, a group of volunteers with Dream a Dream began visiting Ananya Trust regularly. Founded in 1999 by a dozen young people in their 20s who dreamt of meeting the needs of children in ways that appreciated diversity and differences, the NGO Dream a Dream had been built from a loose group of volunteers into a formal organisation by one of the founders, Vishal Talreja.

With a background in business and finance and inspired deeply by a three-month exchange programme in Finland, where he began to think about ways to bridge divisions in caste, class, and communities in India, Vishal began working full time at Dream a Dream in 2002. He recruited professional artists, athletes, and corporate volunteers to offer arts, sports, mentoring, and other life skills programming to children.

Even as much of India's public education system retained an exclusive focus on academics in educating its children, Vishal's day-to-day experiences with young people from backgrounds of adversity had convinced him to remain steadfast in his commitment to offer the kinds of social, emotional, and other life skills that schools and families were not providing. While for-profit learning centres were beginning to develop all over India, focused on "personality development" that taught young adults how to correctly pronounce words and dress for job interviews[17], there were few that were teaching life skills, for free, to young children from backgrounds of adversity at the time.

---

[17] Giridharadas, A. (2011). *India calling: An intimate portrait of a nation's remaking.* Henry Holt and Company, LLC.

By 2002, Dream a Dream was into its third year, having made its own journey from volunteers visiting terminally ill children at founding to later partnering with organisations such as Ananya Trust to focus on providing structured enrichment activities that allowed young people to experience community, caring, and belonging. For Prasanna and his classmates at Ananya Trust, this meant playing games and going on outings with Vishal and Dream a Dream's volunteers to places such as Lalbagh Botanical Gardens, a 240-acre botanical garden with recreational space, in the middle of Bangalore. Prasanna and his classmates looked forward to these outings with "Vishal Sir" and his friends, for the adventures that they were able to experience. Prasanna appreciates that Dream a Dream offered him a chance to explore new places and new activities — those things that he would have loved to do, with abandon, were it not for his family's circumstances. He participated in Dream a Dream's variety of activities, such as computer classes, sports sessions, adventure camps, and summer camps, for the next seven years.

In particular, Prasanna loved playing field hockey with Dream a Dream. Yet, Prasanna's chaotic childhood environment had limited his ability to manage his emotions. It impacted his participation in activities. He recalls that period in his life: "I was a very angry person. If I felt anything went wrong for me, I would hit my friends and hit everyone." Prasanna's behaviour is not unusual as research shows that children exposed to violence tend to have magnified emotional responses and more difficulty effectively adjusting their responses[18]. Even while playing his beloved sport, field hockey, if his

---

[18] McLaughlin, K. (2017). Science Brief: The long shadow of adverse childhood experiences. Blog post. https://www.apa.org/science/about/psa/2017/04/adverse-childhood

team did not play well, Prasanna would hit others on his team with sticks. These incidents would happen so often that he remembers he would always be standing outside the field, in detention, as punishment for beating up other teammates. He recalls that Vishal "knew that I had trouble managing my anger because whenever Vishal would visit the programme, I would not be playing but would be standing outside the field."

Instead of punishing him further, Dream a Dream volunteers intervened with different tactics. His field hockey coach started bringing extra balls with him to practice, directing Prasanna to practice hitting 10 balls into the goal every time he felt himself becoming angry and wanting to hit someone. So, Prasanna slowly learnt to direct his anger at hitting balls and not people. In this and other ways, he learnt to recognise and channel his response to his anger.

[Prasanna training young people for the Street Football Festival, Bangalore, 2016]

The kind and caring staff at Ananya Trust also intentionally guided Prasanna to shift his relationship with learning and with adults, from what he had experienced earlier in other schools. Ananya Trust created an environment where children learn to talk about their emotions, where they have control over what they want to study and where they want to study. It is a non-competitive environment, with no fear and no pressure.

In one incident, a volunteer who was teaching maths kicked Prasanna out of the class when he became unruly. Prasanna had finished the problems he was given quickly and had used the extra time to fidget and joke around with his classmates. Prasanna, having experienced these kinds of directives and punishments from other adults before, left the class. But he was also afraid to return to class.

Dr. Rao pulled the volunteer aside and told him that expelling Prasanna included the unintended negative consequence of excluding him from learning. She reminded the volunteer that it was the adult's responsibility to help children, no matter how children behaved. She suggested that Prasanna likely thought the maths problems to be too easy and was fooling around out of boredom. The volunteer listened to Dr. Rao and apologised to Prasanna for punishing him.

The volunteer asked Prasanna what was bothering him and what he wanted from the class. "This was a surprise for me," Prasanna recalls. "No adult had apologised to me until then, and he was also trying to understand what I wanted out of that class." Prasanna also apologised to the volunteer and told him he would no longer distract the other students. The volunteer gave Prasanna more maths problems to solve than he gave to other students. He also gave Prasanna more difficult maths problems and Prasanna solved those problems easily, as Dr. Rao had predicted.

The adults in Prasanna's life continued to pay attention to him, shoring him up in places where he needed support. For example, Dr. Rao worked with Prasanna's field hockey coach and told him that while Prasanna was one of the very best players, he lacked confidence, and he would always downplay himself, letting one of his friends hog the limelight instead. The coach, then, focused on casually but intentionally praising Prasanna in public, emphasising what a skilled player Prasanna was. Prasanna's confidence grew.

Thus, in these thousands of micro-moments, the adults in Prasanna's life filled in the pieces of self-worth, value, and dignity that he did not even know he was missing. Throughout his time at Ananya Trust and with Dream a Dream, Prasanna received intentional love and care — those things that other adults at his previous school and home were unable to give or did not know how to give.

Prasanna, for example, recalls how he used to visit Vishal sitting in front of a big computer in the tiny room that was Dream a Dream's first office. Prasanna would show up without warning at this office. He would tell Vishal, "I want to have lunch with you today." Almost 20 years later, Prasanna remembers Vishal never asking him why he was there. Instead, Vishal would always stop what he was doing and say, "Yes, let's go have lunch." Vishal would take him to a place with good food and would speak kindly to him; he would ask him how his field hockey practice was going and whether he needed new shoes or anything else. For Prasanna, it was a way of interacting with adults that was different from what he had been used to in his previous schools and at home.

Whenever Prasanna and his classmates shared their positive achievements with Vishal and the other facilitators at Dream a Dream, he remembers that they were "always proud of us." But not everything was so freely given. When Prasanna longed for the new shirts that his classmates had, he asked Vishal for money. Vishal did not ask him why, and he did not tell him that he could not have money. Instead, he would tell Prasanna to type a page from a newspaper in exchange for some spending money. Prasanna would then take three to four hours to type an article as he did not know how to type well. He wondered why he was being asked to type but thought that maybe Vishal wanted to have the article for his own use. But Prasanna discovered later that it was for no other reason than to have him practice typing and to encourage him to learn that money had to be earned.

INFORMATION BOX 2D: THE PRESENCE OF A CARING ADULT

Developmental research reflects what many educators, parents, and caretakers intuitively know: the caring adult has many stabilising and positive effects on children. Having an adult that they trust can safeguard children from the risk of social problems such as aggressive behaviour and bullying, as well as depression.

Meaningful adult–child relationships encompass these five critical aspects: 1) showing young people that they care about them 2) challenging them to become their best selves while providing ongoing support 3) sharing power 4) showing respect and 5) expanding their sense of possibilities and opportunities (Search Institute, n.d.).

According to trauma expert Bruce Perry, research on the most effective treatments to help child trauma victims can be summarised as the following: "What works best is anything that increases the quality and number of relationships in the child's life" (Jay, p.180).

Sources:

Jay, M. (2017). Supernormal: The secret world of the family hero. Hachette Book Group.

Murphey, D., Bandy, T., Schmitz, H., & Moore, K. (2013). Caring adults: Important for child well-being. Child Trends. https://www.childtrends.org/wp-content/uploads/2013/12/2013-54CaringAdults.pdf

Search Institute (n.d.). Developmental Relationships Framework. https://www.search-institute.org/developmental-relationships/developmental-relationships-framework/

A Serpentine Road to Adulthood

Even with these relational and financial supports, however, the temptation to obtain more spending money by using his excellent maths skills tempted Prasanna towards gambling. Each time he went home to his family for the weekend, he would see his father getting drunk and hitting his mother, sending her back to her parents' house. Seeing his father angry, frustrated, and drunk all the time made Prasanna wonder why he continued to go to school instead of helping his family. As he sought gambling games to play outside of school and continued to make a lot of easy money that he could give to his father, Prasanna saw that his father became very happy whenever he received money from him.

After one of these weekends at home, and just before a six-week-long summer break that Ananya Trust has every year, Prasanna did not return to Ananya Trust and continued to find gambling games to play. When his mother asked him why he did not return to school, even after the six weeks had passed, Prasanna lied and told her the school was still having a holiday. His father also did not give him the bus fare to return. So, Prasanna continued gambling, earning about 100 rupees ($1.30 USD) a day by betting. He also got a construction job, earning an additional 50 rupees ($0.66 USD) a day. When he gave his earnings to his parents, they were happier. Prasanna did not feel the need to return to school when he felt he could appease his father's anger with his earnings and help his family have a more peaceful and financially stable life at home.

When the Dream a Dream field hockey coach pointed out to Vishal that Prasanna had been missing practice since the restart of the school after the summer break, Vishal and a Dream a Dream volunteer Shashank rode their motorbikes to Prasanna's neighbourhood to look for him. Not knowing exactly where

Prasanna lived, they walked the neighbourhood, asking people where they could find him. Prasanna was in the middle of a gambling game when one of his friends told him that people were looking for him. Hearing that it was people from Dream a Dream, Prasanna left in the middle of the game to meet them. Instead of scolding and punishing him, as might have been the treatment from other adults in his life, Vishal and Shashank took him out to eat and asked after him. Prasanna was pleasantly surprised. Moved by the thought that he was important enough to be missed and cared about enough to be sought after, Prasanna returned with them to Ananya Trust.

Prasanna stayed in touch with Vishal and Dream a Dream volunteers and staff, even as his time at Ananya Trust ended. Prasanna fully stepped up to provide for his family, when he was 15 years old, to make up for his father who was, by then, debilitated from alcohol abuse. Prasanna completed pre-university college by the time he turned 18 years old and found a job at a company. He worked at a digital media company for two years, learning to use Photoshop and other visual communication tools. When he turned 20 in 2012, he looked for a part-time job to support himself and his family while he studied in university full time. Dream a Dream was in a position to hire him. Prasanna began to work as a part-time facilitator at the After School Life Skills Programme which had, by then, developed into programmes focused on developing life skills using arts and football.

As Prasanna worked for Dream a Dream, Vishal personally financed half of Prasanna's college education, as Dream a Dream was just in its initial stages of building a scholarship programme for its students and employees. When Dream a Dream started to hire young people in 2006 to help with their programmes, the staff realised that if they wanted to retain these young people from unique backgrounds, they needed to have workplace policies that were conducive to their success. These policies included flexible hours, part-time work, opportunities to be mentored, and scholarships to support the completion of college or professional certification programmes.

Dream a Dream currently has a standing human resources policy that gives its staff the opportunity to receive up to INR 10,000 ($130 USD) to further their education. With this kind of practical and financial support, Prasanna was able to finish his bachelor's degree in business and, later, decided to pursue an additional degree in law.

When asked how Dream a Dream helped him, Prasanna reflects, "They [Dream a Dream] made me understand what my strengths are. They built in me the confidence and ability to make good decisions." He says that as he started to get to know his own strengths and interests, "I started to find myself and ask how I can build myself for the organisation, as well as for myself." One of the most important things Prasanna says he learnt was to solve his problems instead of running away from them. He reflects, "I see many children running away if they have any problems. But Dream a Dream told me not to run away from my problems; instead, they told me to stay with the problem and solve it until I see success."

When asked to give an example of how he learnt to stay and solve problems, Prasanna shared a story about asking Vishal which college he should go to. Vishal told him it was important to know his choices and to look at many colleges. Prasanna dutifully researched and visited several colleges, weighing costs, geographical proximity to his home and work, and the environment of the campuses. Prasanna recalls being frustrated by the work he had to do to conduct his own research. He wondered why it was that Vishal did not just tell him which university to go to or even tell him the names of two or three places he should consider. But, later, Prasanna realised that the challenge of solving this problem of deciding which college to go to not only built perseverance but also the practice of considering many factors before making important life choices. Prasanna believes that what he has grown into is the direct consequence of building his resilience in facing, tackling, and solving challenges. "Today, you can see I have not given up on my family. So, now I am still with my family; I'm taking care of them. This [persistence in the face of adversity] is what Dream a Dream filled me with."

Dream a Dream has given Prasanna the chance to explore, take calculated risks, and take on challenges to facilitate his growth and confidence. He decided to stay with Dream a Dream to help young people and support the teachers who help young people. Many others in the programme experience similar kinds of challenges that Prasanna faced in his family. He notes that because of his background, he had a special kind of empathy with the hundreds of thousands of children that Dream a Dream helped. When he "reflected why Vishal Sir had chosen this kind of field, and why Dr. Shashi Rao had built Ananya Trust for [him and his friends]," he realised that he also wanted to help young people. He currently plans on using his law degree to help young people in trouble with the law, taking with him the lessons he has learnt from Dream a Dream to advocate for young people.

Prasanna explains what he finds special about how Dream a Dream works with young people: "First you understand the child. Then give the child what she needs." Applied to his case, Dream a Dream staff understood that Prasanna was angry and empathised with his challenging background that had contributed to this anger.

They knew they needed to coach him and give him opportunities and tools to express his anger in healthier ways. Working with their partners at Ananya Trust, they recognised that each child is different and needs different kinds of interventions at different points. They were able to provide what Prasanna needed. Those provisions varied, according to circumstance — whether it was open, casual, continual praise on the field hockey team or an assignment to type out articles in the newspaper. They included a full-on pursuit of him into his neighbourhood to let him know that he had intrinsic value and worth as a person, regardless of his choices or behaviour. The provisions included actions that showed Prasanna that his supporters from Dream a Dream would support and accompany him in his journey to become who he wanted to be.

Prasanna shared in his interview that he is trying to change his father's alcoholism, but that he has not yet been successful. He now understands his father's behaviour and challenges better and could empathize with him. His father possibly did not have the positive experiences and supportive adults that Prasanna had while growing up. Prasanna's patience and desire to help his father is an indication of the empathy and care for other people that he learnt and saw modelled at Dream a Dream. He persists in this and other efforts to show what is possible for young people from his background, with enough support. Prasanna reflects, "People in my community think that children from vulnerable backgrounds can't achieve anything. They treat us with suspicion and distance and believe we can't do anything. Mainly, I wanted to show them… I wanted to show… that my mother, father, and brother have dignity. I want to be an example for other children from adverse backgrounds."

Prasanna's story shows that with caring and appropriate support, children with multiple sources of adversities in their backgrounds can thrive into their adulthood. As researchers note, while young people who face adversity in childhood can carry too heavy a burden, "adversity does not have wholly negative effects… and can also be pathways to compassion and competence."[19] Those who have struggled "are more likely to be inclusive, or to see the similarities between their own struggles and those of other people, and to feel empathy for those in pain."[20]

The rest of the chapters in this book profile other young adults who have experienced both tremendous adversity and tremendous success through Dream a Dream's caring and consistent presence in their lives. They explain further what these young people have found helpful in enabling them to thrive.

---

[19] Jay, p. 262; Herman, J. (1997). *Trauma and Recovery*. New York: Basic Book, p.201.
[20] ibid.

03 | Designing a Happy Life with Individualised Care and Attention

Sukanya G. V.

[Sukanya G. V., Bangalore, 2018]

Often, the road to a happy life has bumpy beginnings. This was the case for Sukanya G V, a graduate of Dream a Dream. At the time of her interview, in 2019, she was 27 years old and had been working for Dream a Dream for seven years. She currently tracks data of graduates for Dream a Dream at their After School Life Skills Programme. After speaking to graduates and based on the survey data she collects from them, she organises and offers relevant workshops based on graduates' needs and interests.

She is married to Prasanna H, another Dream a Dream graduate and staff member, whom she has known since she was 13 years old when they were at Ananya Trust together. They recently had a baby daughter, and they work to support not only themselves but also their families. Sukanya has finished college and wants to continue pursuing her interest and talent as a designer. Her road to designing for herself this fulfilling, busy, and happy life had a challenging beginning, however.

Missing Care and Attention in Early Childhood

Sukanya attended a school in her neighbourhood until the third standard. She did not do well academically. In school and in her family, she was put down and labelled as "not having the skills to study." In a school system where students sat in rank order based on their academic performance, with the "best" students sitting at the front of the class, she was relegated to the last bench in her classroom. She was mostly ignored by the adults. Other children also saw her as someone to discriminate against. She remembers that because of such discouraging treatment, "I was scared to talk to people; I was nervous all the time."

With her father being an alcoholic and unemployed, the family's finances were not good. They had trouble paying rent and other household bills. Sukanya's father also began to hit her mother. Their relatives blamed her mother for the troubles that their family faced and did not offer help. When her mother realised that they could not afford to pay Sukanya's school fees and also feed the family, her mother made the difficult decision to enrol Sukanya into Ananya Trust. It was a school for children from disadvantaged backgrounds that did not charge school fees.

INFORMATION BOX 3A: ALCOHOL USE DISORDER

A 2019 Indian government report found that of an estimated 160 million users of alcohol in India, at least 57 million Indian, or 5.2% of the population, are dependent on alcohol and need treatment for alcohol abuse. However, only one in 37 people with alcohol dependency are reportedly receiving it. There is a gender division in the number of alcohol users, with 27.3% of all men and 1.6% of women are estimated to be alcohol users.

According to the DSM-5 (Diagnostic and Statistical Manual of Mental Disorders, fifth edition), "alcohol use disorder" is a pattern of use that meets two or more of the following criteria:

- "drinking more than was intended;
- unsuccessful efforts to cut down or quit drinking;
- spending a great deal of time obtaining, consuming, or recovering from alcohol;
- a strong desire or urge to drink;
- drinking that interferes with responsibilities at work or at home;
- interpersonal problems caused by drinking;
- giving up other activities to drink;
- using alcohol in dangerous situations such as driving;
- drinking continues despite health, occupational, or social problems caused by alcohol;
- tolerance to alcohol, or a need to drink more and more;
- withdrawal from alcohol, or physical discomfort when abstaining for long period."

Meeting two or three of these criteria is to have a "mild" alcohol use disorder; having four to five symptoms qualifies as a "moderate" case, and six or more symptoms suggests the disorder is "severe." (American Psychiatric Association, 2013).

Problem drinkers are likely to suffer from related health problems, such as losing their jobs and their relationships, and even dying at an early age (Jay, 2017). The World Health Organization reports that the harmful use of alcohol is a component cause of more than 200 disease and injury conditions in individuals, most notably alcohol dependence, liver cirrhosis, cancers, and injuries. (Jernigan & WHO, 2001)

Sources:

American Psychiatric Association, (2013). Diagnostic and statistical manual of mental disorders (5th ed.). https://doi.org/10.1176/appi.books.9780890425596

Jay, M. (2017). Supernormal: The Untold Story of Adversity and Resilience. Hachette Book Group, Inc.

Jernigan, D. H., & World Health Organization, (2001). Global status report: alcohol and young people (No. WHO/MSD/MSB/01.1). World Health Organization.

The Wire Staff (2019, February 20). 57 Million Indians need treatment for alcohol abuse: Government survey. The Wire, India. https://thewire.in/health/57-million-indians-need-treatment-for-alcohol-abuse-govt-survey

World Health Organization, (n.d.). Management of Substance Abuse. https://www.who.int/substance_abuse/facts/alcohol/en/

At Ananya Trust, Sukanya was pleasantly surprised at being provided with everything she needed, including clothes and even soap. She stayed at Ananya Trust during the weekdays and went home to visit her mother on the weekends. Meaning unique, "Ananya" is located on a coconut grove. The school aims to encourage curiosity in children and allow them to find answers through inquiry, exploration, and experimentation. The staff encourage freedom and responsibility. They work actively to make children feel safe, including providing encouragement to speak their opinions without fear of ridicule.

Begun by Dr. Shashi Rao, with a doctorate in education from the United States, Ananya Trust was created with children like Sukanya in mind. Dr. Rao reflects about how and why she started Ananya Trust:

"One of the things that struck me was the examination systems, which are a means of keeping children out of the educational system, because they don't fit in with our idea of an ideal student, of what children should know, how children should talk, and how children should behave. And if children don't fit into our framework of assessment, then they are considered failures.

It brought me to thinking of all the children in India who are rejected and who are [considered] "failures" and who are thrown out of the educational system, because they don't seem to fit into the mainstream idea of an ideal student.

My question used to be, "Is there something wrong with the children?" But the more I studied, I felt it was the educational system that was failing the children; it was not the children who were failures.

So that's when I had this idea that when I do come back to India, I am going to start a school, and it will be a school for the "rejects," or the "failures" of society that people feel we cannot cope with. It's just a typical Indian backbencher mentality, you know — those in the back are not worth paying any attention to. So that's how the idea of Ananya was born, basically."

Children are grouped by ability and not by age at Ananya Trust. In addition to classroom learning, children are asked to take responsibility by helping keep the premises clean, perform kitchen duties, organise free play, and look after the younger children. Learning comes from engaging in activities and children are given responsibility and power. For example, when Ananya Trust planned a trip, the staff involved children in every decision from where and when to go, for how long, and how much to spend on what. Vishal, as he was developing Dream a Dream, saw that these kinds of activities at Ananya Trust "further strengthened the children's ability to make independent choices, work in teams, resolve dilemmas and tensions, and be decision makers."

INFORMATION BOX 3B: MUTUALLY BENEFICIAL RELATIONSHIP BETWEEN DREAM A DREAM AND ANANYA TRUST

At the beginning, Dream a Dream used to partner with other community-focused organisations such as Ananya Trust, Vishwas, Freedom Foundation, Child Fund Association, BOSCO, Makkala Jagriti, and Sukrupa. These were either institutional care homes, local organisations focused on community engagement in vulnerable communities, or residential schools such as Ananya Trust.

When Ananya Trust began in 1998, it had only 20 children and a limited budget. Dream a Dream stepped in first to donate enough money each month to provide vegetables for all the children. Along with the money came the offer that they would help in any other ways that Ananya Trust needed. With the big dream of providing individualised curricula for each child, but with limited means to do so, Ananya Trust began to approach Dream a Dream for volunteers to teach dance, music, or art — whatever children expressed interest in.

The partnership with Dream a Dream worked well because they were "exceedingly flexible," Dr. Rao recalls, stopping a program if children lost interest, whether it was after two weeks or two months. When children expressed interest in

Contd...

table tennis and hockey, for example, and Dream a Dream volunteers could sustain their commitment to teaching the sports, Ananya Trust teachers would then step in with health and biology lessons about the physical benefits of playing sports and geography lessons about which countries famous field hockey players were from.

Dr. Rao notes, "One of the most common features between Ananya and Dream a Dream is that they, like Ananya, respond to the needs of the children. It was always Dream a Dream responding to our needs, instead of imposing something, saying, we have this program, take it. It was not like that. That was what was very interesting and comfortable for us to work with."

Vishal Talreja reflects, "In the early years, Ananya's pedagogical approach helped Dream a Dream learn and gain valuable insights on how to engage and support children through our life skills interventions. The partnership was complementary and was based on trust, support, and learning from each other. While Ananya created a child-centric safe environment to help children learn, Dream a Dream complemented that with opportunities to develop life skills and get an exposure to the external world. Over the years, Ananya started running life skills interventions of their own, thus helping Dream a Dream phase out and work with other more vulnerable partners. The first 10 years of Dream a Dream's work with Ananya has helped ground and shape a lot of Dream a Dream's own pedagogical practices and vice versa."

Dr. Rao notes that Dream a Dream, while no longer running a programme at Ananya Trust, still absorbs many Ananya Trust graduates in their staff, offering guidance and employment for alumni.

Experiencing Fun, Care, Love, and Empathetic Understanding with Ananya Trust and Dream a Dream

Sukanya had just started attending Ananya Trust at 11 years of age when she first encountered Dream a Dream. This was in the early days of Dream a Dream as an organisation, and she remembers volunteers coming to play with her and her classmates for two to four hours during the weekday, about twice a week.

Starting from 2002, Dream a Dream had partnered with local organisations. As the volunteers went to shelter homes in Bangalore, they quickly learnt that these homes focused on providing basic needs of food, clothing, education, and healthcare, but that young people did not get to experience or learn a broader set of skills such as paying attention, getting along with others, or concentrating for a prolonged time on a project — skills that other children from more privileged backgrounds naturally pick up while playing sports, playing music, dancing, or making art.

Recruiting volunteers from the vibrant, young corporate sector in Bangalore, Dream a Dream conducted art-and-play-based activities on the weekends with volunteers. They engaged young people living in shelter homes or boarding schools like Ananya Trust. Dream a Dream volunteers would teach arts and crafts, play games, and provide snacks. They even started a table tennis programme for the students at Ananya Trust, based on student interest. The interested students would travel by bus to play table tennis in an academy that was 13–15 kilometres from their school and would go to different areas to play, including participating in tournaments. First, they travelled by bus, until one of the Dream a Dream volunteers began driving seven to eight of the students in a car. When Dream a Dream began to offer computer classes in the evenings, the students travelled by car to the sessions.

At the time, whatever life skills children learnt from Dream a Dream were implicit, not yet explicit. For participants, however, spending time with the Dream a Dream volunteers was nevertheless fun. Sukanya remembers enjoying her time during the three years that she was part of it. She remembers Vishal coming to Ananya Trust dressed as Santa Claus around the holidays and giving gifts to the students, for example. Whenever there were special celebrations and events, Sukanya went.

During one weekend, one of the celebrations went on until late in the evening. Sukanya was nervous about arriving home later than when she was expected at home by her parents. Vishal noticed her anxiety and asked her about it. When she told him, he offered her his phone to call home. Remembering that moment, years later,

Sukanya says, "That moment was really surprising to me because no one had offered to share their phone with me; everyone was ignoring me. Uncle Vishal showed me a lot of love. So that made me want to be with Dream a Dream and Ananya Trust more and more." These kinds of simple but concrete gestures of help and attention to her needs and feelings were something she had not been accustomed to receiving until then.

Recounting how she learnt to overcome her background of adversity and other challenges, Sukanya says that it was critical that there were people at Dream a Dream who had backgrounds like hers. She found that her manager, Revanna Marilinga, had gone through situations like hers when he shared his stories with her; his story is told in the next chapter of this book. Sukanya reflects that it was invaluable to have people who knew how to listen well instead of giving advice and rushing to solve her challenges for her. For example, Sukanya shares how Suchetha Bhat, now CEO of Dream a Dream, is a very good listener. The Dream a Dream staff "don't give suggestions; they just listen to us. Having someone there to listen to us makes us feel good," Sukanya emphasises.

As researchers note, "social support is crucial — even a key difference between those who are and are not happy…. In one study of more than seven thousand adults who had experienced early adversities, those who had social support were less likely to struggle with anxiety and depression. And multiple meta-analyses including hundreds of studies and thousands of participants show that, in both children and adults, *what predicts stress after adversity is not the severity of the event but how alone one feels afterward*"[21] (emphasis added).

---

[21] Brewin, C. R., Andrews, B. & Valentine, J. D. (2000). Meta-Analysis of Risk Factors for Posttraumatic Stress Disorder in Trauma-Exposed Adults. *Journal of Consulting and Clinical Psychology* 68 (5). 748-766; Davis,

Researcher Meg Jay notes that two of the most powerful predictors of being able to feel good in adulthood after early adversity is the sharing of secrets and having people who can provide support, with the two often going hand in hand. "Communication creates community," she notes, observing that "sharing our secrets is one way that relationships become closer and more real," and people are most likely to confide in those they can count on[22]. She also cautions that those who open up need and want people "who can be discreet, who can be trusted not to judge or to respond with ignorance."[23] Jay notes, "Those who disclose may be blamed or shamed or rejected or refuted, or they may be discouraged from further honesty. Sharing our secrets can make us feel more connected or more isolated, safer, or more endangered, depending on how others respond."[24] Thus, listening is an intentional act of healing, connecting, and finding community, when done with consideration and intention. Dream a Dream makes it a skill that they teach explicitly to their participants and staff.

L. & Siegel, L. J. (2000). Posttraumatic Stress Disorder in Children and Adolescents: A Review and Analysis. *Clinical Child and Family Psychology Review* 3 (3): 135-154; Ozer, E. J. et. al. (2003). Predictors of Posttraumatic Stress Disorder and Symptoms in Adults: A Meta-Analysis, *Psychological Bulletin* 129: 52-73; Trickery, D. et al. (2012), A Meta-Analysis of Risk Factors for Post-Traumatic Stress Disorder in Children and Adolescents, *Clinical Psychology Review* 32 (2): 122-138; Vranceanu, A., Hobfoll, S. E. & Johnson, R. J. (2007). Child Multi-Type Maltreatment and Associated Depression and PTSD Symptoms: The Role of Social Support and Stress, *Child Abuse and Neglect* 31 (1): 71-84. All cited in Jay, M. (2017). *Supernormal: The Untold Story of Adversity and Resilience*. Hachette Book Group, Inc.

[22] Jay, p.242-3. Cohen, S. (2004). Social Relationships and Health, *American Psychologist* 59 (8): 676-684; Uchino, B. N. (2006). Social Support and Health: A Review of Physiological Processes Potentially Underlying Links to Disease Outcomes, *Journal of Behavioral Medicine* 29 (4): 377-387; Umberson, D Montez, J. K. (2010). Social Relationships and Health: A Flashpoint for Health Policy, *Journal of Health and Social Behavior* 51 (1): S54-S66, in May, p.242-3.

[23] Jay, p. 243; Kelly, A. E. & McKillp, K. J. (1996). Consequences of Revealing Personal Secrets, *Psychological Bulletin* 120 (3): 450-465, cited in Jay.

[24] Jay, p.244.

 **INFORMATION BOX 3C: DREAM A DREAM'S PRACTICE OF LISTENING WELL**

People at Dream a Dream believe that listening well is key to creating connections and working effectively with young people. If someone listens to another with full attention, commitment, and support, the person who is speaking can feel affirmed and important. When young people are accepted and recognised for who they are, they are more likely to feel more comfortable expressing their feelings. They are more likely to explore their own thoughts and feelings to understand who they are. With practice, they are likely to make better decisions about the issues they are facing and find their own solutions to their problems.

Suggested Paired Sharing Exercise from Dream a Dream:

i) Get into pairs and choose who will speak first.

ii) The speaker can speak about anything that means a lot to them or what they are passionate about.

iii) The role of the listener is to listen deeply without making any verbal comments and keeping their body language to a minimum and simply open themselves to their partner without a huge visible response.

iv) Switch and have the listener become the speaker, repeat the exercise.

iv) After both speakers finish, do a short debrief on what it was like to talk, to listen, and what they learnt about themselves through this process.

Sukanya observes that the kindness with which she was treated at Ananya Trust and Dream a Dream was a dramatic contrast to her previous experiences at school, where she was ignored and dismissed if she did not do something as simple as not having her hair tied properly. "However we arrived [or looked] or [behaved], Ananya Trust and Dream a Dream used to take us," she remembers.

The staff at Ananya Trust and Dream a Dream would also encourage students, noting when they did well and telling them to keep trying when they did not. It felt good to be showered with positive attention and have her feelings and talents recognised. Sukanya reflects, "Being from adversity, the thing I was missing was a lot of love and care, but I found them at Dream a Dream and Ananya Trust. I found that I was something and that made me feel good and made me realise that I am also a human being. That made me want to be at Dream a Dream more and more."

[Sukanya at the Life Skills through Arts Programme
organised by Dream a Dream, Bangalore, 2017]

Choosing and Designing a More Expansive, Proactive, Dynamic Life

Sukanya also began going to other places around Bangalore with Dream a Dream, as well as on outdoor adventure camps to Honnemaradu ("Golden Lake") near the Linganamakki Reservoir and the Sharavathi River. In 2004, Dream a Dream began a partnership with an organisation called The Adventurers, led by Ashoka Fellow, S. L. N. Swamy and his partner Nomito Kamdar. On a beautiful campsite on the banks of the Linganamakki, The Adventurers teach children to appreciate nature and develop life skills through outdoor adventure activities. Dream a Dream used to take between 25 to 30 children on an overnight train trip from Bangalore to Honnemaradu for four-day camps. The activities included setting up and running a camp, swimming, trekking, coracling (taking special circular boats local to the region), and camping on islands in the Linganamakki Reservoir. Activities focused on learning teamwork, building leadership, problem solving, and decision making.

One of the activities included solo camping, where specific, safe campsites were designated, and young people were encouraged to spend one night camping alone. They were given a sleeping bag and provisions to start their own fire and cook their own meal. The children were spread across the campgrounds and facilitators patrolled the camp sites to ensure the children's safety. The primary aim of the activity was to develop children's independence and help them overcome fear. Sukanya remembers being directed to sleep alone in the forest and being afraid; she also remembers knowing that Dream a Dream staffers were making sure that they were safe. Sukanya recalls, "The next morning, Vishal came to us and gave us big hugs, which no one had given to us before. Even my mom and dad had not given that kind of love and affection to me, but Vishal showed a lot of love and energy. That hug helped and made me try many more things that I was afraid of doing." Sukanya says that it was those moments that encouraged her to become more confident and more able to trust herself to make decisions and to work independently. By the time she was 14 years old, she was travelling two hours from Ananya Trust to her home on the weekends by herself despite being afraid the first time she did it on her own.

Both Ananya Trust and Dream a Dream encouraged Sukanya and her classmates to explore not only new places but new interests to follow their dreams. She discovered through extracurricular activities with Dream a Dream that she enjoyed *mehndii* (decorative body art, including decorating the hands) and decorating and making greeting cards. As she decorated the halls of the school with her classmates, she was encouraged by her teachers and volunteers. "That's how I got to know that I am very good at designing," Sukanya says.

Both organisations emphasised that while what the students were learning in school was important, identifying students' interests was also important. Dream a Dream further provided a supportive and safe space where Sukanya was encouraged to reflect about what interested her. As she grew older, Sukanya began to explore jewellery and fashion design, drawing on her interest in design. When she was 17 years old, she began making terracotta jewellery and ended up working for Dream a Dream when she turned 20 years old, as a part-time facilitator for the After School Life Skills Programme. She attended college during the day and worked in the afternoons.

She says that many of the parents of the students that she works with put pressure on their children to "study, study, study" when their children might enjoy and be good at other activities like drawing. She sees education as a part of life but not the entirety of living well, and not the only path to success and happiness. She tells the story of one graduate, who also graduated from Ananya Trust, who discovered that she enjoyed dancing and was good at it. Now, she works at the gym, teaching dance and earns a good living. Sukanya called her and asked her to share her journey with students at Dream a Dream's After School Life Skills Programme, hoping to encourage others to identify their passions and see how it might provide a good pathway for a happy future.

Sukanya shares many similar stories of students at the After School Life Skills Programme who are embracing and creating more opportunities for themselves. She speaks about one young man who liked to dance and, with school friends, learnt dancing. He and his friends danced together on the After School Life Skills Programme's graduation day and performed in front of everyone. Another young woman painted *diyas* (oil lamps made from clay with a cotton wick dipped in ghee or vegetable oil) and sold them, learning about marketing, managing her money, and running a small business while also studying. The students also learnt time management. Another young woman learnt to make earrings and sold them, earning enough money to buy her college books.

Sukanya says that like her, many other staff members at Dream a Dream now virtually head their families, supporting not only themselves but also their parents and siblings. They manage their money and their households well, in part, because of the life skills that Dream a Dream taught them. She shares how she learnt to buy things for her family instead of giving them money because she learnt that when she gave money, it was not always used well. While there are no specialised programmes focused on financial literacy and management, every programme at Dream a Dream is focused on giving more agency to children and teaching them practical skills. For example, in the Table Tennis programme which Sukanya was part of, children had to manage a weekly transport and snack budget, before rides were offered by volunteers. This included planning for how much money they needed for bus tickets, how much they could spend on buying a nutritious snack after every session, and other expenses. The responsibilities were rotated among the children from week to week. When they travelled for tournaments, they were given a budget and had to manage the trip with that budget. As they got older, they also had to prepare and submit their own personal budgets.

> **INFORMATION BOX 3D: CELEBRATING A CULTURE OF CHOOSING ONE'S OWN PATH TO SUCCESS**
>
> Through the After School Life Skills Programme, Dream a Dream engages with young people until they complete the ninth standard, so that by the time they reach the 10th standard, they would have the skills to be responsible young adults. At this juncture, in celebration of their new-found independence, Dream a Dream organises a graduation ceremony — an official declaration that participants are now Dream a Dream graduates, well equipped with skills to face the challenges of the fast-changing world. All young people who have been part of the programme for at least one year are included.
>
> During the ceremony, graduates share their stories about questioning conventional paths, re-imagining what it means to be successful, and being confident and unapologetic about who they are. The After School Life Skill Programme encourages participants to question conventional paths and explore their interests by creating space for young people to explore different career opportunities. For example, young people attend Dream Fundays, workshops, and events that give them a broad understanding of the opportunities around them. The sessions are designed to help young people understand their strengths; young people are given an opportunity to apply these strengths in practical ways.
>
> One of the main reasons young people end up following conventional career paths or choices is the fear of being ostracised by family and community. The facilitators at the After School Life Skill Programme act as role models/ambassadors to the young people in the sessions as they share their own journeys of making unconventional choices and choosing unconventional career paths. The sessions in the programme help young people build the skill of standing up for themselves, negotiating different viewpoints, and having healthy conversations with parents to help them understand young peoples' passions that might appear unconventional to more traditional viewpoints.
>
> The graduation ceremony is a culture-building opportunity to bring all young people from across centres together on a common platform to celebrate and become role models for each other in finding out and following their dreams. It is also an opportunity for Dream a Dream's supporters to witness the impact of the organisation's work.

Sukanya summarises her own journey with Dream a Dream as one where the organisation was responsive to her strengths and challenges as a staff member, just as they were responsive to her needs when she was a programme participant. When Sukanya moved from being an After School Life Skills Programme facilitator to apply for the position of being an executive assistant for Vishal, he did not look at her resume. Instead, he suggested that she try out the role for a week. After that week, they decided to have her try the role for a month. She says she appreciated how Dream a Dream gave her time to learn instead of immediately judging her competence and fit with the job. She admits that at the beginning, she was nervous and afraid to talk to new people, including sending emails or booking reservations for Vishal and having to speak to customer service. But slowly, after repeatedly doing the tasks, she became less nervous and more confident. Dream a Dream and Sukanya did decide, however, that the role was not the best fit for her, so they found her the current role of tracking data of the graduates of the After School Life Skills Programme. Sukanya says that she recognises and appreciates Dream a Dream's effort to find her another role instead of just telling her to stop and asking her to leave the position and the organisation.

Designing Her Happy Life

When she became pregnant after marrying Prasanna, her childhood sweetheart from Ananya Trust, Sukanya was able to take some time to read and study by watching videos about how to best support her child. With her child, Sukanya sees herself as growing up, with having less time to waste and to focus more on working, not only at her job but also at home. Her younger sister currently stays with her and helps with the baby, and Sukanya's mother and father live nearby. She says that even when she was on maternity leave, Pavithra ("Pavi"), her manager at the Career Connect Centre and a mother herself, would text her and ask about her baby. She says that Pavithra, whose story is told later in this book, encourages her to bring the baby to the office if she needs to. Sukanya says that kind of care and support gives her energy.

Sukanya is learning to make new decisions and making plans for her day-to-day life that has changed since the arrival of the baby. She is learning how to take care of herself as a new mother and how to continue to take care of her family, with new responsibilities. She says she can feel herself changing, even as she continues to learn and adapt to this new life stage. Her efforts to have a thriving life have a different, more mature focus, such as how to maintain a secure job and arrange to have her baby cared for while she works. But she focuses on moving forward and making adjustments to create a happy life that meets these new challenges and opportunities.

As she has matured, she has drawn from the reflection activities that Dream a Dream encourages in their participants. While she was on maternity leave, she found that she had a bit more time to be by herself, in a quiet place, while her baby took her naps. She reflects that not only is she growing in her management of her time but also in her management of with whom and how she shares her struggles. Before, as a young girl, she would readily trust anyone and go to them with her problems. It was helpful and enabled her to learn many things. But as she has matured, she says she has learnt to think critically about this practice and is teaching herself to not immediately always go to someone else — whether to people at work or to her extended family and friends — when faced with her problems. She finds herself wanting to be less dependent on others, especially those who want her to be dependent on them, or those who might want to take advantage of her vulnerability and use it to fan their own ego and feelings of power over her. She says she is learning to be more careful in selecting the few people who can be trusted with her private struggles — people who were not just going to use what she told them to make themselves look or feel better.

In other words, Sukanya is thoughtfully designing a happy life for herself, even as her life changes with the arrival of a new baby. A happy life, for her, involves not only work, but taking care of her immediate and extended families; it involves managing not only her time but her relationships with others. None of what she is doing has been explicitly taught to her. Nonetheless, the care, attention, and kindness shown to her throughout her youth by the staff and volunteers at Ananya Trust and Dream a Dream have taught her to value her time, her interests and passions, her relationships, her work, her family, and herself, and to think of ways that she could make choices to enable her to design a happy, thriving life.

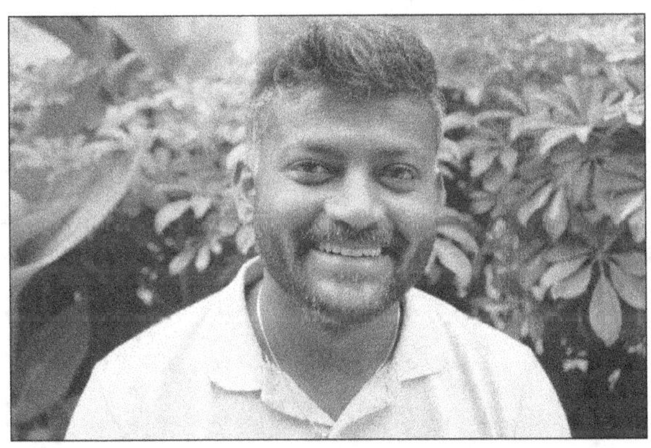

[Revanna Marilinga, Bangalore, 2022]

Sukanya's stories about being relegated to the back bench and ignored at schools has echoes in other graduates' stories as well. Revanna Marilinga was born in a small village in the Mandya district, a largely agricultural area, some 70 miles away from Bangalore. His parents worked for daily wages, so even as a toddler, he was left at home by himself, as an only child. He tried and failed twice in the school selection process. The school headmaster and teachers would visit his village to ask parents about the ages of their children. If the parents did not know the age of the child, the school authorities would ask children to touch their ears. They believed that those who could touch their ears, when asked, were at least five years old and could attend school, but Revanna could not. Thus, Revanna associated the feeling of failing with school, even before he set a foot in a classroom.

When he did make it to school after the third time of taking the test, it was an even bigger disappointment. Not only did his school not allow him to play, but there were active restrictions that he was not used to at home. While at home, he could play, eat, or sleep. But at school, all he felt he was allowed to do was to sit and listen to the teacher.

Without any prior formal learning experiences nor preparation for school, Revanna felt "very weak" and "totally ill-prepared to learn," he recalls. "In the third standard, we were expected to write sentences, but when I was unable to recognise letters, how could I write sentences?" he laments. The response from the school authorities was not to provide him with extra help but beatings from the teachers when he was unable to answer their questions.

Revanna decided that between his apparent inability to learn and the daily painful, tear-inducing beatings from teachers "school was not for me." When he informed his mother that he would not continue his education, his parents said that not going to school was not an option. To his parents, sending him to school was the only way to ensure that they had regular childcare so that they could focus on working and earning their livelihood. His parents insisted that he continue to attend school.

Revanna coped as he could, by walking to school, putting his bag inside the classroom, then running out to play in the field by the school, and then returning home by lunch time. He maintained this routine until the end of the academic year when his parents found out that he was not eligible to take the final examination because of his poor attendance record. When the principal told his parents about Revanna's absences from school, his parents were in disbelief at first. Then they insisted that he attend school, no matter how painful the punishments were. Perhaps his parents wanted him to have more choices than they did, by attending school, or perhaps they thought that the physical punishments were no less ordinary than what they themselves had experienced in school. When Revanna tried to insist that he could help them with their work instead of enduring daily beatings on his knees at school, his parents did not listen to him.

INFORMATION BOX 4A: SCHOOL READINESS

School readiness refers to whether a child has the skills to make a successful transition into school. In addition to some academic basics, school readiness skills also include "self-care, attention and concentration, physical skills (e.g., having the endurance to sit upright for an entire school day), emotional regulation, language skills and play and social skills" (Kid Sense, 2016). Key aspects of this include being able to self-regulate their behaviours and emotions, the ability to articulate and express themselves, and the ability to interact with and negotiate with peers in accordance with social norms.

In the United States, studies have shown that fewer than half of children from low-income households are ready for school at five years of age as compared with 75% of children from moderate- or high-income households (Webb, M. & Dowd K. et al, 2009; cited in Williams & Learner, 2019). Head Start and Early Head Start are U.S. Federal programmes that promote school readiness of children from birth to age five, for families who have incomes below the federal poverty level (10% of the programme participants can also be from families above the federal poverty level, and 35% of the programme participants can also be from families above the federal poverty level but below 130% of the federal poverty level). The programmes enhance the cognitive, social, and emotional development of infants, toddlers, pregnant women, and their families. The programmes help build relationships with families that support family well-being and view parents as "their child's first and most important teacher." (US Government, n.d.)

School readiness can thus be seen not only as the responsibility of children and families but also of schools to receive children and of the community to support optimal early childhood development. The American Academy of Paediatricians issued a technical report about school readiness, for example, that argues that paediatricians have a role to play in school readiness, given their regular and ready access to young children and their families (Williams & Learner, 2019).

Contd...

For a more general discussion about the state of education in India and India-specific data, please see the series of reports issued by the ASER Centre (*https://www.asercentre.org/Keywords/p/371.html*). The ASER 2020 report, for example, notes that households increasingly have the resources with which to support their children's education; in rural areas, for example, more than a third of parents of five- to eight-year-olds had completed the fourth standard or higher (Bhattacharjea, 2021).

Source:

Aser Centre (n.d.). ASER 2020 Wave 1. http://www.asercentre.org/Keywords/p/371.html

Bhattacharjea, S (2021). Supporting young children in the time of COVID. Aser Centre.

Kid Sense. (2016, November 28). *School Readiness. https://childdevelopment.com.au/areas-of-concern/school-readiness/*

Williams P.G., Lerner, M.A. (2019). School Readiness. AAP Council on Early Childhood, AAP Council on School Health. Pediatrics. 144(2): e20191766 https://pediatrics.aappublications.org/content/144/2/e20191766

US Government, (n.d.). Head Start and Early Head Start. https://www.benefits.gov/benefit/616

Webb, M., Dowd, K., Harden, B. J., Landsverk, J. & Testa, M. (2009). Child welfare and child well-being: New perspectives for the national survey of child and adolescent well-being. Oxford: Oxford Press.

Running Away to Bangalore

Disappointed and angry with his parents for not being sympathetic to his physically and psychologically painful experiences at school, Revanna snuck on a passing train to Bangalore, thinking he could find a job in the big city. He was just eight years old. He looked for jobs in different places, but no one would hire him. As he sat in the Bangalore railway station, crying, staff members from BOSCO (Bangalore Oniyavara Seva Coota), an organisation that worked with street children and provided them with shelter and basic education, found him. Founded in 1980, BOSCO takes in about 650 children from the street each year in Bangalore. Revanna gave all false answers to their questions about his background because he did not want to return home and be forced to go to school. His goal was to find work and earn money to prove himself before returning home. He found that at the shelter home, there were basically two groups — one group of children who attended school and another group who chose to work. He also found out that he had to be at least 14 years old in order to work, and that he could not even work part time until then. He stayed in the shelter home, not attending school. As he observed the children going to school, he noticed that those children participated in activities outside of school. Not only did they attend school from 8 o'clock in the morning to 4 o'clock in the afternoon, but they also went to cultural activities in the evenings and played sports. Wanting to go on field trips and play sports with them, Revanna finally overcame his fear of going to school and told the counsellors at BOSCO that he wanted to go to school.

INFORMATION BOX 4B: STREET CHILDREN IN INDIA

In 1994, UNICEF estimated 11 million street children in India, a figure considered a drastic under-estimation of the actual figures (Ikram, 2018). According to the UNICEF report in 2000, which is the most recent figure available, there are 18 million street children in India, which is the highest in world street children's data (UNICEF, 2000).

UNICEF (2000) defines street children as children in difficult circumstances who are living on the streets. There may be multiple factors that lead children to live on the streets. Some may have been abandoned by their families; others may have been sent to cities from rural areas with the hope that they would be able to support the family in coming out of intense poverty; still others may have run away from dysfunctional institutions and homes that did not meet their needs.

It is difficult to estimate the number of street children. However, attempts have been made. One of the studies estimated 45,000 street children in Bangalore, out of which 25,000 were homeless (Bose, 1992). Nonetheless, it can be said that the number of street children is significant enough to demand a policy-level change to cater to the challenges and needs of such children.

Contd...

Sources:
Bose, A.B. (1992). The Disadvantaged Urban Child in India, Innocenti Occasional Papers, Urban Child Series no. 1, International Child Development Centre, Florence

Ikram, M. (2018, October 25). Street Children – Statistics, Their Lives and Why We Have to Care, https://inbreakthrough.org/street-children-statistics-lives/

UNICEF (2000, November 1). The state of the world's children 2000. UNICEF. https://www.unicef.org/reports/state-worlds-children-2000

Discovering a Passion and Talent for Swimming and Learning Not to Give Up

When Revanna started going to school in Bangalore, he discovered his love for sports. Father Cyriac, the director of the BOSCO Centre, firmly believed that sports could help the children at the centre. BOSCO had partnered with different sports coaching academies for cricket and swimming and established a partnership with Dream a Dream for field hockey and table tennis. Revanna tried cricket, but found he was not very good at it; he tried field hockey and found the same thing. He tried table tennis a couple of times but had no success. He remembers that throughout his many attempts at different sports, "there were no judgmental statements" made by volunteers and staff when he could not play well. He recalls, "When I failed hockey, nobody scolded me, no one beat me. When I failed cricket, though they had put more effort into coaching me than they had for other players, they did not express their disappointment. They gave me space to find a sport that was suitable for me."

That process of trial and error in an environment that centred on him as a young person discovering his talents led Revanna to try swimming. Not only did he learn to swim but discovered that he was excellent at it. Revanna was selected with 24 other young people to be coached to learn how to swim every weekend by another BOSCO organisational partner. After those sessions, he was selected to receive coaching every day for two hours during regular school hours. He swam with the Basavanagudi Aquatic Centre for five years. Even with just a basic swim gear sponsored by the coaches that he found embarrassing to wear in front of others who were outfitted in more expensive and better gears, Revanna ended up being selected to travel and represent the club and the state of Karnataka in swimming competitions for five years.

In order to continue to participate in sports, he kept up his studies and attended school. He participated in other Dream a Dream activities, such as Dream Fundays and Outdoor Adventure Camps, learning life skills along with his classmates and having a fun time playing. He recalls that he gained confidence, such as being more comfortable speaking in front of others, not only in his native language but also in English. For example, he rejected at first an opportunity to co-host Dream a Dream's annual celebration event because he was insecure about his ability to speak English in front of others. But Dream a Dream staff did not give up and persuaded him to prepare by reading from a script. They practised with him for a week. By the time of the event, he was able to speak in front of donors and other stakeholders. Revanna recalls, "I was so confident that my stage fear and fear of speaking in English disappeared. It changed my life." With his English skills that he was continuing to work on even at the time of this interview, at age 29, Revanna hosts visitors from abroad, has spoken at multiple conferences, and has led multiple teams from Dream a Dream to Wales, Brazil, and elsewhere. Reflecting on all the support that he received while trying different sports until he found swimming and the other guided challenges that Dream a Dream helped him to overcome, Revanna says, "I learnt not to give up."

> **INFORMATION BOX 4C: THE BENEFITS OF PLAYING SPORTS**
>
> In 2005, Dream a Dream was running 16 different arts and sports programmes. But in 2006, they decided to narrow the activities to teaching life skills through football and creative arts. The decision was borne out of necessity as several of the programmes were easily disrupted due to the lack of coaches or venues. But football could easily be played anywhere and creative arts could be taught in schools. They had learnt over the years that sports was a useful activity to teach life skills such as cooperation, conflict resolution, teamwork, communication, and perseverance. Researchers have documented the physical, psychological (positive attitudes, self-efficacy, resilience, reduction of anxiety, etc.), social (sense of belonging, empowerment, cooperation, etc.), lifestyle, health, and cognitive (problem-solving, working memory, goal setting, and planning) outcomes of physical education (OECD, 2020).
>
> Among children who have been through adverse childhood experiences, those who were involved in team sports during their adolescence were associated with less depression and anxiety in young adulthood. Aside from the positive effects of staying physically active, the interpersonal aspect of team sports often leads to better social interactions and better self-esteem. Group sports also have an inherent element of accountability, which often leads to important and simple forms of social support (Klass, 2019).
>
> **Sources:**
>
> Klass, P. (2019, July 8). Team Sports May Help Children Deal With Trauma. New York Times. https://www.nytimes.com/2019/07/08/well/family/team-sports-may-help-children-deal-with-trauma.html
>
> OECD (2020). Making physical education dynamic and inclusive for 2030: International curriculum analysis. Paris. https://www.oecd.org/education/2030-project/contact/OECD_FUTURE_OF_EDUCATION_2030_MAKING_PHYSICAL_DYNAMIC_AND_INCLUSIVE_FOR_2030.pdf

On Staff with Dream a Dream

About two years into staying at BOSCO, Revanna had the opportunity to return to his village to see his family. But because he had given false information at the beginning and because he had forgotten the name of his village, they had trouble finding out where he lived. But eventually, the BOSCO staff were able to find his village. When he returned, he found out that both of his parents had passed away. "My life is over," Revanna thought. His extended family were there, so he stayed with his uncle and aunt for a little while, but he quickly realised that he was being treated differently than his cousins. So, he decided to return to BOSCO and to Bangalore, where he felt he had received more support than he did in his village.

Revanna found that with a different teaching method at BOSCO than his village school, he did better at school, particularly in maths. Volunteers from different organisations who came to teach maths would encourage Revanna and his classmates. When he was able to get a job at a hotel and worked part time for two to three years, he was able to practice counting money. Whenever there was a maths competition, he used to get the maximum number of points. Because he had initially entered the third standard when he arrived in BOSCO, to learn basic reading and writing skills, even though he was over age, he skipped the eighth and ninth standard to take the 10th standard examination. With targeted tutoring, he passed his exam. As BOSCO expected its students to live independently after the 10th standard, Revanna moved to another centre. There, however, the resources for continuing to play sports were not the same. As he continued his studies in pre-university college, he started to look for a part-time job and for ways to continue his sports career.

At an annual marathon race in Bengaluru, Revanna participated with his friend Manju, hoping to find a sponsor for his competitive running career. There, he found Vishal, who asked after him. Vishal had first met Revanna nearly eight years ago when he had visited BOSCO on weekends for different Life Skills programmes with other Dream a Dream volunteers. Vishal had met Revanna during an art workshop, helping the boys connect with their dreams and draw their dreams on paper. Vishal remembered Revanna's drawing as being particularly riveting as he drew an army officer saluting the Indian national flag. Vishal remembered Revanna saying that he would like to be an army officer and that he loved the movie actor Rajnikanth, and he loved to eat biryani. Through his encounters with Revanna over the years, Vishal had noted Revanna's zeal, drive, leadership, emotional stability, and resilience.

When Vishal met Manju and Revanna at the marathon, and they mentioned that they were looking for a job, Vishal asked them to come to the Dream a Dream office for a conversation about their dreams and aspirations. Revanna shared that he had a dream to work with young people using sports to teach life skills. He said he strongly believed that children who come from vulnerable backgrounds have impressive talents and skills, but they are not getting any chance to showcase them. He said, "Sports has changed my life; I want to use sports as a medium to inspire young people and youth." Shortly after, Dream a Dream offered them part-time facilitator roles in the After School Life Skills Programme, and Revanna was able to finish his bachelor of arts degree while working at Dream a Dream. Even though he felt he had no idea how to behave during a job interview, Revanna found himself hired.

Many years later, Revanna shared with Vishal that he did not even have the money to take a bus from the BOSCO Centre to the Dream a Dream office to attend the interview; he had walked nearly 7 kilometres to get there. For the first month, until he received his first salary, Revanna did not have enough money for bus and food, and on some days, the only meal he would eat was the lunch brought by Vishal from his home that he shared with team members. He sighed with relief when he received his first salary at Dream a Dream. Vishal says that this first experience of hiring alumni and listening to their stories helped Dream a Dream recognise and understand some of the contextual challenges their graduates faced; he and the staff could then design organisational policies that supported more alumni to join as staff. For example, Dream a Dream began to include travel allowances and financial support for staff to continue their studies among other offerings that benefited graduates.

Dream a Dream decided to hire their own graduates as staff to give "power to community leaders to solve their communities' problems by using community resources," says Vishal. Dream a Dream had, by then, developed a philosophy and culture through practice — they practice non-judgement, do not punish, and do not use hurtful words towards children. They found that it was more challenging to find sports coaches who could readily practice those behaviours and that most external people they hired tended to teach more sports skills than life skills. By hiring and training their own facilitators, who were often alumni of the programme, however, they found they were able to prioritise the teaching of life skills and support young people and youth to thrive in their life.

Dream a Dream also believes that youth from the local community are the best people to understand the community problems and solve their problems. For example, one of the activities Dream a Dream supports is creating playgrounds and community spaces for young people. Under Revanna's leadership, a few youths from the Roopenaagraahar community picked the need for a playground as an issue they wanted to solve. They identified an empty space where lots of garbage was dumped into the empty land. They spoke to local leaders, political leaders and school leaders and cleaned up the garbage and created a safe community ground where people could play and conduct sports activities. Since the establishment of a clean and safe shared space, the community ground has been used by many school sports activities and sports tournaments. Dream a Dream also uses that community ground to conduct life skills sessions.

Hiring alumni facilitators ensures that they practice four of the big ideas of Dream a Dream:

1. When we develop life skills within us, we can develop life skills in others.
2. When we learn through experience, the learning lasts a lifetime.
3. We all respond well to caring and compassionate adults.
4. We all have a valid desire to be seen and heard. (Dream a Dream, n.d.)

In his role as Dream a Dream's facilitator for the After School Life Skills Programme in football, Revanna would take children to the field outside schools, and while external football coaches conducted technical skill sessions for two hours, Revanna would lead reflection circles about life skills. As he ran these sessions, Revanna noted his own discomfort when he saw other coaches scolding children for making mistakes during football practice. Revanna knew that the children who came to Dream a Dream programmes were often scolded or beaten by parents and teachers, as he once had been. He had valued, as a child, Dream a Dream's warm, non-judgmental, and kind environment even more than the technical sports skills they taught. He wanted the children to experience the same supportive and caring relationship with adults that he knew they would not get otherwise. He shared his thoughts with his manager. True to Dream a Dream's culture of receptivity to feedback, after internal discussions, they decided to facilitate the football sessions with Dream a Dream-trained facilitators instead of outsourcing technical coaching to others. So, Revanna began to facilitate the football sessions himself.

INFORMATION BOX 4D: DREAM A DREAM'S PRACTICE OF SELECTING STAFF WHO CAN VALIDATE THE EXPERIENCES OF YOUNG PEOPLE

Currently, 40%–60% of the Dream a Dream staff are graduates of the programme, like Revanna, who are able to show the patience that they themselves were shown when they were programme participants as children. Dream a Dream hires not only passionate but also compassionate people who can listen with empathy and without judgement. This is because young people often go through experiences that need to be understood. The most effective way to do this is to listen with care as young people process these experiences for themselves.

Having their experiences validated strengthens programme participants' trust in the teacher or facilitator and supports a culture of healthy communication. Invalidating behaviour, such as scolding, dismissing, or trivialising the challenges young people face, can cause issues such as making it more difficult for young people to identify their own feelings; it may create shame, feelings of worthlessness, and high levels of fear and anxiety. These feelings, when internalised, can lead to chaotic relationships, uncontrollable expressions of emotions, an inability to trust adults, and avoidant behaviour (Kennedy & Pearson, 2007).

Source:
Kennedy, F. & Pearson, D. (2007). The Dream Mentoring Manual: Life Skills Development for Youth from Vulnerable Backgrounds.

[Revanna with Dream a Dream young people during Spoorthi Football Tournament, Bangalore, 2013]

Learning to Lead

In 2014, Revanna was selected as a young leader for the FIFA World Cup 2014 football festival supported by Street Football World Network. He was able to take a group of children from Dream a Dream to Brazil to represent India. Dream a Dream was among the 40 NGOs invited from around the world that used football as a medium for social change. Revanna recalls it as another "life-changing experience, a huge turning point" for him, not the least because of the challenges he had to face and overcome. For example, when they were preparing the Dream a Dream team to travel overseas, they found out that the young participants did not have any documents that were necessary to obtain passports, such as birth certificates and proof of address. Revanna frantically contacted authorities such as the Bruhat Bengaluru Mahanagara Palike (BBMP) office that is the responsible administrative body for Bengaluru. Through it, Revanna learnt in real time, under tremendous pressure, how to navigate bureaucracy and work with government officials.

Revanna was also part of the festival design team and played a big role in the execution of the festival with the hosts. It built his confidence to know that he had the skills to lead a global event with others. The trip abroad was also an eye-opening experience for him. On whether he would enjoy going on future trips, Revanna says that while he would enjoy it, he would prefer that others from Dream a Dream go, as he wants others to experience what he learnt and gained from the trip. His answer was in alignment with the admirable leader that Revanna has become and the traits that he had seen modelled by others at Dream a Dream.

It was 2009 when he began to work for Dream a Dream, and for the next 10 years, he continually increased his responsibilities, starting as a field coordinator, then becoming a programme facilitator, anchor, and then associate manager. His love of spending time with the children participating in the programmes has driven him to spend extra time with them, dropping children off at their homes if sessions run late, or visiting their homes to understand their families and their lives. Having continually exceeded expectations and being a supportive colleague in the organisation, he rose rapidly at Dream a Dream. Now, at 29 years old, Revanna manages the entire After School Life Skills Programme for over 5,500 students, across 28 schools, with 40 facilitators and six full-time staff. Revanna has also been instrumental in building the next-generation leadership at Dream a Dream through his work with young people like Vishnu, Ranjith, Pallavi, Manja, and many others who look up to him for guidance, advice, and validation.

As a manager, he has learnt to consider everyone's perspectives, including the perspectives of donors, facilitators, other staff, and Dream a Dream as an organisation. He continually reflects on his knowledge about his strengths, such as his tendency to always move towards accomplishing new goals. "I cannot sit quietly," he says. "I will set a new milestone every time I achieve a goal, so the next goal is always bigger and further away." It was this kind of thinking that led him to believe that being a facilitator limited how he wanted to influence the lives of the young people with whom he worked. He found himself asking, "Why do the children I teach have to wait for Revanna to smile? Why do they have to wait for a Dream a Dream class to laugh and have fun? Why can't they smile, laugh, and have fun in their regular classes?"

He did not keep these questions to himself; rather, he posed them to others on staff, including Vishal and Suchetha. These kinds of conversations among staff led to the development of the Teacher Development Programme (TDP) that would enable teachers to learn the skills to create the space in which children could feel safe, laugh, and have fun. The staff also began developing a parent coaching program in 2018, knowing that along with the teacher's, parents' role in the day-to-day happiness of children is important. Dream a Dream is now planning programmes to equip parents with life skills.

But they also know that there are other issues to solve. When Revanna hears about the stories of the children he works with, he knows that many of them come from single-parent households or households where both parents work from early morning until late at night. Children are not able to share their feelings because of the absence of adults around them; moreover, parents do not often know what the children are thinking, feeling, and experiencing as often the only time they may see their children is when their sons and daughters are sleeping. Revanna understands these issues and knows that the Dream a Dream facilitators fill in an important gap in children's lives.

What Revanna and other Dream a Dream staff intuited about the importance of providing children with caring adults has been substantiated by research. Researcher Meg Jay writes the following about the positive impact of having positive relationships with adults for young people: "In the National Longitudinal Study of Adolescent Health, a study of more than twelve thousand individuals, what most protected at-risk teens from poor outcomes was feeling connected to a parent or a teacher or a mentor. In another longitudinal endeavour, this one a fourteen-year study of nearly seven hundred diverse youth and their families, it was parents, friends, teachers, mentors, relatives, and lovers who were the 'lifelines' that saved those who found themselves swimming against the current. In more research, tracing the lives of three hundred teenage mothers over seventeen years, the support of parents or significant others made it more likely for these young women to excel at school and in work." (Jay, 2017, p.290)[25]

Revanna reflects that as a manager, he takes care to not just instruct his staff but to inspire them and act as a role model for them. When he plans events like the Life Skills Day, an annual day in November that celebrates Dream a Dream's work with life skills, he asks his team about what they want to do and how they could take the activities "to the next level" while keeping the children at the centre. They weave each other's ideas to form a coherent plan for the day. He listens to the staff as they share personal and professional challenges and successes.

When asked to name his biggest current challenge in managing and leading, he laughs and says that the biggest challenge is that at 29, he is "too young" for the role. He also speaks about the need to become better at speaking and communicating and that he is seeking coaching and mentoring from Suchetha Bhat, the current CEO of Dream a Dream. He adds that as a manager, the work can be stressful sometimes, but that he has realised over the years that getting angry or shouting at people does not help. Rather, he has learnt to identify the issue or problem, and then ask what kinds of skills or attitudes are missing that have contributed to the creation of the challenge. He then asks how he can help bring awareness about the issue to the people who are involved. He says he knows not to blame himself or others but to create safe spaces in which they could discuss and make good decisions. He says that Vishal

---

[25] Cited in Jay, M. (2017): Resnick, M. D. et. al. (1997). Protecting Adolescents from Harm: Findings from the National Longitudinal Study on Adolescent Health, *Journal of the American Medical Association* 278 (10): 823-832; Cairns, R. B. & Cairns, B. D. (1994). Lifelines and Risks: Passages of Youth in our Time. New York: Cambridge University Press; Furstenberg, F. F., Brooks-Gunn, J. & Morgan, S. P. (1987). Adolescent Mothers in Later Life. New York: Cambridge University Press.

and Suchetha have helped him with their mentoring and coaching by asking him reflective questions such as "What is the real issue here?" and then standing by and supporting him with his decisions. "There is no fear of failure," Revanna reflects. His mentors and coaches have helped him to "take great learning from failures with the request 'Don't do these things again.'"

Revanna also acknowledges that he has at times, perhaps focused too much on work, at the expense of his personal life. "I can forget about my personal life. I need to marry and enjoy my life [instead of] being fully in a work, work, work mode," he says. "If there was free time, everyone else would go to the movies, or chat with a friend. But when I had free time, I would run away to the Dream a Dream office. I didn't see it as a job; I enjoyed playing football, rugby, table tennis, and field hockey with children. It was more fun for me to completely commit to caring about these people. It was easy to do as Dream a Dream people were never judgmental; they never disappointed me, and they always listened to me. I wanted to learn from visionaries like Vishal, Bobby, and Rakesh. I also met people like Geeta, an English teacher, who taught many graduates from BOSCO. While other schools asked for documents such as birth certificates from children, she didn't ask for them, which was a good thing as we didn't have any, having run away from home. Even though she was retired, she continued to come to BOSCO to hold English classes for children. Meeting and knowing these kinds of people really motivated and inspired me to continue to work for Dream a Dream. I know that I missed some parts of life, such as my family, parents, my parents' love and care, or having a girlfriend, because of the choices I made. But I feel like I made good choices in the area of helping other people to thrive. I'm very, very proud of graduates like Pallavi, who takes care of her father and the rest of her family. When I hear Manja's story or Vishnu's story, I am reminded of the impact of what we do." (Pallavi, Manja, and Vishnu's stories are included later in this book.)

Revanna recalls that when he was in high school and doing very well in sports, he had a dream of winning a gold medal for India in the Olympic games. It did not happen, but he believes that when he joined as a staff member of Dream a Dream, the dream came true, in that he and Dream a Dream are enabling everyone to achieve gold medals in their chosen areas of passion. He believes that Dream a Dream exists to allow children to follow their own passion, "not Dream a Dream's passion." He believes: "Leadership is not hidden with a single person." And he is committed to ensuring that Dream a Dream nurtures many leaders like himself.

05 Learning to Make Good Decisions through Dream a Dream's Mentoring Programme

Vijay Bhaskar S.

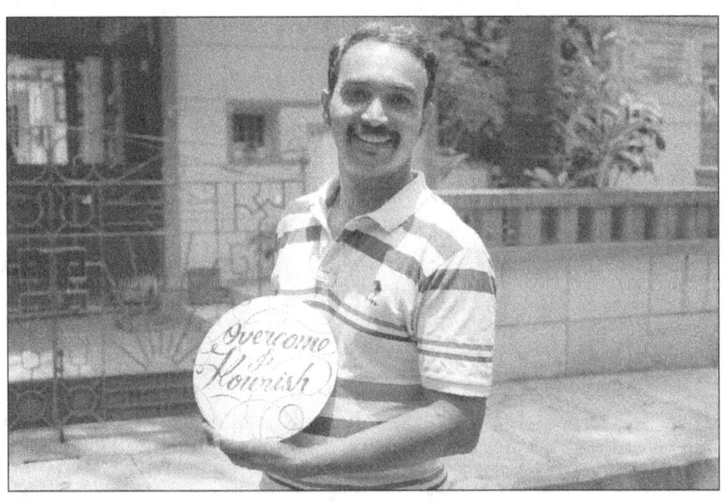

[Vijay Bhaskar, Bangalore, 2022]

Just as Revanna had run away from home to find a job in Bangalore to support his family as an eight-year-old, other young children in Bangalore live with a crushing awareness of their families' financial needs. Some work in terrible conditions to support their families. Karnataka is India's primary producer of silk thread, with the town of Ramanagaram in Bangalore Rural District housing the largest cocoon market in Asia[26].

---

[26] Human Rights Watch, (2003, January 23). Child slaves abandoned to India's silk industry. https://www.hrw.org/news/2003/01/23/child-slaves-abandoned-indias-silk-industry#

The production of silk depended on bonded children, usually under the age of 14, as late as 2003, when Human Rights Watch issued an 85-page report "Small Change: Bonded Child Labour in India's Silk Industry.[27]" According to this report, between 60,000 and 100,000 children worked twelve or more hours a day, six and a half or seven days a week in Karnataka's silk industry, enduring physical and verbal abuse. They often suffered a variety of health problems, working in crowded, damp, and poorly ventilated rooms with poor lighting that lead to vision problems and injuries to the hand.

Starting as young as age five, they earn from nothing at all to around Rs. 400 (USD $8.33) a month, some or all of which is deducted against loans taken by their families, ranging from about Rs. 1,000 to 10,000 ($13 to $132 USD). The children are usually Muslim, Dalit, or from lower castes. As of 2003, in Bangalore Rural District, no one has been convicted of some 10,000 cases of bonded labour that the Karnataka state government identified in 2000 and 2001[28].

Stitched clothes were considered impure during rituals in ancient India, and the sari follows this Hindu philosophy of purity by allowing the wearer to drape woven cloth over the torso and legs[29]. A sari weaver since he was little, Vijay was afraid he would be punished severely after making a big mistake in one of the saris he was weaving. So, Vijay ran away from home when he was about fourteen years old, in 2004. After wandering for about three days by himself between Bangalore and Mysore, he was taken in by officials and was taken to BOSCO. He knew that he had a better opportunity to study at BOSCO, so with his parents' permission,

---

[27] ibid.

[28] ibid.

[29] Nandan, J. L. (2017). *Pukka Indian: 100 objects that define India.* Roli Books.

he stayed at BOSCO for the next seven years. It was there that he began to participate in Dream a Dream's programmes.

> **INFORMATION BOX 5A: HOW CASTE-BASED DISCRIMINATION CONTRIBUTES TO BONDED LABOUR**
>
> According to Human Rights Watch (2003), Dalits and low-caste Hindus are most vulnerable to bonded labour for the following reasons:
> 1. Upper castes expect Dalits will perform free services.
> 2. Dalits are typically landless and, therefore, economically dependent on their employers. Economic dependency keeps them from reporting atrocities against them.
> 3. Upper castes can levy social and economic boycotts against Dalit communities who try to assert their rights.
> 4. Upper castes dominate local political bodies, the police, and the judiciary, bonded labour vigilance committees, and child labour committees that are supposed to enforce existing laws about bonded and child labour.
> 5. Discrimination against Dalit children in school encourages them to drop out and be sent to work.
>
> **Source:**
> Human Rights Watch, (2003, January 23). Child slaves abandoned to India's silk industry. https://www.hrw.org/news/2003/01/23/child-slaves-abandoned-indias-silk-industry#

When he was interviewed for this chapter, Vijay was 29 years old and had been married happily for five years. He proudly showed off the photo album of his wedding, with photo after photo of the happy day and their families. When we joked that he must have been happy as we could easily see that he had put on weight since he had gotten married, he grinned and agreed. He had been a manager and cashier at a branch of a large ice cream shop chain called Corner House for five years. He says he works diligently, six days per week, in 8- to 12-hour shifts. He had gotten the job after earning a bachelor's degree in business management.

Vijay has dreams of owning his own home on his own land and his own store — perhaps a food chain store — before he starts having children with his wife. He has dreams of his wife taking care of the business so that she "could be her own boss," with him as a guide, based on his experience of working at Corner House. The dream of owning his own home and land and working for himself is important to Vijay, given his and his family's background of always having had to scrape by on low wages determined by stingy employers, and living and moving from dwelling to dwelling, whenever a landlord raised the rent or decided to kick them out.

Learning to Manage Anger

Vijay is talkative and charming and speaks easily about himself and his life. He pokes fun at himself, and it seems surprising that he admits that he used to get easily angered by small things, such as other boys teasing him. Vijay was always on alert and tense, so much so that one of his friends shared that when they greeted Vijay, his standard response used to be, "What? What do you want?" rather than a simple hello spoken in return.

When I question him about his anger, Vijay deflects the question at first and jokes that he used to be angry because he was from Andhra Pradesh, where he grew up eating the region's spicy food since childhood. The spicy food made him have a "spicy" temper since he was young, he explains. But all jokes aside, he admits that if he had not learnt how to express his anger appropriately, with help from Dream a Dream, he would not have become a good manager, friend, husband, or a member of the society. "If I don't overcome my anger, I cannot be a good manager, I cannot be a good cashier, I cannot be a good friend. And I cannot be a good husband to my wife, and I cannot be a good person to the society," he observes.

For example, as a cashier, and now as a manager, he has to interact with many people who might be explosively irate about a mistake, whether perceived or real. It would have been easy for him to react, with anger, and find himself in violent situations or even find himself fired for handling an incident poorly. But Vijay says he makes sure to think before he speaks, and he tries to understand people better, even when they upset him. He makes decisions carefully, without being purely driven by his emotions, taking some time to make important ones, like when he decided to continue his education on his own and earn a living.

He learnt many skills related to managing his emotions at BOSCO and Dream a Dream. When Dream a Dream came to BOSCO to offer various programmes, Vijay went to their overnight outdoor adventure camps and participated in their field hockey and table tennis programmes between the ages of 14 and 17, playing hockey about two to three times a week. He ended up playing in hockey tournaments at the district level, representing his school.

There were two hockey coaches, and Vijay remembers how they taught him and his classmates to "respect" the sport. This meant taking care of their clothing and equipment and being prepared for each practice and game. Vijay says, "Without the equipment or shoes, I was not even allowed to enter the field." Along with respecting their equipment, they also learnt to respect other players as they played. These lessons were a far cry from his time working as a saree weaver, when the few skills he had learnt included avoiding getting into trouble as physical abuse and disrespect clouded his days. Vijay played hockey until he graduated from pre-university college, at which time he focused on his college education, using the same habit of respecting his study materials, his classmates, and his teachers.

Between the years 2004 and 2007, when Vijay was learning from Dream a Dream's programmes, Dream a Dream was just starting to undergo a big shift in the design of their programmes. From 2006 to 2009, it distilled its programmes from 16 different arts and sports interventions to two after-school programmes — football and creative arts — with teaching life skills as the goal and football and the arts as the paths to reach that goal.

The redesign drew in part from Vishal's reflection that many of the young people Dream a Dream worked with did not have the skills that other children would pick up naturally from having experiences of adults telling them stories, singing songs, making art, and from cooperating with each other to develop their physical strengths while playing sports. "The experiences of being neglected prevented certain developments from happening," Vishal observes. Dream a Dream refocused on the goal of equipping youth from disadvantaged backgrounds to acquire the life skills they needed through sports and creative arts.

[Vijay (middle row, fourth from the left) after an interschool hockey tournament, Bangalore, 2005]

Thus, Vijay was a participant in an early version of what later became Dream a Dream's After School Life Skills Programme, including the Dream Hockey Programme and the Dream Mentoring Programme, all of which focused on teaching social emotional skills. Vijay says that learning social emotional skills was his favourite part of the programme from Dream a Dream. It was where he learnt how to manage his emotions better. Some of the skills he believes he has learnt are good decision-making, controlling the expression of his emotions, and thinking before acting. He appreciates how the programme allowed him and others to share their feelings and to learn to be understanding of other people and their situations.

For example, Vijay was given a leadership role of taking younger children to early morning practice sessions. They had to wake up as early as 5 a.m. and be on the ground by 6 a.m. He was the eldest in the group and was given the task of ensuring others were there on time. When some children would inevitably be late, he would get angry and show it in his body language, looking stern, frustrated, and tense, and wanting to quit. Looking at his response, the children would arrive even later to the practice. After seeing calmer approaches being modelled by his hockey coaches and with mentorship, his response evolved. He stopped being reactive and began being more accepting and listened more to the children, to earn their respect and care. From wanting to quit that leadership responsibility, he modulated his response to the point where young people began looking up to him and started arriving on time.

Before attending Dream a Dream programmes, Vijay would argue with almost everyone almost all the time, getting into fights, but through the Dream a Dream, he learnt to think about whether it was necessary to argue. When he did feel he needed to argue, he learnt how to do it in a healthy way, rather than in anger. He admits with laughter that his acquired ability to be patient in conversations has helped him in his relationship with his wife. Speaking in a tongue in cheek manner, he notes that his wife has a lot of curiosity about many things, and he has cultivated some of the patience to answer her many questions.

Benefitting from Dream a Dream's Evolving Approach to Healing, Trauma-informed Care

Vijay was also a beneficiary of another programme that had just been developed when he was part of Dream a Dream. In 2006, a Dream a Dream employee had by chance met two English clinical psychologists, Dr. Fiona Kennedy and Dr. David Pearson, while travelling on a bus. Dream a Dream had been working on developing a mentoring program, and in 2007, these two researcher–practitioners of psychology came to Bengaluru for 10 weeks to observe Dream a Dream's work and contribute where they found need.

As soon as Fiona and David met some of the young people from shelter homes with whom Dream a Dream was working, they were struck by the extent of the medical condition known as "failure to thrive" exhibited in the programme participants. Failure to thrive describes children who do not meet the developmental milestones in accordance with standard growth patterns. It is usually measured through height, weight, head circumference, and other physical attributes. While failure to thrive can be caused by lack of food and nutrition, it is also caused by neglect, trauma, abuse, and abandonment — conditions that many of Dream a Dream's young participants such as Prasanna, Sukanya, Revanna, and Vijay faced while growing up. The physical effects include shorter-than-average height and smaller-than-average physique.

While these symptoms are clearly visible, David, a child and adolescent psychologist, saw the physical symptoms and recognised that the Dream a Dream participants also exhibited less visible cognitive and emotional symptoms such as attachment issues and inability to calm down and self-regulate. "There was knowledge about how the lack of food and nutrition can lead to stunting and failure to thrive, but David thought it was really important that people also understand how lack of love can lead to developmental delays," Fiona recalls.

Vishal, from his own experiences of observing children from shelter homes, agreed with them. "In a shelter home, kids come running and hug you," Vishal says, providing an example of a developmental gap he often witnessed. "They will try to become friends with you immediately. A child growing up in a privileged home will not typically go running to strangers; they usually hide behind their parents. Those same children who come running and hug you, when they are 15 or 16 years old, it is not easy for them to make healthy relationships. They have what's called *confused development* — when they form physical relationships as kids, they feel that is the only way to relate to others. They grow up with this narrative, and when they grow up and are physical with a stranger, they get an adverse reaction and don't understand why."

With the desire to share their knowledge as experienced researchers and psychologists and the desire to help the social and emotional development of Dream a Dream participants, David and Fiona created and taught the first version of the Mentoring Programme that year. The Mentoring Programme involved matching a young person with a sensitive adult who would act as a stable and caring presence in the young person's life. Fiona recalls the following about the training that they offered to mentors:

"David spoke about the effects of adversity, and I spoke about the skills needed to relate to young people who are dealing with these problems. I kept a specific focus on not solving problems for the young person; we saw the negative effect that problem-solving could have on the potential relationship between young people and mentors. It was challenging for us to tell the mentors to not solve problems for their mentees, as the mentors were young professionals; they had resources and ideas, and they wanted to solve everything. The young people got overwhelmed by [all the advice thrown at them] and would get scared and not return," says Fiona.

Fiona and David designed the Mentoring Programme to focus on the mentors' skills of validating young peoples' feelings, thoughts, and situations, and holding a safe and non-judgmental space, where the young person could feel seen and heard. Fiona and David focused the mentors' attention on understanding the circumstances around a young person's behaviour, rather than immediately judging a young person's behaviour as good or bad. They spoke with mentors about using their relationship with mentees to help them change their environment so that better choices could be made.

Fiona recalls, "I remember watching Vishal's face when David was talking — Vishal was amazed by these concepts... Vishal had been counteracting the problem without knowing what the problem was; he was intuitively addressing the issues, but he didn't know that. Our knowledge and understanding, combined with Vishal's systems knowledge — suddenly, we had a framework!" The principles of how to support young people that David and Fiona laid out in the Mentoring Programme provided the soil from which all of Dream a Dream's subsequent programmes blossomed.

Even though Vijay experienced the Mentoring Programme at its initial stages, it had a powerful impact on him, and he remembers it, over a decade later. His assigned mentor was Vikrant P M, who was a software engineer. Vikrant took him on outings on the weekends, away from BOSCO, and Vijay enjoyed those opportunities very much. His mentor even invited Vijay to his wedding and kept in touch with Vijay by e-mail when Vikrant moved to the United States. He helped Vijay set up his first email account.

Vijay remembers those times with his mentor fondly and remembers that his mentor also helped him to make thoughtful choices, including deciding to come back to Bangalore to continue his studies, even after he was expelled from BOSCO and sent home to Andhra Pradesh in the 11th standard. BOSCO had strict rules, but Vijay kept breaking them to go home to visit his parents frequently. BOSCO also did not allow its students to have a phone, but Vijay managed to get a second-hand phone and used it. As the disciplinary issues piled up, when Vijay was caught with his phone, he was told to leave the school.

But Vijay kept in touch with Vikrant even in Andhra Pradesh. It was because of these conversations that Vijay understood that he needed to continue his formal education to become successful. Vikrant had told him that if he wanted to change his life, one way he could do it was through coming back to Bangalore and completing college. When Vijay was confused as to how, Vikrant helped him think through how he could take a part-time job to fund his studies. So, once Vijay arrived back in Bangalore, he found a part-time job as a security guard for Rs. 3,500 rupees ($46) a month and stayed in his friend's place for a year while continuing and completing education.

Planning for the Future

Currently, Vijay does not have any debt and has been saving ever since he started working. He does not want to go into debt, even to achieve his dream of owning a house and a business. He said he learnt how to manage his money and carefully plan through Dream a Dream and BOSCO. They taught him to only buy things that he really needed and wanted, rather than spending his money on impulse purchases.

 **INFORMATION BOX 5C: THE NEED FOR FINANCIAL LITERACY SKILLS**

The Organisation for Economic Cooperation and Development (OECD) defines financial literacy as a combination of knowledge, skill, awareness, attitude, and behaviour which are needed to equip an individual to make healthy financial decisions in life (OECD, 2018). According to a report by Global Financial Literacy Excellence Center, only 24% of the Indian adult population is financially literate (GFLEC, 2021). In comparison to other emerging economies, the financial literacy rate of India is the lowest mainly because of the absence of awareness and capacity-building training on understanding finance (Garg & Singh, 2018).

The government is trying to improve the financial literacy of the people as it requires them to take quality financial decisions and enhance their financial well-being. An average middle-class family or students studying in low-cost private, or government schools are not aware of the basics of financial initiatives. There is a need for financial education for students and graduates at the grassroots level and inculcate financial education into the main curriculum and real-life practices and train the teacher to implement this at the classroom level. (Roy, 2020).

Sources:

Garg, N., & Singh, S. (2018, January 08). Financial literacy among youth, from *https://www.emerald.com/insight/content/doi/10.1108/IJSE-11-2016-0303/full/html*

Global Financial Literacy Excellence Center (GFLEC), (2021, September 23). Research. from *https://gflec.org/research/*

OECD (2018), *OECD/INFE Toolkit for Measuring Financial Literacy and Financial Inclusion.* http://www.oecd.org/financial/education/2018-INFE-FinLit-Measurement-Toolkit.pdf

Roy, S. (2020, September 20). The Importance of Financial Literacy in India., from https://streetfins.com/the-importance-of-financial-literacy-in-india/

He also learnt the value of being self-sufficient and being responsible for himself from Dream a Dream. For example, when Vijay left BOSCO, it was clear to him he had to be independent and own up to whatever choices he was making in his life. While he had a safe space in BOSCO, what he felt was lacking was the support system for him where he was cared for and understood. So, while leaving BOSCO should not have been advised as the best option, he was ready to take responsibility for that choice and make the extra effort to work part time and fund his education on his own. A careful and thoughtful planner, he admits he would not have known how to take care of a baby if he and his wife had a child immediately after they got married. He says he wants to save enough money to buy a house before he has children.

Vijay believes Dream a Dream provides the much-needed opportunities to children and helps them build good futures for themselves. He believes Dream a Dream gave him opportunities that other children in his situation might not have had, by offering enrichment programmes like field hockey, and through these activities, teaching him and the other students life skills. Added together, the exposure to sports, Dream a Dream's staff, and carefully trained mentors enabled him to learn how to manage his emotions, delay gratification, and make good choices to create a promising future for himself and his family.

06

Benefitting from Dream a Dream's Partnership with PYE to Learn to Teach Others

Sneha Deepa

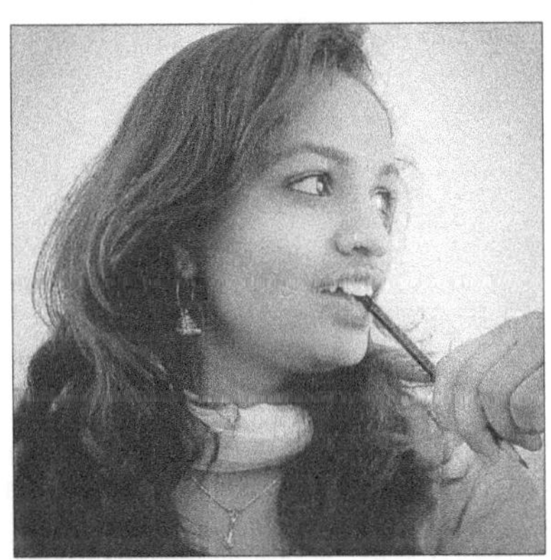

[Sneha Deepa, Year Unknown]

Just as Dr. Fiona Kennedy and Dr. David Pearson helped Dream a Dream grow its mentoring programme so that Vijay and other participants could benefit from it, Partners for Youth Empowerment (PYE) helped Dream a Dream develop its After School Life Skills Programme using the arts so that participants like Sneha Deepa could benefit from it. Sneha bubbles over with joy as she describes how she is living in Hubli (officially known as Hubballi[30]) as a music student and music teacher.

---

[30] Hubli is the second largest city in Karnataka. Dharwad, a city 20 kilometres away, is considered its twin city. In 2017, the Indian government included Hubballi-Dharwad for a smart city project to develop infrastructure in the twin cities.

At 21 years of age (at the time of the interview in 2019), she also teaches dance part time to young people. She moved to Hubli from Bengaluru, about 375 kilometres away, about a year ago, to pursue her music studies. When she was living in Bengaluru, she had started participating in Dream a Dream's After School Life Skills Programme in the creative arts since the age of 14. She went on to work as a creative arts facilitator for Dream a Dream for one and a half years when she was 18 and 19 years old. It was from those experiences that she grew as a teacher, she says; Dream a Dream also nurtured her dream to become a singer one day.

Learning to Dream

Sneha had wanted to become a singer ever since she was little. But she had no idea of how to reach her goals. She remembers that there were organisations that offered singing lessons in her neighbourhood, but she only sang in school. Singing was not seen as a career for Sneha by those around her. Most of the adults with whom Sneha shared her interest in pursuing singing as a career dismissed her dreams. They advised her that she needed to concentrate on her studies because a career in singing would be unstable and would not enable her to make a good living. Sneha lacked the presence of an adult who could mentor her in her dream of becoming a singer.

INFORMATION BOX 6A: GROWTH MINDSET

In *Mindset: The New Psychology of Success* (2006), researcher Carol Dweck bridges developmental, personality, and social psychology to argue how individuals' beliefs about their own abilities inform their behaviours and can ultimately predict the outcome of their endeavours. She compares the differences between what she calls a "fixed mindset", where an individual believes intelligence to be static, and a "growth mindset", where an individual believes that intelligence can be developed.

Dweck argues that success can be influenced by whether people believe that their abilities can change with effort. For example, someone with a fixed mindset may easily give up and avoid challenges and label their efforts "useless". In contrast, someone with a growth mindset is more likely to embrace challenges and persist to overcome challenges. Someone with a growth mindset is likely to look at effort as a way to gain expertise. That person would also learn from criticism and find motivation from others' success, in contrast to those with a fixed mindset who ignore negative feedback and feel threatened by others' success (Popova, 2020).

Sources:

Dweck, Carol (2006). *Mindset: The new psychology of success*. Ballantine.

Popova, M. (2020). Fixed vs. Growth: The Two Basic Mindsets That Shape Our Lives. https://www.brainpickings.org/2014/01/29/carol-dweck-mindset/

It was not until she took part in Dream a Dream's After School Life Skills Programmes that Sneha experienced encouragement from others to sing. In addition to allowing her more freedom to express herself than when she was at school or at home, Dream a Dream facilitators encouraged the participants to sing, even if their words were wrong or even if they did not quite know the tune. "They would say, 'If you are wrong, that is not a problem,'" Sneha recalls. This encouraged Sneha to sing "everywhere". "Whether wrong or right, I expressed myself by singing wherever I could," she adds. "I used to love staying with Dream a Dream more than going home." Along with other participants interviewed, Sneha remembers the snacks that Dream a Dream offered. "They also gave us snacks to eat after class, and I still love that."

INFORMATION BOX 6B: MASLOW'S HIERARCHY OF NEEDS AND THE IMPORTANCE OF PROVIDING SNACKS TO PARTICIPANTS

Almost every single Dream a Dream participant interviewed mentioned how much they remembered and appreciated being given snacks. For many, given the financial constraints at home, snacks were rare treats, and they loved and looked forward to the biscuits, bananas, apples, dried fruits, and juice provided by Dream a Dream. They noted that snacks were provided even if there was no special occasion, like a holiday.

Dream a Dream began to provide snacks as a key part of their programme simply because the staff felt the children would be hungry by the time the session was over in the evening, recalls Suchetha Bhat. "It was never expected that a gesture which was meant for convenience would mean so much to the participants," she notes. Over time, Dream a Dream heard from donors and partners that there were many instances when participants told them that they attended Dream a Dream only for the snacks. "It serves as a reminder for us of the extent of the adversity that our participants come from," Suchetha adds.

In the 1932 paper "A Theory of Human Motivation," psychologist Abraham Maslow argues that human beings have a number of needs that can be arranged in a hierarchy, with some needs being more basic than others. Maslow's hierarchy of needs is often presented as a five-level pyramid, with physical needs (air, water, food, rest, and health) being the most basic and foundational needs to be met. Security needs (shelter, safety, and stability) come next, then social needs (being loved, belonging, and inclusion), ego needs (self-esteem, recognition, and power), and then the need for self-actualization (development and creativity). Even as Dream a Dream's programmatic focus is on providing social, ego, and self-actualization needs, the organisation recognises that those needs are better met if they are built on providing physical needs of food and security needs of safety and stability for its participants as well.

Source:

Maslow, A. H. (1943). A Theory of Human Motivation. *Psychological Review, 50*(4), 370–396. *https://doi.org/10.1037/h0054346*

As a student in the After School Life Skills Programme, Sneha also remembers being asked to think about her goals and dreams and to express them using drawings and pictures. Classmates would try to name the emotions of the person in the picture, helping them to develop their abilities to "read" other peoples' feelings. Once her classmates found out through her drawings that she wanted to become a singer, they encouraged her to sing and would volunteer her to sing in front of them whenever an opportunity came up. "She knows how to sing; she can sing!" they would say. Sneha sang in classrooms, and then her classmates encouraged her to sing in front of bigger audiences.

Sneha was not the only one who was encouraged to follow her dreams. Her classmates encouraged each other to follow their dreams. Sneha feels that Venkatesh, her Dream a Dream facilitator, was key to building relationships in which young people felt comfortable to share their thoughts and feelings. "He spent a lot of time with us, not only teaching us but spending time connecting with us, so we could open up to him. Like half of the time, he spent teaching us skills, and in the other half, he would just talk to us and spend time with us," Sneha says.

Unbeknownst to Sneha, Venkatesh had been trained in facilitation using the Creative Empowerment Model (CEM) developed by Partners for Youth Empowerment (PYE). A chance encounter in 2009 between Vishal Talreja, Dream a Dream's co-founder, and Charlie Murphy, PYE's co-founder, during a breakfast meeting for Ashoka Fellows at Oxford University had led to a years-long partnership between the two organisations. Vishal and Charlie, in 2005, had both been awarded the prestigious Ashoka Fellowship that honours "leading social entrepreneurs" who "champion innovative ideas that transform society's systems, providing benefits for everyone"[31].

As they shared each other's work, they found instant synergy between Dream a Dream and PYE, which had developed an innovative arts-based approach to create transformative learning experiences for young people. A year later, Charlie along with

---

[31] Ashoka, (n.d.). Ashoka Fellows. [Blog Post] https://www.ashoka.org/en-us/ashoka-fellows

his colleague and senior PYE trainer, Nadia Chaney, arrived in Bengaluru to spend five days with Dream a Dream. Recalling his first experience with PYE's approach with young people, Vishal reflects, "There was just so much alignment" between the two organisations. Realising that both organisations "used play and art as media to engage young people," Vishal saw potential in learning from Charlie's decades of experience as a facilitator and from PYE's CEM approach. Both the organisations jointly raised money to bring PYE to train Dream a Dream's entire team on the CEM the following year, in 2010.

As Charlie, PYE's other co-founder Peggy Taylor, and Nadia made repeated visits to Bengaluru between 2010 to 2015, the Dream a Dream team worked with them to adapt PYE's facilitator training that had been developed primarily for a North American audience to the Indian context. Nadia, for example, lived and stayed with Dream a Dream practitioners for about seven weeks every year while leading basic and advanced levels of facilitation training. Vishal recalls the PYE trainers "had a much deeper body of knowledge and experience. We were like sponges soaking it all up. PYE helped us to understand what happens when you accept young people the way they are… and what happens when you allow both facilitators and young people to take creative risks." PYE helped Dream a Dream understand and name what had only been until then an intuitive approach to supporting young people[32].

Vishal explains why encouraging young people to take creative risks is so central to their programme: "Creative risk is when a young

____

[32] Nalani, Andrew (2020). Organising partnerships for innovations in youth empowerment: A case study of how the Creative Empowerment Model transferred from one organisation to another to support life skills development across continents and cultural contexts. Unpublished manuscript.

person or adult moves beyond their comfort zones and towards their learning zone. It's about stepping out of what they have always believed about themselves to exploring a new belief or idea. For example, a participant may move from believing 'I am not creative' to 'I am creative.' Creative risk-taking includes facing a creative challenge, responding to it through a form of creative expression, receiving appreciation from the group, and experiencing increased self-knowledge that they can, in fact, do something they did not believe they could do. As the level of creative challenge slowly increases throughout a programme, the individuals and the group as a whole are able to learn more about themselves and access inner resources such as resilience, courage, and vulnerability, thus adding depth to the process of transformation."

Learning to Open Up and to "Empty Her Bowl"

Thus, by the time Sneha joined Dream a Dream as a programme participant in 2012 as a 14-year-old, she was experiencing the authenticity and empathy that were central to PYE and Dream a Dream's approach to facilitation. From Dream a Dream's activities and supportive interactions with facilitators and classmates, Sneha learnt how to speak in front of people more confidently and do those things that would make her and her classmates happy. Before, she had not had many opportunities to share with others, trusting only a few close friends. Reflection times that followed activities allowed participants to share with each other what they had learnt, what they liked, how they felt, and what made them think and feel that way. "Then, we slowly started to implement what we had reflected and thought about changing in our lives," Sneha says.

Observing Nadia and Charlie's approach, what stood out to Vishal was that they were people who embodied care as they facilitated skilfully. When one participant, for example, berated himself for not being able to colour his nametag well, Nadia took the name tag as her own, as a gift. The participant became more confident when he saw that what he thought he had done so poorly was considered fit to use by Nadia. He began to be much more aware of how he denigrated himself and took on a kinder approach to himself and to others[33].

Working with facilitators who had learnt to teach with kindness and receiving all of the opportunities to share her thoughts and feelings during the After School Life Skills Programme, Sneha started to talk more at home. Her mother noticed the change and told her, "You were very silent before; but since you have joined Dream a Dream, you have become so much more talkative." Her mother even complained that "it was all Dream a Dream's fault." Sneha laughs as she remembers telling her mother, "You should be happy that I am opening up to you."

Sneha feels that being able to express what she is feeling inside helps her to move forward in accomplishing her goals and dreams. Sharing her feelings, whether they are negative or positive, helps her and others around her to be aware of what she is thinking and feeling, and to "empty" herself, so new thoughts and feelings can come in. She believes these practices help her learn new skills, and she explains it very succinctly: "If the bowl is empty, then we can fill it with more ingredients." With these life skills and tools of communication, she believes she has gained happiness, friends, and the courage and motivation to achieve her goals.

---

[33] ibid.

INFORMATION BOX 6C: THE BENEFITS OF CREATIVE ARTS

Creative arts play a significant role in the development of young people. A study by Harvard Graduate School of Education's Project Zero, *The Qualities of Quality: Understanding Excellence in Arts Education*, found that quality arts education can also improve creative thinking, which can positively impact society (Seidel, S. et al, 2009). In the employment sector, too, creative thinking is in demand. The World Economic Forum's 2016 Future of Jobs report included creativity as one of the top five skills workers would require by 2025 (WEF, 2016).

Creative arts also build a strong relationship between creative expression, exploration, release, and the healing process. (Stuckey & Nobel, 2010). Especially for young people from vulnerable backgrounds, creative art practice has shown significant support to young people's mental and emotional well-being; for example, there is correlation between creative arts school attendance, motivation to learn, and increased confidence in school context (Sellman, Cunliffe, & Stickley, 2012).

Researchers Bower & Carroll (2015) write the following: "Dance and arts activities have been found to promote social and emotional growth through independence, self-esteem, and initiative (Blomfield & Barber, 2011; Soares & Lucena, 2013) …. Vulnerable high school students who were involved in a combination of extracurricular activities (e.g., organised sports and volunteering) were three times more likely to go onto college according to these researchers (Peck et al., 2008). For some students, fields other than academics may be the only space where they learn important problem-solving life skills and experience recognition for success (Feldman & Matjaske, 2005)."

Sources:

Bower, J. M. & Carroll, A. (2015). Benefits of getting hooked on sports or the arts: Examining the connectedness of youth who participate in sport and creative arts activities. *International Journal of Child and Adolescent Health, suppl. Special issue: Places and spaces: The domain of adolescence* 8(2), 169-178.

Seidel, S., Tishman, S., Winner, E. Hetland, L. & Palmer, P. (2009). *The Qualities of Quality: Understanding Excellence in Arts Education.* Project Zero. Harvard Graduate School of Education.

Sellman, E., Cunliffe, A., & Stickley, T. (2012). Working with artists to promote mental health and wellbeing in schools: An evaluation of processes and outcomes at four schools. *Qualitative research in arts and mental health: Contexts, meanings and evidence. PCCS Books.*

Stuckey, H. L., & Nobel, J. (2010). The connection between art, healing, and public health: A review of current literature. *American Journal of Public Health, https://doi.org/10.2105/ajph.2008.15649*

World Economic Forum (2016). The future of jobs: Employment, skills, workforce strategy for the fourth industrial revolution.

Teaching Others

Sneha wanted to share what she had learnt from Dream a Dream with others. After her 10th standard, when she had completed her school leaving examination, she approached one of the facilitators at Dream a Dream, Shilpa, to ask if she could come and work for Dream a Dream. Shilpa told her that the minimum age requirement to be a facilitator was 18 years, so Sneha patiently and impatiently waited until she turned 18 years old. Then, she went back to Dream a Dream, applied, and became a part-time creative arts facilitator with the After School Life Skills Programme.

As a facilitator, she worked at Lord's Convent School, where boys and girls studied separately and were not allowed to talk or touch each other. Along with the senior facilitator who had been at the school for five years, Sneha tried to bridge the divide between boys and girls and advocate for gender equality. For example, she brought a few girls to mixed gender activities that Dream a Dream facilitated and that took place out of the school. She continued the work when she went on to become a facilitator at the Siri School. Even though there was limited outdoor space, given that the school was located on the main road, with buses speeding by, Sneha tried her best to teach children within the confines of the school. Fellow facilitators and her managers noted that she interacted well with school management and communicated well with the children in the local language, creating a comfortable space for all.

One aspect of the Dream a Dream approach is to ask the facilitator to understand the local context of the children and school environment and to be understanding, non-judgmental, and empathetic towards local customs and norms. For example, the first step for Sneha was to listen, observe, and understand the history behind the gender-based policies in Lord's Convent School. This helped her build trust with the teachers and school leadership before she could bring in practices to change these belief systems. In Siri School, Sneha understood the constraints of the physical environment and instead of complaining about it, she accepted the reality of the situation and adapted the curriculum and approach to still create the best experience for her students.

After being a creative arts facilitator, she also trained to facilitate football sessions. She was hesitant to approach Dream a Dream staff to say that she wanted to become a Life Skills football facilitator, but because she had learnt creative arts as a student and had already been a creative arts facilitator, she wanted to try something new. However, her fears were unfounded as Dream a Dream listened to her request and selected her to attend a seven-day Premier Skills Football Training in Mumbai with the then-manager of After School Life Skills Programme, Revanna. Revanna had noticed that while Sneha had been enthusiastic about becoming a football facilitator, she had had no previous sports facilitation background. He waited until he found a training camp for football coaches and went with her. Sneha was nervous because there were not many people she knew, and she would be speaking Marathi, a new language for her, where she was unsure of her accent. But she ended up having a good experience with a roommate who was very friendly towards her.

After she returned, as part of the project, she had to form a football team and train younger people in what she had learnt in Mumbai. A few of the junior year students at Mount Everest English High School were already going through the football programme at Dream a Dream, so she formed a team with six of them. Girish and Maheshwara, two other Dream a Dream facilitators, also helped with coaching. Revanna then selected her again to go to Delhi for four days, for the Goals for Girls programme, where she, along with Girish and Maheshwara, was a coach for the girls' football programme. Revanna had hopes that this experience would better prepare her to become a football facilitator at Dream a Dream. It was another example of how Dream a Dream staff met young people where they were and supported them to grow into who they wanted to become — in Sneha's case, it was an After School Life Skills Programme facilitator who evolved into a football facilitator.

Singing towards Her Dreams and Encouraging Others to Follow Their Dreams

As Sneha was developing her skills as a facilitator for both creative arts and football, she was also growing as a singer. As Sneha began singing in more public places and in front of larger groups of people, more people started to recognise her as a singer. Groups at her college asked her to sing for different cultural events. But she did not yet have formal training. Her mother, who was now very familiar with Sneha's dreams (with Sneha frankly sharing what she wanted to explore), happened to work at Sri Sathya Sai Vidya Kendra Institution, a residential school based in Muddenahalli with a branch in Hubli. She had moved there to take a job after Sneha's father passed away suddenly from a heart attack about a year after Sneha had started working for Dream a Dream. Her mother felt safer at Hubli as a woman living alone.

The school had a well-regarded performance arts programme, and Sneha's mother showed the principal a video of Sneha singing and asked if she could attend the school and become formally trained. The principal agreed, and Sneha moved to Hubli to be with her mother and start to train formally. The students at the tuition-free residential school come from all over Karnataka to study and participate in extracurricular activities such as singing and dancing.

While she trained in Hubli, Sneha also began to teach young children how to dance and sing, applying what she had learnt as a facilitator with Dream a Dream. "I learnt to be patient while working at Dream a Dream," Sneha recalls. "I used to hit or scold children if they irritated me or if they made me feel uncomfortable." But when she saw how children reacted to her scolding — they became sad or ran away from her — she learnt to manage her emotions and control her reactions better. She reflects that perhaps she used to be silent at school because of teachers who might have acted as she did, taking out their stress on children. "I saw myself in many children," she says. The realisation inspired her to make more efforts to listen to her programme participants.

Sneha also learnt to incorporate activities into her teaching. In typical schools, a teacher "only explains what is in the lesson, just writing on the board or drawing a few diagrams," Sneha explains. In contrast, Dream a Dream facilitators not only explain a concept but also give participants the opportunity to use what they have learnt immediately. "The facilitators would give us a chance to understand it more clearly, giving the opportunity for students to make personal connections so that there are feelings and emotions associated with what we learnt," Sneha recalls.

 **INFORMATION BOX 6C: THE IMPORTANCE OF LEARNING SELF-REGULATION**

Just as Sneha learnt to monitor her reactions to her students, research shows that people can exercise control over their feelings, actions, and thoughts (Bandura et. al.,1995). This involves regulating one's own behaviour and engaging in self-reflection, noticing and learning from surroundings and people, and other skills. The ability to self-regulate can help individuals influence their surroundings and circumstances with their actions (ibid).

There are different types of self-regulation. Emotional self-regulation helps children manage how they express and experience emotions. Behavioural self-regulation helps children control their actions.

Researchers have found that self-regulation skills can develop with practice and can be taught in the classroom. For example, playing simple games, such as Simon Says, is one way to help children note and manage their impulses (Golinkoff et. al., 2014).

Sources:

Bandura, A. (1995). *Social foundations of thought and action: A social cognitive theory*. Englewood Cliffs, NJ: Prentice Hall.

Golinkoff, R. M., Hirsh-Pasek, K. & Rajan, V. (2014, August 14). Self-regulation: Just as important as learning your ABCs and 123s [Blog post]. https://www.huffpost.com/entry/selfregulation-just-as-im_b_5675896

Sneha also learnt to be more creative with children, learning by experience that it takes practice to teach them well. With the other facilitators at Dream a Dream, she learnt to be more social and say more than just "hi" and "bye" as other staff members took the initiative to come up to her, greet her warmly, and talk to her with patience, kindness, and respect. It helped to have other facilitators model the kind of behaviour that she could emulate while working with her students.

Sneha believes that for many young people like her, memories of school are mostly about getting physically punished for making mistakes, doing a lot of homework, and sitting still, even when they did not understand what was being taught. According to Sneha, Dream a Dream facilitators, who are trained in PYE's Creative Empowerment Model adapted to the Indian context, create a different kind of space for young people. Dream a Dream facilitators lead with their smiles, listen to young people, express care, and build authentic relationships with those they teach. Thus, children primarily remember feeling good about themselves, being treated with respect and being given the space to experience learning at their own pace. It is this kind of positive feeling, confidence, and happiness about learning that she hopes to pass on to the students whom she is teaching now.

07

Learning the Life Skill of Interacting Well with Others in Dream a Dream's Safe Spaces and through Experiential Learning

Ayesha Bibi

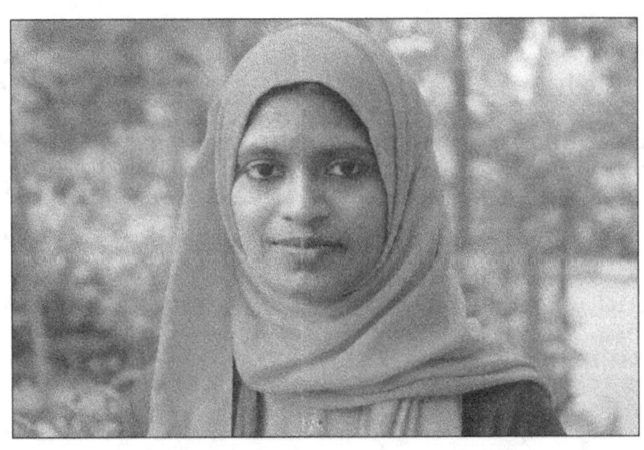

[Ayesha Bibi, Bangalore, 2022]

Ayesha is currently pursuing an MBA degree at T. John Institute of Management and Science in Bangalore, India. She describes herself as "not shy" and that she "loves" meeting new people and finding out more about them and what they like. "I usually like to spend time with people," she says. Others at Dream a Dream echo her words, describing Ayesha as "bold, articulate, and [as] someone who takes initiative." "She is like a magnet," another Dream a Dream facilitator says. "If she decides on something, she sticks with it until she has finished it and achieved her goals." But she was not always like this.

From Shy to Social with Dream a Dream's Safe Spaces

Ayesha had been painfully shy when Dream a Dream came to her school when she was in the seventh standard. The friendly Dream a Dream facilitators who explained their programmes to the students even before classes formally began, however, captivated her. The facilitators let the students know that they could decide whether they wanted to join the After School Life Skills Programme and could choose either creative arts or football. Ayesha had been interested in painting and the arts since childhood, so this unquenched thirst pushed her to want to try their classes despite her shyness. It also helped to see that the facilitators acted like her friends, rather than stern disciplinarians. Ayesha says that although the facilitators were adults, they carried themselves in a carefree way, "like children". Their friendly and warm mannerisms contrasted with her teachers' who demanded seriousness and respect from the students and who emphasised on the power difference between them.

As someone who was curious to try new things, Ayesha wanted to try football, after she finished the creative arts programme in the seventh standard. She had only seen football played on the TV in the FIFA World Cup. She thought of it as a game that foreigners played. But she wanted to try it, so she joined the After School Life Skills Programme for football during the eighth standard. She enjoyed the new learning that came every day with playing football. Describing herself as shy in those days, she remembers not knowing many boys. But because football practices were co-ed, she not only learnt football but also got to be friends with boys. "After football, I got to know them, and I was enjoying their company rather than maintaining stereotypes I had about them," she recalls.

She also grew out of her shyness through after school activities with Dream a Dream. After each session, held once a week, the facilitators would ask the participants what they had learnt that day. During games, to score goals, the team also needed to set up strategies and that involved sharing opinions and thoughts. Ayesha did not speak at first because of her shyness and just listened to everyone, even though she was the only one who did not share her views. As she saw that people who spoke were not criticised or punished, she slowly began to open up to others. She started to share what she enjoyed and what she had learnt.

As she started to share her ideas about how to score goals in football games and how to work together as a team, she worried about how her thoughts would be received. But her tentative, initial words were greeted with encouragement from both her fellow classmates and the facilitators. She gradually learnt to express what she was feeling, without overly focusing on what others were thinking. She focused instead on trying to communicate well and framing her ideas about strategies so that her teammates would be persuaded and would know how to execute the moves she suggested. She found it helpful that others were also sharing their views, and that the facilitators explicitly told the students that they should be respectful when others were speaking. The facilitators encouraged the group to try to understand what others were saying and see issues from their perspective. The facilitators also stressed that they were a team, and that in a team, every person should play his or her part. Ayesha found after a while that her fears about speaking up had slowly disappeared.

[Ayesha and Manikanta, another Dream a Dream participant, speaking as part of a panel discussion at the Dream a Dream Change the Script conference in 2019, with the Honourable Henry De Sio, former Chief Operating Officer for the 2008 Obama Presidential Campaign]

Learning the Life Skill of Interacting Well with Others: Expressing Emotions and Communicating Well

Drawing on their training rooted in Dream a Dream's Mentoring Programme developed in partnership with Dr. Pearson and Dr. Kennedy and the After School Life Skills Programme developed in partnership with PYE, Dream a Dream facilitators were creating a special space for Ayesha to express herself, in ways different than in other parts of her life. When Ayesha was younger, she used to say what she wanted to her parents, but as she grew, she noticed that she shared her feelings with her parents less and less frequently. She thought that if she complained to them about a teacher, they might blame her and say that it was her fault that her teacher had treated her a certain way. When she did share her thoughts and feelings, it was with one or two close friends; she did not share anything other than greetings with others. Ayesha remembers being very deferential to her teachers, never expressing herself if she had a different opinion.

But with more practice with the Dream a Dream after school programme, and learning the life skill of interacting with others, including expressing emotions and disagreements in respectful and effective ways, she found herself sharing more with her parents and with a greater number of friends. She also learnt to share her feelings appropriately with her teachers. She had begun to express her opinions without fear: "Ma'am, this thing, I don't like it." She had not done that before her time with Dream a Dream. But learning explicitly how to interact with others — how to share, how to frame a scenario or a problem, so that those listening to her would understand her — helped her become more confident in expressing what she was truly thinking and feeling.

As Ayesha developed these skills and feelings of confidence during her time with Dream a Dream programmes, she found herself taking a leadership role in organising a Teacher's Day party for the teachers at her school, when she was in the ninth standard. On Teacher's Day, 5th September of each year, Indian students celebrate and show gratitude to their teachers. Often, schools host events such as talent shows. This was not something Ayesha would have been able to do as a shy student in the seventh standard when she was usually the last in her group to speak up. She had learnt from Dream a Dream that being a leader is not about performing in front of others, showing off, having power, nor gathering attention; instead, leading was about completing tasks well and helping teammates finish their tasks and face any challenges they might have.

Learning the Life Skill of Interacting Well with Others: Teamwork

Ayesha remembers one Dream a Dream activity from the seventh standard that helped her learn to interact better with others. The assignment was to search for and gather leaves from plants. They were to dip the plant leaves in paint and make prints from them on A4 sheets. The students were divided into groups, with five members in each group. The A4 sheet was to have the prints of the leaves of all five members of the group. But the A4 sheets were small, and everyone wanted their leaf print to be the one on the top, the one most visible to others. One of the members of Ayesha's group was very insistent, and they ended up not completing the task because one person would not let them print their leaves unless her leaf was the one highlighted.

The facilitator intervened and suggested a way in which all their leaves could be highlighted. The facilitator reminded her that they were a team and that they should work to understand each other and respect others. If a team member wants her leaf to be highlighted, they should work to find a way to accommodate her request, as they should work to accommodate other team members' requests. Ayesha understood that what the team member wanted was what everyone else also wanted, and that there was nothing wrong with that. "I learnt the true meaning of teamwork then," Ayesha says. "It's not about you; it's about everyone. It's about respecting all and everyone's views and what they want."

Ayesha feels that the activity and the reflection time worked well together to elicit learning. With just the activity and no intervention from the facilitator and the time to reflect, they would not have had the opportunity to come to the realisation. With just abstract advice from the facilitator and no activity and genuine reactions from teammates, they would not have understood the lesson either. The activity and the reflection session made it so that the time was not just about making the leaf prints but about how to work well as a team and how to manage themselves and others' desires in satisfactory ways.

Ayesha compares the activity to the way in which she was taught in school, which was mostly by tests. If they were to solve problems in groups, it was so that one person could teach others in the group how to solve a problem. The focus was only on "bookish knowledge". In groups, they would share their knowledge until the tests came, after which they went their separate ways thinking "I have taught her this problem; whether she is able to learn it or not is her problem. I have explained it to her; I am done with my responsibility." There was not much of a follow-up to make sure that the material was learnt by everyone in the group. The focus was on just sharing what they knew for tests, not about what they were thinking or feeling. At school, even the group work would be geared towards preparing for individual tests, rather than solving a shared problem together or making something together.

INFORMATION BOX 7A: THE BENEFITS OF EXPERIENTIAL LEARNING

One of the well-known theories of learning is experiential learning or learning by doing. "What I hear, I forget; what I see, I remember; what I do, I understand," is a well-known saying from the Confucian scholar Xunzi. Experiential learning proponents echo this idea by observing that one of the ways to learn things is to have experiences.

Researcher David Kolb (1984) established the experiential learning theory model, building on the work of philosophers and psychologists such as John Dewey and Jean Piaget. The theory includes four stages: 1) concrete learning 2) reflective observation 3) abstract conceptualization 4) active experimentation. Learners can enter the cycle at any of the stages. Experiential learning in the classroom often involves the opportunity to immediately apply or use knowledge, work in teams, and time to reflect on what has been learnt and experienced.

Sources:

Kolb (1984). *Experiential Learning: Experience as the Source of Learning and Development.* Prentice-Hall.

Western Governors University (2020, June 8). Experiential learning theory. https://www.wgu.edu/blog/experiential-learning-theory2006.html

Learning to Interact Well with Others by Sharing about Their Lives, Not Just Their School Work

Ayesha also remembers Dream a Dream facilitators as the students' "go-to people", with whom they could share any challenges they were facing, including those not directly related to academics. The kind of safe space that facilitators created at Dream a Dream naturally invited students to share what happened in school, or anything that was troubling them.

"I would wait for the facilitators to arrive, the entire day, so that I could share my problems," Ayesha recalls. "As soon as they would arrive, I would tell them, 'This happened. That happened, like I fought [with my friends], or the teacher has given me this assignment." The facilitators understood "our interests and mood," she says. The problems that the students confided with the facilitators included instances of teachers scolding them for not doing an assignment and parents scolding them for not eating properly. If they quarrelled with friends for reasons that seemed silly in retrospect, it was nevertheless a big thing for pre-teens and teens at the moment, "like the world has fallen apart." Ayesha recalls, "So, for an entire day, we would wait for the facilitators to share our problems, so that they could give guidance or help us patch up with our friends."

Even if the facilitators could not immediately "solve" a problem, they would engage the students in activities that "turned our sadness into our happiness," Ayesha explains. They would sing and dance; there were rituals or structured activities that they did each time, such as checking in about how their day was and what they had learnt. They also learnt to see each day as a new day and a new beginning. Ayesha would reflect with these questions: "What did I learn today? Did I waste a day? Or did I learn something?" She still asks herself these question as part of her habit of reflection.

INFORMATION BOX 7B: DREAM A DREAM'S PRACTICE OF UNCONDITIONAL ACCEPTANCE OF PARTICIPANTS

Suchetha Bhat notes that Dream a Dream facilitators are trained to accept young people for who they are, without any judgement or restrictions. Unconditional acceptance is usually a completely new experience for young people who have always been judged and restricted throughout their lives. Suchetha believes that facilitators understand that acceptance is the first step towards any change. By unconditionally accepting young people, facilitators create a safe relationship that allows young people to openly share the challenges that they are facing.

Vishal Talreja notes that while growing up, young people are filled with the desire to explore; they express curiosity, frustration, confusion, and a host of other emotions as they learn to know themselves and the world around them. As they go through these emotions, young people get closer to a trusting adult and sometimes want to move away from that adult (see figures 7A and 7B below). As young people go through these experiences of connection and disconnection, Dream a Dream believes that the role of the adult in their life is to engage with them with acceptance, care, trust, empathy, respect, safety, and non-judgment.

This philosophy forms one of the core tenets of Dream a Dream's approach. Dream a Dream believes it is one of the critical components that help young people thrive. Young people interviewed for this book commented over and over again on how much they valued this aspect of the facilitators they encountered at Dream a Dream.

When facilitators model acceptance, young people can move towards acceptance of their own situation, from being fearful of showing shortcomings, fearful of their future, fearful of expressing themselves, and fearful of failure. Young people can then work on action plans with the facilitators to address their challenges proactively.

By modelling unconditional acceptance, facilitators help young people understand themselves better and be more empathic to the needs and feelings of those around them. By helping young people accept their challenges but not allowing the challenges to define their future, Dream a Dream facilitators encourage young people to follow their passion and help them understand that whatever career path they choose has value and can be celebrated.

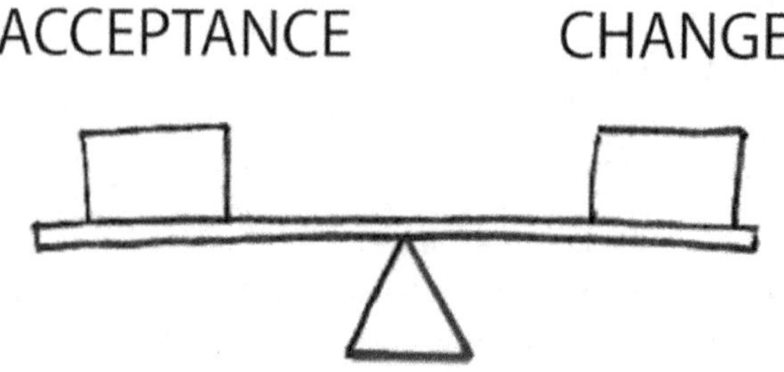

Figure 7A: Dream a Dream's Approach to Validating Young Peoples' Experiences

Vishal has found that working with young people towards their transformation is a balancing act. He notes that Dream a Dream staff have found that the more they "learn to accept young people for who they are, without judgement, the higher the possibility that they will learn to trust their supporters and build the capacities needed for change." For instance, Vishal explains, "When a young person steals something, we know that the behaviour is wrong, and we want to change that behaviour. However, just telling them that what they did was wrong is not going to cause change albeit it is going to push away the young person because they will feel judged. They will continue to steal, but now they will no longer share that with you. If, however, we first establish trust with the young person, understand why they stole, what triggered the behaviour, what was the context of the behaviour and validate their sharing, without necessarily endorsing their behaviour, it will help the young person trust the adult more. From that space of trust, we understand the core issues (which could be hunger, extreme poverty, seeking acceptance with their peer group, lack of impulse control, bad company, etc.), and then, we can create alternative pathways to address the behavioural issues which will help a young person transform."

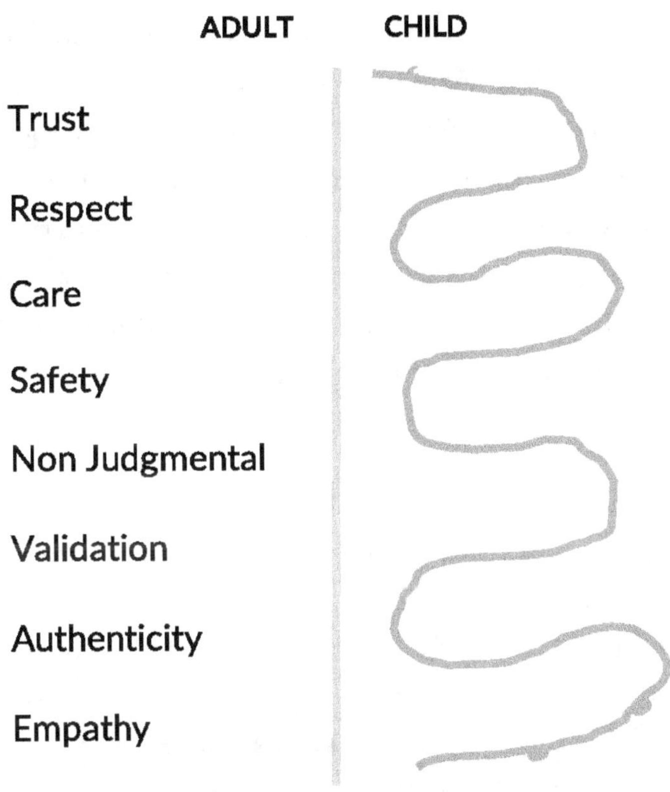

Figure 7B: Dream a Dream's Visualisation of the Role of Adults in a Child's Life

"Growing up for all young people is a constant balancing act of getting closer to an adult and moving away from an adult, trusting an adult and distrusting them, having moments of clarity and moments of confusion. When they are going through these ups and downs of life, what they need is the presence of at least one adult who is like a rock-solid straight line — an adult who brings trust, respect, care, safety, validation, authenticity, empathy, and a non-judgmental approach to their relationship with the young person. As the young person makes mistakes, knowing that they have an adult they can trust and connect with makes a huge difference in helping them make healthy choices and learn to change," Vishal adds.

Vishal's insights from decades of practice mirror that of scientific studies. The National Scientific Council on the Developing Child, for example, notes, "Whether the burdens come from the hardships of poverty, the challenges of parental substance abuse or serious mental illness, the stresses of war, the threats of recurring violence or chronic neglect, or a combination of factors, the single more common finding is that children who end up doing well have had at least one stable and committed relationship with a supportive parent, caregiver, or other adult."[34]

Applying the Lessons Learnt from Dream a Dream to Guide Her Future

Ayesha attended the After School Life Skills Programme for creative arts and football for three years, from 2010 to 2013. She started when she was in the seventh standard with creative arts, then transitioned to football for eighth and ninth standards. But the lessons she learnt from those years carried her through other challenges she faced later in life. She remains connected to Dream a Dream and uses the lessons she learnt from the programme to help her plan her future.

For example, Ayesha's childhood dream when she was in school was to become a cardiologist. But she could not score the 85% passing standard in her school leaving examination that she needed

---

[34] National Scientific Council on the Developing Child (2015). Supportive relationships and active skill-building strengthen the foundations of resilience (Working Paper 13). Cambridge, MA: Center on the Developing Child at Harvard University. Retrieved from wwwdevelopingchild. harvard.edu

to pursue science in college; she scored a 76.48%. For a short time, she felt she had lost her dream, and with it, herself. But she also remembered that Dream a Dream had taught her that "you can do anything; the thing is, you have to believe in yourself." The loss of her childhood dream was painful for her, but Ayesha also knew that she could make the best of the situation, if she believed in herself.

After graduating from university with a bachelor's degree in commerce, Ayesha saw that an MBA could lead her to a good job and financial independence. She chose to study business administration for her master's degree. She is currently thinking about becoming a financial analyst or entering the human resources field. The courses she took on entrepreneurship, basic computer skills, and accounting from Dream a Dream's Career Connect Centre were useful to her. Even though she lives far away from the Centre, she travelled an hour and a half each way to take the classes, as much for the warm facilitators and the classmates as she did for the content of the courses.

Reflecting on her experiences with Dream a Dream, Ayesha likens the organisation to an "invisible door". She says, "If you step through that door, your life will change. You will not be the same person that you were earlier." She values Dream a Dream for encouraging participants to embrace their dreams, whether big or small, regardless of their backgrounds or cultures. She believes they encourage participants to become aware of the potential each of them holds. To her, life skills such as teamwork, the ability to see from another person's point of view, openness, and having confidence are essential to thriving in a world that is constantly changing.

One of the core tenets of Dream a Dream's work is the relationship between the facilitator and the young person, in which the facilitator holds space for the young person's journey and discoveries. According to the founder of the Centre for Holding Space, Heather Platt, "Holding Space means that we are willing to walk alongside another person in whatever journey they're on without judging them, making them feel inadequate, trying to fix them, or trying to impact the outcome. When we hold space for other people, we open our hearts, offer unconditional support, and let go of judgement and control"[35] Ayesha not only learnt to break out of her shyness in the safe space created by her Dream a Dream facilitators, but she also learnt the life skills to relate well to others. With the skills and support that Dream a Dream provided, she is continuing her journey with confidence.

---

[35] Platt, H. (2019, August 17). What it means to hold space for someone. Uplift. https://upliftconnect.com/hold-space/

08 "My Past is Not My Future; My Failures are Not My Future": Learning from Dream a Dream's Arc of Transformation

Afreen Begum

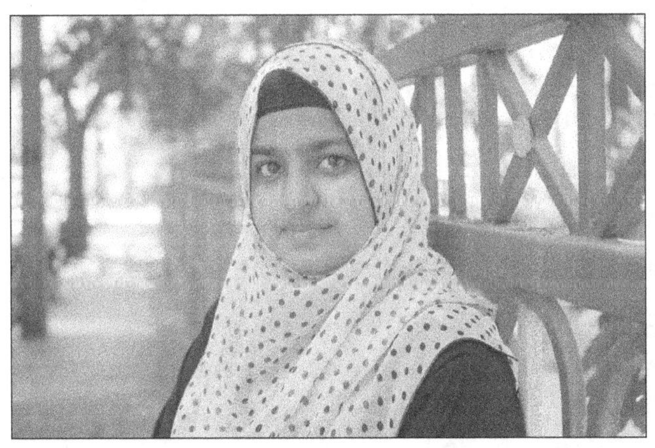

[Afreen Begum, Bangalore, 2022]

Like Ayesha, the very first day with Dream a Dream stands out in Afreen's memory, seven years later, and she remembers it with a smile and a laugh. She recalls that Dream a Dream facilitators gave them a snack. "We asked, 'How much should we pay, sir?' We asked because we had never received free snacks from our school. It was not even a special day — just a normal one. We really enjoyed that day, and it was a brilliant moment that I still remember."

When interviewed in 2019, Afreen was a 20-year-old student, in her second year of earning a bachelor's in science degree.

She also worked part time as an After School Life Skills facilitator for Dream a Dream and had been doing so for one year. She aspires to take the civil service exams and work for the Indian Administrative Services[36] after graduating, or work in software, depending on her family's circumstances. Afreen first encountered Dream a Dream when she was 13 years old, in the seventh standard, at Blossom Public School through the Dream a Dream creative arts After School Life Skills Programme. Participating in Dream a Dream programmes helped her overcome self-defeating beliefs and even bullying from others and led her to believe that she could do anything.

Little did Afreen know at the time, when she was greeted with snacks, that what Dream a Dream was offering was just part of the first step in a transformative process she would undergo through the programme, like other participants profiled in this book. Providing snacks, among other aims, enables Dream a Dream facilitators to signal to participants that they are entering a space that is different from what they have been used to. It shows care and concern about the participants' physical well-being. It allows participants to relax and have fun. It also indicates generosity and hospitality. It is part of the first step of the Arc of Transformation, Powerful Beginnings: Building Trust and Engagement.

---

[36] The civil services examination is considered one of the most competitive examinations in India. The success probability is less than 1% as only a few hundred are selected out of more than a million applicants. For example, out of approximately 1,100,000 applicants in 2018, 758 were selected after a preliminary screening, a main examination, and an interview. Information taken from:

Purushothaman, K. (n.d). *Understanding the competition in civil services examination* [Blog Post]. *https://www.civilserviceindia.com/current-affairs/articles/competition-in-civil-services-examination.html*

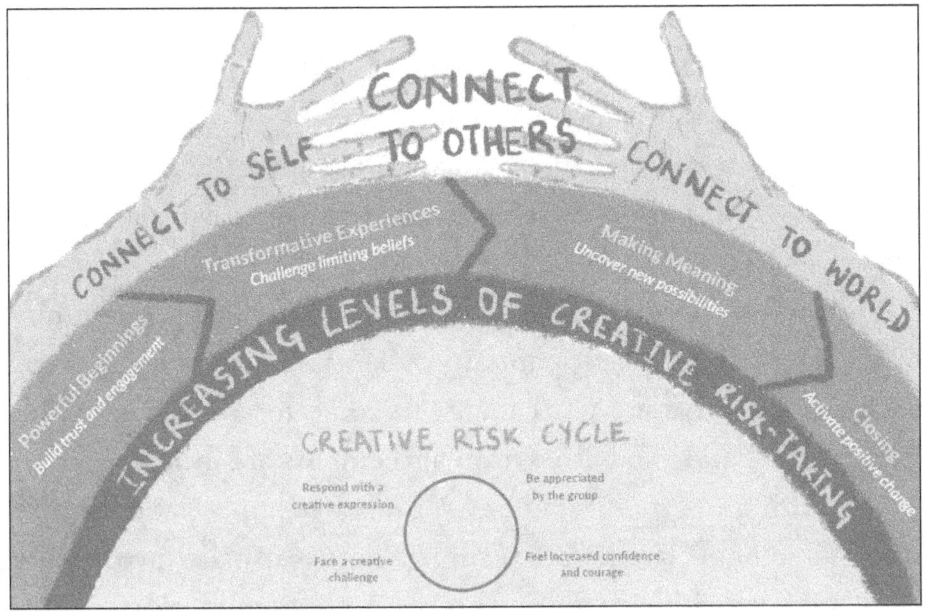

[Dream a Dream's Arc of Transformation]

Experiencing Dream a Dream's Arc of Transformation, Step One: Powerful Beginnings to Build Trust and Engagement

Based on Dream a Dream's long-term partnership with PYE that began in 2009, Dream a Dream adapted a facilitation framework called "The Arc of Transformation" (AOT). It is a framework for creating a safe and supportive group environment in which participants can take creative risks and access resources that allow them to respond to and create new opportunities and overcome challenges[37]. The first phase of the AOT is to develop trust between

---

[37] The information included in the description of the Arc of Transformation include two sources: 1) Dream a Dream, (n.d.). *The arc of transformation: A guide to using the arc of transformation*; and 2) Dream a Dream & PYE, (n.d.). *The arc of transformation: A facilitator's guide to designing creative learning processes that develop life skills and empower personal and social change.*

facilitators and participants as Dream a Dream staff believe that learning happens more effectively when participants feel psychologically safe enough to participate fully. As explored and discussed in Ayesha's chapter, Dream a Dream facilitators make a deliberate effort to create spaces that feel safe for participants in all aspects — physical, social, and emotional.

Facilitators begin to build a shared learning community of trust by asking participants to make personal introductions. Facilitators encourage participants to come to an agreement on shared goals and establish group agreements about norms, such as consenting to establish an environment of appreciation rather than judgement. Dream a Dream facilitators usually incorporate arts-based activities in this process. For example, participants may be asked to perform mime to share their hobbies, mirror each other's actions, or describe how they are feeling by using metaphors.

While allowing for creative risk-taking in the way the participants show up for these activities, there is no judgement if a participant does not wish to participate or is not yet ready to take a creative risk. The facilitators know that for someone just showing up is a creative risk; for someone else, it may be speaking in a group, and for another, it might be making themselves seen in the group when they perform an activity. Each participant's journey is unique and is celebrated. The establishment of a safe space, trust, and engagement does not end with introductions, but continues throughout the life cycle of a Dream a Dream programme.

Like other Dream a Dream participants who were interviewed, Afreen remembers how patient the Dream a Dream facilitators were. Even if the students were mischievous, the facilitators would address the misbehaviour gently, and describe how they wanted the students to behave, instead of scolding or physically beating them, as was the case often in schools. Shobhana and Ravi were facilitators during Afreen's first year at Dream a Dream, and Ravi was her facilitator for two more years, through Afreen's ninth standard. Ashwini, another facilitator, took Shobhana's place for those last two years. These long-term relationships with the same facilitators helped Afreen develop trust and close relationships with all of them.

Afreen speaks about Ravi: "From the first day until our graduation day, the last day, he was there with us. No matter the situation, no matter how we felt, he was always there to support us. We used to say, 'Sir, we want this; we don't want this.' He would respond, 'Okay, tell me whatever you want; we'll do that only.' Whatever problem we faced, he was always there to support us. He was like a pillar to us. And no matter what we did, how much we screamed, he would just tell us, 'Don't shout. Please be calm, be patient.' He would never say a bad word. He would never scold us. He was such a fantastic person. I cannot even compare him with anyone." Both the opportunities to learn things that she found useful in her life and the warm kindness of the facilitators made Afreen look forward to Dream a Dream classes.

Experiencing Dream a Dream's Arc of Transformation, Step Two: Transformative Experiences to Uncover Limiting Beliefs

The sense of comfort and security created by Dream a Dream helped Afreen and other Dream a Dream participants to engage in a "transformative experience" — an activity or a set of activities that help students to surface and question self-limiting beliefs or assumptions. The experiences can be simple, such as inviting participants to tell a story in front of others and having the storytelling be greeted with positive affirmations. If the participants believe that "I am not creative" or "No one likes to listen to me" or I'm not interesting to others" or "I cannot speak in front of other people," those beliefs would come to be questioned with repeated experiences suggesting that those beliefs may not be correct. According to Dream a Dream staff, many of these beliefs have come from the messages participants pick up in their home, communities, and schools by other adults who judge and label these young people.

In this way, Dream a Dream helped Afreen to overcome a long-standing fear of speaking in front of people. Earlier, she would shake even if it was just one person she had to speak before. She would talk only to her friends, whom she knew, never to strangers or people she had just met. But with support from her friends, teachers, and Ravi, her Dream a Dream facilitator, she gradually gained enough confidence to speak to people she did not know. Dream a Dream activities engaged her to speak in front of just one person, then two, then three, and then more and more people. Now, she is comfortable speaking in front of a thousand people. She has even learnt to go on stage and perform. She wonders why she was so afraid when she was younger. "Why should we be afraid? We are all human beings," Afreen reflects. According to Vishal Talreja, the experiences were designed to be transformative in the way they challenged existing belief systems and helped participants create new identities and narratives about themselves.

Experiencing Dream a Dream's Arc of Transformation, Step Three: Making Meaning and Identifying New Possibilities and Step Four: Activating Positive Change

Afreen honed her reflection skills further through other activities with Dream a Dream. The third step of the Arc of Transformation is "Making Meaning: Identifying New Possibilities." Reflection is central to this step. In addition to immersing themselves in experiential activities, participants are encouraged by skilled facilitators who pose questions that ask participants to step back from an activity and carefully think through and name the thoughts and emotions they experienced. Reflecting with others provides the opportunity to learn from others' reflections as well.

Reflection naturally leads to the fourth step in the Arc of Transformation — "Activating Positive Change." Based on what they realised about themselves and their actions through reflection, participants make commitments to how, where, and when they will put their new realisations into practice in their lives. Speaking their commitments aloud to others in a group as the last step of learning experience with Dream a Dream reinforces the sense of having a supportive community that encourages its members to make positive changes even as the learning moment ends. A participant may move from 'I am not creative' to 'I am creative', for example. The fourth step helps them use this new identity to shape a new reality for themselves. In this case, the commitment may be to trust themselves more with their creativity in life situations or develop a creative practice and to learn to trust and act upon their creative instincts.

The key to the impact of 'Arc of Transformation' are the following big ideas: 1) young people learn best through experiences; 2) the impact of transformative experiences stay with young people for life as the memory makes a place in the body, mind and heart; 3) transformative experiences happen when compassionate adults hold space for journeys of young people through trust, safety, care, non-judgment, respect, and dignity among others; 4) every individual has a valid desire to be seen and heard; 5) as we cannot design when transformation will occur for a young person, it is imperative that we design each engagement within the AOT framework and support with positive affirmations when the transformation does occur; 6) the framework is in the shape of an arch as it helps participants move over to the other side of the arc, and then, they cannot go back to who they were before the experience. The new identity stays with them and becomes part of how they show up in the world.

Afreen remembers doing an activity with Dream a Dream called "Blind Drawing"; it allowed her to reflect and consider positive changes to her behaviour. One afternoon, when the students had gathered in the assembly hall, Dream a Dream facilitators asked them to draw one of the paintings on the wall without looking down at their paper and without lifting their hand off the paper. They were then asked to draw the same painting again, but this time, with eyes only on the painting and never on the paper. Then, they were asked to draw the painting for the third time, but with their eyes closed and without lifting their hands. Afreen says that she began to realise the importance of making an effort to concentrate during the activity.

With prompting to reflect on her experience, the activity also became more than a simple exercise in drawing or concentration. Afreen realised that she was, in fact, not paying as much attention to her teachers or to her parents when they spoke or gave her directions. She thought, "Oh, I wasn't really looking carefully, and I can't remember what I just saw; next time, I am going to look more closely and pay more attention and really try to remember." The lesson carried over to her classes, so she consciously tried to focus more intently on what her teacher was saying. Even at home, she found herself making effort to listen to her mother. The immersive experience of engaging in an activity and self-reflection enabled Afreen to make a conscious decision to change her behaviour that a lecture or scolding likely would not have achieved.

The Core of The Arc of Transformation: The Creative Risk Cycle

Central to the Arc of the Transformation is the "Creative Risk Cycle," which is part of each step of the Arc of Transformation. It involves facing a creative challenge, responding to it through creative expression, receiving appreciation from the group, and experiencing increased self-confidence. As participants repeatedly engage in the Creative Risk Cycle, they grow in their ability to meet challenges with courage, their ability to be resilient and recover from setbacks, and their determination to continue to grow and learn from new opportunities and experiences. Vishal, who helped to adapt the PYE approach, believes repeatedly facing creative challenges "builds a new muscle and the constant practice helps keep that muscle strong and agile."

For example, the Creative Risk Cycle conditioned Afreen to seek out new activities and explore her interests. After being part of Dream a Dream After School Life Skills Programme, she expanded her creative pursuits by participating in inter-school cultural performances and competitions that included folk dance, folk songs, mime shows, and mimicry. Her school also used to celebrate Islamic Day and would host *Na'at* (poetry in praise of the prophet Muhammad) singing sessions. Afreen began participating in these events as well. She performed folk dances with her friends in a group and performed mimicry by herself. Even though some teased her about it calling her *"deewani"* and *"pagal"* (Hindi words for "crazy"), she would take it positively, thinking that others were uncomfortable with themselves that she had the courage to try something that they did not know how to do.

Repeated engagements of the Creative Risk Cycle, where she tried new activities and received encouragement from other participants and facilitators, had strengthened her sense of self. Her ability to reflect let her figure out which words to listen to and which to ignore. "I never fought with them," she recalls about the other students who would tease her. Others also made fun of her for caring so much about cleanliness, calling her "Swacch Bharat," a government initiative for cleanliness. But Afreen would say to herself with determination, "Whatever they say to me, I know what I am."

ⓘ INFORMATION BOX 8A: THE PREVALENCE OF BULLYING AND TEASING

Physical bullying is a big concern in schools across India. A systematic review of research literature about bullying in India found that bullying perpetration estimates ranged from 7% to 31% and bullying victimization ranged from 9% to 80% (Thakkar, van Geel, & Vedder, 2020). Bullying can be physical, verbal, social, or relational; it can be direct or indirect, but all forms cause emotional and psychological harm (Malik, 2014). Childhood experiences with aggression, such as physical discipline (e.g., spanking or domestic violence) are positively associated with bullying (ibid).

The National Center on Safe Supportive Learning Environments (NCSSLE) in the United States recommends that schools adopt trauma-informed approaches to create safe and supportive learning environments to reduce and prevent bullying (USDHHS, 2020). These steps include:

1. Educating school staff about trauma and its effects
2. Promoting physical and emotional safety in relationships and the environment
3. Reducing trauma-related triggers in the school environment
4. Considering trauma in all assessment and protocol behaviour plans
5. Ensuring students and families have a voice, choice, and empowerment

Sources:

Malik, A. (2014). Understanding the Potential Bully. *Indian Journal of Youth and Adolescent Health*. 1. 3-6. *https://core.ac.uk/reader/230826624*

Thakker, N. van Geel, M. & Vedder, P. (2020). A systematic review of bullying and victimization among adolescents in India. International Journal of Bullying Prevention. https://doi.org/10.1007/s42380-020-00081-4

U.S. Department of Health and Human Services, (2020, May 19). Bullying and Trauma [Blog Post]. https://www.stopbullying.gov/bullying/bullying-and-trauma

"My Past is Not My Future"; Negative Comments and Disappointments are Not Reasons to be Despondent — Lessons Learnt from Dream a Dream

From the Dream a Dream After School Life Skills Programme, Afreen learnt to confront limiting beliefs and uncover new possibilities even in the face of challenges. It helped her to overcome another negative incident during her school days. In her school leaving certificate exam, she had scored very good marks, and all her relatives praised her. But during her second year of pre-university classes, Afreen failed one subject. She says that she felt like "finishing myself." People taunted her to the point where she felt that she could not even leave her home. Even though her parents were supportive, other members of her family teased and made fun of her.

But Afreen told herself, even in her lowest moments, "Why should I give up? What have I done? I just flunked one subject. I'll write it again; I'll write the test again." She studied, retook the test, and passed. She showed her relatives, "See, I have cleared it."

"Failure is not at all the end of your life. It is the first step to success," Afreen reflects. She said that Dream a Dream facilitators always encouraged participants to never ever give up. Though the message came from multiple sources over the years while she was at Dream a Dream, she remembers one incident, when she was in the eighth standard, in 2013. There had been a widely publicized rape case in which the victim killed herself. Afreen remembers discussing the case with other girls and with her Dream a Dream facilitator, Ashwini. "If someone does something negative to you, you should fight back. It is not the time to die. It is not the end. If you die, the ones who hurt you will only live freely, with no one to question them. So, that was the moment when we learnt that failure is not everything; we still have more to learn," she says, recalling her discussion with other girls at Dream a Dream. Suchetha notes that Dream a Dream facilitators encourage participants to avoid victim shaming and remind them that if someone does something negative to them, it is not their (the victims') fault. Dream a Dream provided time and a safe space to discuss events that were happening in the world and what they meant to them and how they wanted to live their lives; it helped Afreen and other teens to reflect and discuss openly and thoughtfully current and other immediate events that concerned them.

Experiencing the Arc of Transformation and the Creative Risk Cycle also gave Afreen ample practice in gaining a mindset of not letting disappointments leave her despondent. As a National Cadet Corps (NCC) member, she was selected to attend a 10-day Republic Day camp. NCC is a branch of the Indian Army that has an extracurricular program in colleges. Afreen was hoping to be selected to the final camp, in Delhi, which would mean that she would not only meet the Prime Minister but that she would be marching in the Republic Day parade, a huge, nationally iconic event that takes place every year on 26 January. Unfortunately, however, she was not selected because of her height, which, at 5' 2," was two inches shorter than the required height of 5' 4." She was disappointed, but again, she remembered to not let it drag her down into the depths of despair.

She knew there were other opportunities if only she were to continue looking. For example, from her Dream a Dream days she remembered going on field trips to nearby businesses, to learn about different career options available to them. One such trip was to Dell and another day was spent at Microsoft. People from the Indian Institute of Technology (IIT) would also come visit the school; they would inform the students about the different professional pathways available to them. According to Afreen, such opportunities rounded out Dream a Dream's focus on life skills such as overcoming fears, challenges, and disappointments and were very helpful in instilling in her the belief that her future was full of different possibilities. Dream a Dream provided opportunities to learn from a variety of sources that contrasted and complemented her school curriculum, which was traditional and focused only on what was outlined in textbooks.

"She Can Do Anything in Her Life"

With Dream a Dream, Afreen also became more self-assured about solving her own problems and making decisions before asking someone else. "Before coming to Dream a Dream, even if I had a small problem, I would ask my mother, 'Mama, I have this problem; please solve this. But now, even if I have a big issue, I try solving it by myself without telling my mother," Afreen says. She claims that she "can literally say that my past is not my future, and I am very happy about what I left" in terms of things like the fear of speaking to people, lack of focus, lack of confidence to solve problems and to make decisions. In fact, as she learnt to make her own decisions, she chose to apply to work for Dream a Dream without telling her mother. When she showed her mother the offer letter from Dream a Dream, her mother was very surprised.

Afreen had decided to apply in part because she wanted to help her father, who had a stomach ulcer that required four surgeries. When she was in the 10th standard, he was in a very critical condition, and the doctor had told the family that her father was likely in his last days. As the older child in her family, with just a younger sister, and a mother who also did not work because of problems with her back, Afreen wanted to work so that her father could stop going to work as a helper in a hardware shop. She knew that she loved working with children, so she wanted to try becoming a Dream a Dream facilitator.

[Afreen Begum at Dream a Dream's Art for Resilience event, 2021]

Her decision to work while she was studying meant that Afreen was the first girl in her extended family to work while going to school. Growing up, Afreen had felt that all the praise had gone to a cousin who had a black belt in karate and was a national football player. Afreen felt she had very few things that she could be proud of, even though her parents were very supportive of her. After she began working part time, however, her extended family members began to praise her, saying, "She can do anything in her life." For Afreen, it felt like it was the first time her success was being recognised by others in her family.

"I have always felt that it is not just an organisation that helps students graduate. But it is a platform that enables young people to lead and live their lives independently," Afreen says of Dream a Dream fondly. With what she has gained from her time with Dream a Dream and how she was able to transform her attitudes and gain life skills, no failure, no matter how small or big, seems to be able to stop her from continuing to make decisions with confidence in pursuit of her dreams.

09

Facilitating Dreams — The Critical Role of Facilitators

Bharath Kumar M.

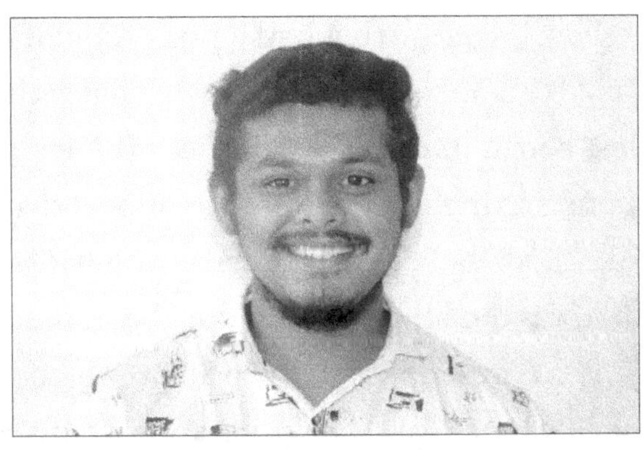

[Bharath M. at Dream a Dream office, 2019]

At 22 years of age, Bharath works as a delivery person for Swiggy, a delivery app popular in India. He has been at his current job for a year and a half, after holding a sales position at a mobile telephone company for six months. His colleagues see him as a responsible, respectful young man.

Just eight or nine years ago, however, he was a very different person. According to Bharath, as a child and teenager, he was "not at all a good person…, in behaviour and all. I got into street fights and fights in colleges. I drank alcohol; I smoked. Everyone scolded me, both at home and at school." When he had asked for a bike and his family did not give him one, Bharath stole one. Bharath got into fights daily to "maintain his reputation" as a fighter in college and was even expelled along with four of his friends, during his first year at a pre-university college, for hitting his principal under the influence of alcohol. Two of those friends are now in jail. Bharath himself got sent to police stations at multiple neighbourhoods within Bangalore because of his fights, which he was sometimes paid for.

His relatives would say, "He will become a thief; he will go to jail; he will not live for very long." Even though he had scored a 90% in his 10th standard SSLC examination (school leaving examination), he deliberately chose a college that had a poor reputation in terms of students being able to smoke, drink, and even chat with friends while sitting on the last bench in class. He did not even try for his second PUC examinations, having gotten into recreational drug use by then and thinking of school as being secondary to having fun. Bharath used to think that was the kind of "freedom" he wanted and needed.

He laughs as he describes his priorities, which had changed dramatically since then. Now, he focuses on doing well at work, earning money, and helping his family. Now, his friends say, "Bharath is a good person. He is working, and he is supporting his family." His relatives, too, have good things to say about him: "Bharath has changed completely. We are not able to believe how much he has changed." How did such a transformation happen?

Changing, Step by Step, with Support from Dream a Dream

Bharath was 16 years old, in his first pre-university class or 11th standard, when Dream a Dream facilitators came to Sree Venkateshwara PU College (SV) College. According to Mahesh M, a Dream a Dream facilitator, Bharath was part of a "horrible" group of young people who were very difficult to teach. Nevertheless,

Dream a Dream persuaded the principal to help enrol a few of these challenging young people in programmes at Dream a Dream's Career Centre. When the group arrived at the Career Connect Centre for classes, Bharath would saunter outside to smoke at the front of the building. He would return only to pick fights with other students, wanting to be seen and noticed, but only knowing how to express the need negatively by causing a ruckus.

He only started to go to Dream a Dream because his friends went there; however, he completed a basic computer course in three weeks. But as he continued to come to the class, he noticed that perhaps Dream a Dream might be different from his prior educational experiences. For example, he and his friends did not get into trouble as they used to, even though they behaved just as poorly.

When another facilitator substituted for Mahesh, their regular Dream a Dream facilitator, just for a day. Bharath and his friends goofed around at the back of the room, bored, and whispered to each other while the facilitator spoke. The substitute facilitator became upset when they did not listen to her asking them to be quiet. She ordered them to step out of the room. Bharath and his friends spoke back to her, resulting in raised voices and a fight. Another facilitator intervened, but to the surprise of Bharath and his friends, the person who intervened only reprimanded the facilitator. The intervening facilitator advised their substitute facilitator to not become upset at the students but to modify her practice.

Bharath was surprised that they were not scolded. He still carries the memory of that incident from eight years ago because it was the first time he did not get into trouble for creating a disturbance in the class. In fact, the facilitator apologised to him and his friends for asking them to leave the room. Her apology caused Bharath to feel remorseful as he reflected on how he had behaved.

The incident was a demonstration of Dream a Dream's values and philosophy of taking responsibility as facilitators for the positive engagement of the participants. Dream a Dream staff believe that if students are not positively engaged, it may be because there are other factors at play. For example, in Bharath's case, he had had very few to no positive engagements of any kind with authority figures in educational contexts. Bharath and his friends also thought the activities to be boring and they had been given too much time to be passive, rather than active.

Thus, Dream a Dream facilitators design lessons with a variety of active engagement strategies in mind. They encourage participants to share in small and big groups to foster emotional and relational connection. They encourage laughter and demonstrate a sense of humour themselves. A session might include practising English by sharing each student's favourite activity to relax, a moment when they felt sad, or what they do to cheer themselves up.

Dream a Dream has centred its pedagogy on active engagement, use of art and play, and understanding their participants from the beginning. At the very start of the organisation, they worked with young children who were addicted to drugs. At an outdoor camp with young people addicted to substances, when a facilitator asked why they used drugs, one of the youths answered, "You do not really want to know the answer." When the facilitator encouraged a response, the 14-year-old explained, "Look, I live on the street. I eat rotten and disgusting food that other people have thrown away. The only way I can eat that kind of garbage is after I have drugged myself, so I do not smell it and it does not disgust me. At night, boys from gangs or other homeless people abuse me. Policemen have beaten me with clubs in the middle of the night to chase me away from where I was sleeping. The only way I can get through the night is when I'm drugged so that when I wake up in the morning, I do not remember what happened to me at night."

Vishal realised early that this is the reality in which young people who come to Dream a Dream live. He reflects, "Who am I to judge his choice to take drugs? What right do I have to decide what is right and wrong? I must respect his choice, out of a deep and intimate acquaintance with the circumstances of his life. Only then, perhaps, can I try to drive change. It's a long process." Even now, 20 years since the organisation's founding, Vishal maintains, "We are far from understanding the full context. We are still peeling more and more layers of the problem"[38] our children face.

Dream a Dream facilitators, thus, actively practise empathy, trying to understand why students might be acting in such a way. Mahesh, for example, tried to see beyond Bharath's poor choices. Rather than seeing his disruptions and fights with other students as signs of poor character, Mahesh identified them as Bharath's need to be seen and respected as a young man. Mahesh began to explicitly praise Bharath, both publicly and privately, whenever he saw any signs of positive behaviour from Bharath. Other facilitators made the same effort as they interacted with him.

Mahesh also took the time to sit with Bharath one on one, informally, and listened to Bharath talk about his family and his interests. Mahesh also shared his own history, which was like Bharath's story in terms of having had difficulties with getting along with his parents. Mahesh had grown up in a rural village, working on a farm with parents who were not formally educated. He lived in a hostel and stayed with friends when he did not have a place to go, not having a strong connection with his parents. When

---

[38] Dream a Dream. (2019, May 23). An interview with Vishal Talreja by the Haaretz [Blog post]. https://dreamadream.org/about/item/410-an-interview-with-vishal-talreja-by-the-haaretz

he earned his master's degree in social work, he first worked as a children's counsellor but was not satisfied at his first job, feeling like just a cog in a machine.

By chance, he started working at Dream a Dream. When he attended a Dream a Dream camp as a counsellor, he began to think about his own journey and experiences, turning the questions on himself. "When have I empathised with others? When have I listened to others well? How can I value other people?" Mahesh admits, "I have hurt my family and parents by not listening to them and not respecting them." He then made explicit attempts to connect and bond with his parents and saw that his parents responded positively to his overtures. As his parents started to trust him, they shared more of their thoughts and feelings with him. Mahesh said that as he began to be more intentional about practising empathy, respect, and listening to others, and as he gave himself permission to explore his strengths and interests, he saw that his personal and professional lives both changed in positive ways. The experiential approach that he saw at Dream a Dream camp, which was a dramatic difference from the theoretical discussions he found in universities, made a lasting impression on Mahesh. "I remember all the fun moments from my camp experience," Mahesh says, "but I can't remember my lessons from college."

Mahesh was able to bring these experiences and reflections about what made for impactful learning into his facilitation with young people. Mahesh shared honestly with Bharath the ways in which he regretted the negative relationship with his parents and the ways in which he tried successfully to change it. Bharath also saw the ways in which Mahesh tried to make the class fun and engaging and create the conditions for students to explore their interests and strengths. Bharath began to open up to others under the positive attention from the facilitators. As Dream a Dream incorporated opportunities for students to share their personal struggles in safe spaces, in addition to learning English and basic computer skills, Bharath also had the chance to listen to other students' stories. He listened to other participants explain how their lives had changed to the point where they were receiving respect from others. Respect was what he yearned for, after years of hearing negative comments about his behaviour at home and school. Listening to others also made him realise that he was not the only one with problems, struggles, and challenges. Bharath recalls, "I thought only I had problems, but when I joined Dream a Dream, I heard everyone telling their stories and thought, 'Okay, I am not the only one who is poor; everyone is poor. Why should I act like this [when others in similar situations don't]?'" It made him want to consider changing his life for the better as he saw others had.

As Bharath was taking small steps to change his ways, he got into a fight, in one of the toughest situations of his life. He was paid by some people to beat up those they named. One of these fights led to his getting 17 stitches and ending up at a police station. His father, tired of repeated calls from the police about Bharath, refused to bail him out this time. A low-wage garment worker along with his wife, with just a couple of years of formal education, his father had hung his hopes on Bharath being able to finish his education and making something of himself.

Disappointed by Bharath's repeated troubles inside and outside of school and with the law, his father told him, "You are not my son. From this day onwards, don't come home. In my mind, you are dead." The people who had paid him to fight came and got him released, but by then, he also had another case filed against him by the police.

To avoid getting into further trouble, Bharath left home and went to live with his cousin, at the insistence of his mother, about 19 kilometres away, in Marathahalli. It was a positive change of sorts in that his move away from his neighbourhood meant that he could move away from the negative friendships and start anew. Bharath had built up a reputation in his neighbourhood so that if anything happened, the police would routinely visit him at his house, even though he had not been involved. He admits that moving from his neighbourhood turned out well for him.

Throughout the incident with the police and his father, Bharath kept in touch with his mother by phone and would visit Mahesh who was three kilometres away at KR Puram (Dream a Dream Career Connect Centre), even though he was no longer attending Dream a Dream programmes. He felt drawn to Mahesh because of his non-judgemental acceptance and because Mahesh was authentic and transparent about who he was and what he had struggled with, in ways that allowed Bharath to connect with him. Mahesh also allowed Bharath to listen in on his sessions with Dream a Dream students.

As students shared their stories, Mahesh would reflect with Bharath and remind him again that he was not the only one with problems. Mahesh told Bharath that fathers are gifts. He advised Bharath to listen to his father and try accepting whatever his father said, for three days, instead of arguing or fighting with him. He also suggested that Bharath speak with his father even though his father would not speak to him and to start giving to his family part of what he earned at his job. Mahesh's experience with his father was similar to Bharath's, so this encouraged Bharath to listen to his advice, which yielded good fruit. Bharath now speaks regularly with his father, who also respects and listens to Bharath's suggestions.

According to Vishal, behavioural change is a long-term commitment that starts with small steps, and good facilitators like Mahesh recognize this. The staff of Dream a Dream also recognise that due to adverse childhood experiences, it is likely that young people like Bharath will make attempts to change, will fail, and might also give up. Vishal believes that what the Dream a Dream staff have learnt over the years is that what the youth need is constant support, encouragement, and the encouragement and the opportunity to try for the second, third, fourth, fifth, sixth, or seventh time, without being disappointed with or giving up on themselves, or seeing supporters give up on them.

At about the time of the incident with the police, his mother was diagnosed with diabetes and was hospitalised for her sickness. Concerned about her son, Bharath's mother had burst into tears and said, "I will die." The doctors recommended that she avoid stress, and this motivated Bharath even more to change his behaviour dramatically, to reduce her stress. He spoke with Mahesh when his mother was in the hospital and asked him to help him change his life.

With all these interactions, Mahesh noted that Bharath appeared to be increasingly enjoying his time at Dream a Dream. One weekend in December, when the staff had to move offices, Bharath voluntarily came to help and spent time lugging boxes. Bharath also responded favourably whenever Dream a Dream staff contacted him about different events. When the opportunity came to attend a Dream a Dream outdoor experiential camp, Bharath took it. The participants did not know each other at the beginning of the camp, but within three days, they "felt like family," as Bharat recalls. At the camp, Bharath enjoyed being without his phone and social media contact, and he made friends during camp that he still keeps in touch with. He met another Dream a Dream facilitator, Ravi, who also built a good rapport with Bharath after noticing that Bharath would sometimes separate himself from the group during camp and go off to think by himself.

INFORMATION BOX 9A: DREAM OUTDOOR EXPERIENTIAL CAMPS

The Dream Outdoor Experiential camps are designed using the Creative Community Model developed by Partners for Youth Empowerment (PYE Global). The camp is a three-and-a-half-day residential experience designed to take young people and adults through a transformative journey of self-discovery. The model uses experiential techniques for participants to understand themselves, think creatively about challenges they face, and build supportive communities by learning through the arts and having fun.

The camp focuses on four primary goals:

1. To understand ourselves
Dream a Dream believes that through understanding our identities, strengths, and roles, we begin to discover an inner compass through which we can make better decisions and are able to lead lives that we can be proud of. The camp provides the space for all participants to understand themselves, their own journeys, and to take that awareness forward in their lives.

2. To learn from each other
Learning from each other encapsulates critical life skills of teamwork, empathy, listening, and sharing. Dream a Dream considers the ability to learn from others as important because people live in a social world where there is abundant possibility. To be able to appreciate and acknowledge others and build on one's skills in a mutual learning environment is a key component of the camp.

3. To learn to lead to build community
One of the key skills that is focused on within the camp through the experiential process is to take initiative and strengthen one's leadership skills. The ability to take initiative is not only integral through the three and half days at camp, but an important skill to continue to cultivate once the participants leave the camp and go back to their lives in their respective communities.

4. To have fun
Learning through fun is one of Dream a Dream's foundational goals. By creating an environment of joy and sharing through creative experiences, Dream a Dream hopes that participants know that learning remains life-long and joyful.

In one of the camp activities, the participants were encouraged to write on paper the things in their lives that they did not want to continue to do or carry with them in order to lead peaceful lives. During the three days at camp, Bharath did not smoke nor drink any alcohol despite his inability to spend even a minute without drinking or smoking before then. Camp was a dramatically different place for him where no one pressured him to drink or smoke in contrast to his neighbourhood, where everyone encouraged him to drink and smoke. Bharath wrote that he did not want to continue smoking and burned the piece of paper, along with other campers. He quit and has not smoked since. Mahesh was impressed that in spite of Bharath's initial difficult behaviour, he possessed an underlying innocence, goal-orientation, and a desire to do well. Mahesh noted that after just a few conversations about the dangers of smoking, Bharath decided and followed through successfully. According to Mahesh, Bharath also tried to persuade his friends to quit smoking and always maintained a good rapport with his network of friends. He was, in fact, a natural leader.

Bharath recalls about this time in his life, "Day by day I learnt how to behave…. The facilitators helped me learn life skills." Life skills for Bharath included how to speak respectfully to and with elders and to remain patient and "keep cool."

There were also Dream a Dream activities that encouraged participants to reflect on ethics and rules and the consequences of the choices that participants make in their everyday lives. The teaching was done in the context of what seemed to Bharath like radical equality between students and participants. Vishal notes that while Dream a Dream does not have specific activities related to ethics, the facilitators are trained to hold space for reflections about ethics, values, and consequences when participants move in that direction. For example, it might come up during a reflection session that smoking and drinking is bad. The facilitators ask questions about consequences and implications around choices to ensure that multiple, diverse views are shared, without providing simple solutions, and that perspectives are shared without judgement. Young people are encouraged to think critically and make their own choices. Bharath notes, "Teachers at Dream a Dream are not like teachers at school; socially, we cannot tell who is a student and who is a facilitator. We are so friendly… the staff will share everything there."

The Dream a Dream staff also helped Bharath re-orient his life in other ways. When Bharath expressed his interest in getting a job to support his family, for example, the facilitators encouraged Bharath to take more job skills-related courses at the Career Connect Centre. They helped him practise for his first interviews and helped him get a job at Airtel, a large telecom service provider for India. Bharath worked more than eight to nine hours a day at his job once he was determined that he had a goal he wanted to achieve.

Mahesh also spoke with Bharath's parents regularly, asking after them and asking about how Bharath was doing at home. He also shared some positive things about what he noticed about Bharath at the Career Connect Centre. Mahesh noticed that when he first began to speak with Bharath's parents, they had many things to complain about him. But as time went on, they began to have more and more positive things to say, even stating recently that Bharath was doing well. The positive reports from Mahesh to his parents likely influenced their attitude and behaviour towards him to be more affirming. The positive feedback that Bharath directly received from the Dream a Dream facilitators also likely started a virtuous cycle where negativity slowly transformed into more positive interactions and behaviours from him.

Even though Mahesh currently works with the Teacher Development Programme with Dream a Dream, at a different location and has moved from the role of facilitator at the Career Connect Centre at KR Puram, Bharath keeps in touch with Mahesh, speaking with him at least two to three times a month, if not every week. If Bharath has any doubt, confusion, or disappointments in his life or he needs advice, Dream a Dream is the first place where he would go. Dream a Dream staff tell their participants that family, work, education, or other life issues are all welcome to be discussed. Bharath knows that he will receive valuable ideas, and that any issues he might have would go away if he spoke to Dream a Dream, and he would leave feeling more at peace.

[Bharath at the annual Celebrating You event organised by the Career Connect Programme, 2018]

When asked about his dream for five years from now, Bharath said that he wanted to pay off the loans he has obtained to buy land, build a home, and to be with his mother. He believes it is everyone's dream to have a house, so their family would sleep well at night. Otherwise, he spends his free time as any other young person, watching movies (his favourite is *Rangathalam*) and playing songs on his phone, living with the freedom that comes from having work that helps him to support a family, about whom he cares. He is glad to have friends and mentors who support him, as he lives his life, day by day and step by step. Bharath is continuing to learn to sort out his challenges as Dream a Dream supports him to do so, as they do for thousands of young people every year.

10

Changing the Trajectory of the Next Generation

Ranjith M.

[Ranjith M., Bangalore, 2022]

Involvement with Dream a Dream can not only change the lives of children but that of their families as well. Ranjith's story is an example. Ranjith, at the time of his interview in 2019, was a 23-year-old football facilitator for the After School Life Skills Programme who had been with Dream a Dream in various capacities for 12 years, more than half of his life.

He first encountered Dream a Dream as a student in the After School Life Skills Programme for rugby, in 2008, when he was

12 years old. He has been working at Dream a Dream since 2012, when he was 17 years old. Even though he came from a big family, where his father had seven brothers and his mother had five brothers, Ranjith was the first person in his family to pass the 10th standard and continue to obtain a pre-university college certificate, when he finished 12th standard. Dream a Dream and its child-centred practices played a critical role in changing his trajectory and that of his family's.

Recognition from Dream a Dream

Aside from his love for sports, for which he was well-known to his teachers, Ranjith described his younger self as "lonely" and "silent." But he enjoyed playing kabaddi, a contact team sport popular in India and other parts of Asia, featured in professional leagues and the Asian Games, in which India often dominates.

When Dream a Dream came to his school, the Round Table School, offering rugby, Ranjith initially was not interested in playing the sport. But the promise of having a sports uniform, snacks, and new shoes piqued his interest. With his father being a fruit seller and his mother working as a domestic worker, money was tight. There was not much extra for new shoes or snacks. He was selected to join the team after try-outs. Immediately, in the first week, he was named as the "Best Player of the Week" and received a certificate. That kind of public recognition motivated Ranjith, and he wanted to continue. He received the "Best Sportsman" award for three weeks in a row, distinguishing himself from 250 other young people. He also received the "Best Tackler" award. Ranjith recalls, "I was very weak academically and went through school unnoticed. But when I received the award, the school asked me to stand in front of everyone and hear everyone's applause. I felt so happy to be recognised."

Ranjith's engagement with rugby continued with further positive reinforcement. During the fourth week of his participation, a tournament was organised among ten schools and a selection process to join the team was initiated. His school selected him, and even though they lost the tournament, Ranjith caught the rugby fever. He worked hard for the next three years playing rugby and ended up playing in the national tournament in Delhi — his team was placed fifth among twenty-five or so teams in the All-India Under-16 National championships. He enjoyed the friendships, positive energy, and teamwork skills that playing the game helped him develop.

[Ranjith playing rugby in a Bangalore club tournament, Bangalore, 2021]

INFORMATION BOX 10A: USING POSITIVE REINFORCEMENTS TO CREATE POSITIVE CHANGE

Dream a Dream encourages facilitators, teachers, and school leaders to use positive reinforcements, including creating platforms to help recognise every child. This practice comes from Dream a Dream staff members noticing that when children grow up in poverty, they are often taught, intentionally or unintentionally, to be invisible. Dream a Dream staff members note that children often lack the presence of a caring and compassionate adult in their life, with parents living in constant stress and unable to offer the time and attention that children need. Staff also note that children do not have a voice in their household as most of the decisions are made for them without taking their views into consideration as elders are seen as decision-makers.

Dream a Dream facilitators also note many children who participate in their programmes are pushed to become adults at a very early age and are asked to take on the responsibility of the family such as earning an income, taking care of household chores, and taking care of younger siblings while parents are at work, resulting in the emotional needs and well-being of the child taking a back seat.

One of the early insights in Dream a Dream's approach has been that "every child has a valid desire to be seen and heard" and how can supporters' engagement with them to create a safe space where children are seen, heard, and validated. It can start with simply remembering their names, listening to their stories, acknowledging them, validating their presence in the programme and noticing positive behaviours that can be recognised and celebrated. These practices demonstrate to the children that 'they matter' and that others 'see and hear them'.

Further elaboration on Dream a Dream's practice of using positive reinforcement can be found in the mentoring manual written by Dr. David Kennedy and Dr. Fiona Pearson.

Source:

Kennedy, D. & Pearson, F. (2011). *The dream mentoring manual: Life skills development for youth from vulnerable backgrounds.* ISBN 978-81-922631-0-06

A Steady, Listening Presence from Dream a Dream Facilitators

Dream a Dream's After School Life Skills Programme in rugby and the facilitators remained a steady presence during what turned out to be a turbulent childhood for Ranjith. His father lost his source of livelihood due to an accident and resorted to comforting himself by drinking alcohol. As he drank more, there was more fighting between his mother and father at home. With his father not bringing home an income, there was less money at home. This meant that sometimes Ranjith would go hungry. His parents were so busy with their lives, too, that there was not much positive interaction with Ranjith or his siblings. "My parents did not listen to us," Ranjith recalls. "They only came home to cook, eat, and sleep; that is all." Ranjith, too, only went home to sleep as he spent his entire day at school, studying or playing. "No one was there to listen to my thoughts, my ideas, my feelings, or my hunger at home," he recalls.

For example, when his rugby team was placed fifth in Delhi, he came back home, excited to talk to his parents about his travels and his team's success. Moreover, his photo was in the newspaper that day with the rest of the team. But his mother was not happy after fighting with his father and did not respond to him with approval and encouragement as he would have liked. Ranjith remembers being angry and disappointed with her to the point of being depressed and in tears.

When he went to school, however, his teacher noticed the photo from the newspaper, and he put the photo on the school bulletin board. He also invited Ranjith to speak about his experience with everyone at the school assembly. Ranjith said he finally felt happiness with that recognition. Not only did the positive attention strengthen his confidence, but he also noticed that teachers' attitudes toward him changed. "I felt supported by teachers who encouraged me to also put some effort into studying."

INFORMATION BOX 10B: IMPORTANCE OF PUBLIC RECOGNITION FOR YOUTH

Personal or professional recognition for positive behaviour is important for young peoples' socio-psychological development (Law, Siu & Shek, 2012). It promotes identity formation and enhances their moral reasoning and social perspective (ibid).

Unlike other intervention models, where problems are identified by adults and children and young people are the objects of interventions, positive recognition for actions that young people choose to take allows the children and young people to take ownership of their own situations. This is a key strength of positive interventions as the role of children and youth is more action oriented. They are perceived as active agents, who are ready and capable to foster the well-being of themselves and the others around them. It is about having a say while living as a community together, where children and youth are empowered as knowledgeable, active, and self-respecting members of their environments. (Hakli, Korkiamäki & Kallio, 2018).

Sources:

Law, B. M., Siu, A. M., & Shek, D. T. (2012). Recognition for positive behaviour as a critical youth development construct: Conceptual bases and implications on youth service development. *The Scientific World Journal, 2012*, 1-7. doi:10.1100/2012/809578

Häkli, J., Korkiamäki, R., & Kallio, K. P. (2018). 'Positive recognition' as a preventive approach in child and youth welfare services. *International Journal of Social Pedagogy*, 7(1): 5. DOI: https://doi.org/10.14324/111.444.ijsp.2018.v7.1.005.

Ranjith also knew that he could share his challenges with his Dream a Dream facilitator, Revanna Marilinga, a Dream a Dream graduate. When Ranjith entered the 10th standard, having Revanna as someone who could listen to him became very important as he faced three big events in his life. Ranjith fell in love with a girl; finances became a bigger problem in his family with his father losing his job; and he faced the decision of whether to continue with his education after the 10th standard.

As Ranjith was making the decision, Revanna asked him why he wanted to leave school and stop learning. Ranjith told him that he decided that he wanted a full-time job, instead of going to school, because he thought that it would enable him to continue to play sports. Sports had always given him the recognition he craved, and with a new girlfriend, Ranjith wanted to show her and her family that he could be good at something. However, Revanna helped him explore multiple choices that Ranjith could make, including the implications of each choice. Revanna told him that he could also consider a part-time job, which would allow him to continue his studies and play sports. He shared what he thought would happen if Ranjith left his studies and what would happen if he did not. He also shared stories of different people who chose to continue their education and those who chose to stop their education. Revanna told him that the decision was up to Ranjith, but Ranjith felt that he got a good understanding of the consequences of his choices after speaking with Revanna.

Revanna's guidance of Ranjith demonstrates one of the other core principles of Dream a Dream's approach: to not influence young peoples' choices and decisions, imposing an adult's perspective. Dream a Dream believes each individual is unique and has his or her own story and journey and that the organisation's role is to be there for them. The facilitators see their role as comprising of listening, validating, not judging, and helping the participants to think through their choices. Dream a Dream staff intentionally give space for programme participants to make their own choices, even if they are different from the choices the staff would have made. They do this with the belief that guided autonomy helps build critical thinking skills, resilience, and the confidence to make decisions for themselves throughout their lives.

Ranjith's first choice for a job was to work for Dream a Dream as a part-time facilitator, something he had shared with the staff since he was in the ninth standard. But at the time, Dream a Dream did not have any openings. So, Ranjith applied for a part-time job at McDonald's and KFC, and when he got a job at McDonald's, he gave his earnings to his parents, saving some to spend on himself. He also applied to a government pre-university college, where he could play sports.

While Ranjith was making important life choices about his career and future, he also wanted to support his community. He joined with Vishnu Reji, another Dream a Dream graduate, and other rugby players from Dream a Dream to start a community initiative in their neighbourhood. They taught rugby to younger boys and girls in their free time, helping them get a chance to play a sport and learn life skills. Even though they had no money, they scraped together 10–20 rupees ($0.13– $0.26) among themselves every day to provide snacks for the young players, knowing how important snacks had been for them when they were children. Ranjith had such a natural rapport with the children that when Vishal visited one of these community sessions at a public playground and interacted with a few children, one of them, no more than 10 or 11 years old, excitedly shared with him that when he grew up, he wanted to be like Ranjith.

Others too noticed Ranjith's ability to connect with children. As Ranjith shared his experiences of working the night shift at McDonald's with Revanna and showed him his hands that had been burnt while frying food, Revanna invited him to support him in the field while offering the After School Life Skills Programme in football. He noticed that Ranjith had a flair for facilitation. Children enjoyed his company and listened to him. Because Ranjith came from a similar challenging background as the programme participants, he was readily able to offer empathy and patience.

Ranjith's generosity in buying what he could to share with the young rugby participants had also caught the attention of the

Dream a Dream's staff. When an opening came up, they offered Ranjith the opportunity to go through the recruiting process to become a facilitator. When the staff formally asked Ranjith if he wanted to join Dream a Dream, Ranjith's biggest dream of joining and giving back to the organisation that had given him so much, came true.

Learning to Support Himself and to Support Others

Ranjith worked as a facilitator in the After School Life Skills Programme for two years. At the same time, he was participating as a learner in spoken English, basic computer, and money management classes at Dream a Dream's Career Connect Centre. He struggled the first year, as learning to be a facilitator was challenging, even with his natural gifts at being able to connect with children. For a facilitator, he was very young. He was just 18 years old, and physically, he looked even younger. Some children, and even principals and teachers, would not take him seriously. One of the teachers even said, "This boy looks like one of our students. What change can he bring about in them when we haven't been able to make a difference in them after so many years?" But Ranjith persisted.

The first school where he worked as an After School Life Skills facilitator had many students who were continually failing to pass the ninth standard. The fact that they had repeated the standard so many times meant that many students were older than Ranjith. This made Ranjith feel anxious and insecure. In addition, Ranjith had to learn a whole new set of skills in facilitating a life skills curriculum and not just a sports curriculum. Ranjith worked on both challenges and persevered to overcome them with help.

For example, he worked on his language skills to sound more mature and worked on his body language and dress to look older. He also built his general knowledge about facilitation and life skills, and he spent a lot of time with the teachers and principals to build his credibility as a facilitator. He also took individualised training sessions from the After School Life Skills Programme manager and other senior facilitators at Dream a Dream. In this way, Dream a Dream did not give up on him and did not fire him, but kept supporting him and encouraging him to learn and grow.

After a year at a government school, he moved to become an After School Life Skills Programme facilitator at a low-cost private school. Facilitating at this school was a different experience as he found that the teachers and principal were very strict. He did not have the same kind of freedom as he did at the government school as a facilitator. However, the children were very creative and showed initiative and were easy to lead. The only drawback was that the traditional culture of the school hindered the children from showing their creativity and initiative. Ranjith worked with the children to enable them to interact across genders, and this led to many more girls signing up for the Football After School Life Skills Programme.

Ranjith also worked closely with the teachers and principal. He stayed late after every session to name individual children's interests and the potential they have if allowed a bit more freedom. Eventually, Ranjith was able to convince the school staff to allow the children to put on a school event that was completely organised and led by the students.

The reputation of the Dream a Dream After School Life Skills Programme spread with the successful event. It led to three more schools in the neighbourhood asking Dream a Dream to work with them. Gradually, teachers at this school changed their behaviour and learnt to integrate empathy, care, and trust in their approach with students in their classroom. The success he experienced at the school is a memory that Ranjith cherishes, even as he recalls it during our interview.

Ranjith found that he could understand the young people and what they needed in terms of support as they came from backgrounds like his. He wanted to do for them what Revanna had done for him when he was younger — providing unending patience, unconditional support, and acceptance of him just as he was, with room to grow.

Currently, Ranjith mentors After School Life Skills facilitators by modelling the relevant skills for building relationships in schools and for supporting young people. Less experienced facilitators reach out to him for support and advice; he has a reputation among them for always having ideas for new activities and icebreakers to use in sessions. He also introduces Dream a Dream's work to teachers and to parents, to help them understand what Dream a Dream is trying to do with and for young people.

He is an active volunteer, coach, and champion for rugby with the Karnataka Rugby Football Union and participates in many community outreach events. He is currently coaching women players who are under age 20 to prepare for the Karnataka State Rugby tournament as a State Rugby coach. He has been instrumental in getting many girls admitted into prestigious colleges in Bangalore on sports reservation and helping them join the college rugby team and even encouraging a college to start their own women's rugby team. He hopes to create an NGO using the power of rugby to develop life skills and to also train parents and teachers with the skills of facilitation.

There has been no stopping Ranjith in his quest to change the trajectory of his life. In 2020, when the world was in the throes of a global COVID-19 pandemic, Ranjith along with his friends Vishnu and Nasrulla invested in starting a local food shop, Shawarma Adda, in Bommanahalli and became entrepreneurs. Ranjith also used the lockdown to learn a new skill as a tattoo artist and is now a professional tattoo artist earning anything from Rs. 4,000–15,000 per artwork that he creates. Ranjith is thriving.

With his job, he is supporting his two younger brothers — one is studying at the Industrial Training Institute and another is studying for a bachelor's degree in business administration. When his father had an accident and lost his job, Ranjith made sure that he received the healthcare he needed, and he took on the responsibility of supporting his family financially. He continues to contribute his income to his family. His parents are happier now, and while he did not talk to them for a few years, he has mended his relationship with them. He speaks to them almost every day, sharing something about what happened that day. Ranjith feels that he is now receiving the love, care, and support that he had missed from his parents in his childhood. Even the wider community around his family praises him in front of his parents. "My parents have become supportive of my career and have started to believe in my dreams and goals in life," Ranjith says.

Exposure to New Experiences and Support Opens New Possibilities and Choices

Without Dream a Dream, Ranjith believes he would have stopped his education after the 10th standard, and that he would not be playing sports. He imagines he would have gone into working as a manual labourer or would be just roaming the streets, aimlessly, without goals or plans. He says this is what his cousins and friends, who grew up in similar circumstances, are doing now.

Pondering over how he has changed over the dozen years he has been with Dream a Dream as a participant and an employee, Ranjith says that the trips for sports that took him away from his neighbourhood introduced him to lifestyles that were different than the ones he saw in his surroundings while growing up. The exposure to different environments led him to ask questions and aspire to be and to do more than what he saw growing up. He now wants to be a role model for young people and to be for them the kind of mentor he did not have when he was a child.

Many young people with whom Ranjith grew up believed that they were supposed to stay where they were and remain where they were comfortable. Young people would say to him, for example, "No one in our family studied beyond a certain standard; we won't study beyond that either." But as Ranjith went to different neighbourhoods to play rugby matches, he saw that there were many ways to live. Some children came in cars to play rugby, others had Nike and Adidas shoes, still others wore expensive shirts. Ranjith found himself thinking, "Why are our shirts ordinary? Why don't we wear shoes like that? Why don't my parents have that kind of money? Why does my father live the same life as my grandfather? Why hasn't there been any change over the generations?" He began to think, "I want to be able to buy shoes like that. I want to build and change myself. I want to study and go to college. I want to change things for my children. I want different things for my children. If I study, then my children are more likely to study." He decided that he did not want to follow the usual path of staying where his family was. He said he wanted to be "special" and do "new things". He became determined to provide more choices for himself and his family.

Through Dream a Dream, he also learnt not to put himself down and not to be discouraged in the face of challenges or problems, particularly in the face of the financial struggles that his family faced and the fights the financial challenges caused between his parents. He knew from playing rugby, physically one of the toughest games to play, that facing big opponents was part of the game, and that it required hard work. He also knew from the life skills he learnt through rugby that if he could face his challenges and overcome them and if he made good choices, he could build a beautiful future.

Ranjith learnt the value of treating everyone equally and being treated equally at Dream a Dream. As a result, Ranjith felt safe at Dream a Dream. "Whether we were weak or strong, they treated us equally," Ranjith says about the facilitators at Dream a Dream. There were no put-downs and everyone was positive towards him. All staff, from Vishal onwards, acted as role models for each other. This modelling inspired the young people to also behave in a similar way. Ranjith believes that the culture of respect and positivity is so strongly rooted in Dream a Dream that it goes beyond one person or a group of people. When I ask him what would happen if Vishal stepped down as CEO, Ranjith replies that the organisation would go on. "Life skills are in everyone's head," he says, and Dream a Dream is not dependent on a single person, having grown into its value-based identity after twenty years.

Learning through Stories

Ranjith also mentions that he thinks the stories he heard at Dream a Dream helped him think through different choices, challenges, and opportunities he encountered in life. The stories were instrumental in strengthening him. Explaining how the stories were able to do that for him, he says that in the narratives, he saw how people faced problems or stepped away from them and how they struggled with issues like his, how they faced their anger or fear and/or experienced happiness or confidence. He believes that as he works with young people, it is easier to teach them through stories than it is to tell them directly what he wants them to understand. Young people find stories inherently engaging, and Ranjith sees stories as powerful means of communicating with young people.

Ranjith shares a story about Vishal from Dream a Dream's initial days as an example. Vishal did not have much money, but he wanted sketch pads and crayons for children with whom Dream a Dream worked. He took other Dream a Dream volunteers to Chamrajpeta, a local area, where there were several stationery shops. He and other volunteers approached the shop owners and asked for donations, after which they were able to bring back sketch pads and crayons for all the children. From that story, Ranjith learnt how there was almost always a way to resolve challenges, even with limited resources, so that young people are happy.

He also notes that it was not just stories themselves that were important to him, but that he was listened to when he told his own stories at Dream a Dream. The story about his disappointment and anger with his mother for not listening to him when he came back from Delhi from the rugby tournament is something that he shares regularly with parents and teachers when he is explaining what Dream a Dream does for children. "Even though my mother neglected me, and I wanted to stop everything and leave, my teacher and Dream a Dream facilitator gave me space and listened to my problems. Their making space for me and listening to me motivated me to continue to achieve more things."

He emphasises to the parents and teachers how important it is to just listen and not give advice to children when they share their challenges. He encourages the young people he works with to tell him stories, even as he tells them stories, as a "give and take." As he tells his own stories, they feel closer to him, and they in turn, want to tell him more of their stories. Mutual vulnerability and equality create a safe space.

 **INFORMATION BOX 10C: LEARNING TO MANAGE ANGER**

Anger is an emotion that includes irritation, distress, and pain. It can evoke a fight or flight reaction. Excess anger can take a toll physically, mentally, and cognitively (Yadav, 2017). The common reasons for anger in students are unjust treatment, attacks on their personality, and unfair criticism (Kisac, 2009). Research studies show that interpersonal rejection can also contribute to aggressive behaviour and anger management issues (Leary, 1970). While anger management techniques and methods are common, the readiness of the individuals to address it is the most important factor in learning to manage it (Howells & Day, 2002).

Dream a Dream Activity to Help Participants Manage Anger — Paper Bag Puppets
This is an activity for identifying and expressing emotions visually.

Instructions:
1. Give everyone a paper bag and ask them to hold the bag while they listen.
2. Say, "Everyone feels angry sometimes. Most of us have a hard time knowing what to do when we get angry. Sometimes we yell, sometimes we fight, and sometimes we freeze. What else do we do when we're angry?" Pause and ask participants to share their answers. Write them down on the board or chart paper.
3. Say, "Why do you think we get angry? When we're angry it might mean, for example, that we're not getting something that we need." Pause and ask participants for their answers. After the discussion, say, "Today and tomorrow, we are going to practice understanding what happens when we get angry. Using puppets, we are going to understand which need is not being met when we are angry in different situations."
4. Say, "Think of a story of a time when you were angry. Make a puppet that looks the way you felt at that time. This is not a puppet of you! It's a puppet of the way that you feel."
5. Say, "Think about your story. What colour did you feel? Red? Black? Blue? Did your eyes feel big, or wet, or hot? Was your mouth open or closed? Whatever you were feeling make it bigger. Make your puppet look angry."

Tip: As the facilitator, go around and help the youth translate their stories into puppets by asking questions about how they felt and helping them translate those feelings into shapes and colours.

6. Put up a list of feeling words like angry, hurt, sad, disappointed, frustrated, and lonely. Make sure youth know what each one means.

7. When participants are done with their puppets, ask if anyone can share a story (you may have to share yours first. Be sure that you do not share a story that will frighten the young people and tell a story that they can relate to) using their puppet's voice.

8. Listen to the volunteer's story and then reflect back to them, "Do you feel hurt (or sad, or lonely, or whatever the feeling is that you hear in the story)? Do you need some space (or a hug, or someone to listen, or whatever you hear in the story)?" If that is what the volunteer is feeling, they can say "Yes," in their puppet's voice. "I am hurt, and I need some space," or they can say, "No. I'm not hurt. I'm angry, and I need to run away." It doesn't matter what they say at this stage, there is no judgment, just help them to identify the feelings and the needs.

9. Thank the volunteer for their courage in telling their story and tell the others "we will be using these puppets to make plays tomorrow."

Reflection Circle:
First, ask what happened. What was it like to remember your story and make a puppet out of it? Ask the youth volunteer, what was it like to tell your story to the group and have your feelings reflected. Listen carefully as they are sharing.

Sources:

Howells, K., & Day, A. (2002, October 12). Readiness for anger management: Clinical and theoretical issues. *https://www.sciencedirect.com/science/article/abs/pii/S0272735802002283*

Kısaç, İ. (2009, March 18). Anger provoking reasons on high school and university students. https://www.sciencedirect.com/science/article/pii/S1877042809003905

Mark R. Leary, J. (1970, January 01). Interpersonal Rejection as a Determinant of Anger and Aggression - Mark R. Leary, Jean M. Twenge, Erin Quinlivan, 2006. https://journals.sagepub.com/doi/abs/10.1207/s15327957pspr1002_2

Yadav, R. L. (2017, January). ANGER; ITS IMPACT ON HUMAN BODY. https://www.researchgate.net/publication/328065633_ANGER_ITS_IMPACT_ON_HUMAN_BODY

Ranjith does a lot of reflecting while he is commuting on his bike. He thinks about his day — the happy things, the sad things, the positive things, and the negative things. He thinks about whether he is making good choices. He has a lot of dreams and imagines having a family of his own. When he has children, he says, he would invite them to talk about whatever they want to, even if it is about a first boyfriend or girlfriend. He wants to be a supportive presence, explaining different choices and options to them, but not deciding things for them. He wants to be able to recognise their strengths and their weaknesses. "I will not create dreams for them," he says. "I will not think in terms of 'My kids will become like this or like that.'" He wants to be a role model for them, and to support them as they create and follow their own dreams as they work to understand the community, the world, and their lives.

"My parents did not care for me, and they did not talk with us and did not support us like that while my brothers and I were growing up. When I suggested anything to them, they would be afraid first, and thus would not encourage me to act or take risks." As a result, "I was stuck. I did not venture outside. I missed too many things in my childhood. But when I came to Dream a Dream, I went outside, and I explored. I will give my children what I did not have. Very big dream, right?" Ranjith laughs as explains his dreams for the interview. But his dream goes further. He says, "I'm thinking this not only for my children. I want this for ALL children." He continues to speak to teachers and parents, day in and day out, sharing his story, with the belief that they would support the young people around them in the ways that Revanna and others at Dream a Dream did for him.

Providing a Basket of Knowledge and Opportunities to Young People through the Career Connect Centre

Pavithra KL

[Pavithra KL at the Dream a Dream office, Bangalore, 2022]

As Bharath, Ranjith, and other participants' stories show, influential staff members with lived experiences are a key component to Dream a Dream's success in working with young people. As strong as Dream a Dream's programmes are, the people who oversee and run them are the cornerstone on which the programmes are built. There is a common saying in community organising work "people over programmes," and Pavithra KL's journey with Dream a Dream, paired with the story of the development of Dream a Dream's Career Connect Centre, illustrates how this principle manifests itself in the organisation.

In fact, in addition to Vishal, Suchetha, and Revanna, the Dream a Dream staff member who is mentioned the most by those interviewed for this book as an inspirational and supportive leader is Pavithra. It is no wonder that Pavithra, known to her friends and colleagues as Pavi, is the Associate Director of Innovation Labs, which includes the Career Connect Programme and After School Life Skills Programme. Dynamic and warm, she was 29 years old at the time of my interview with her in 2019. She had been with Dream a Dream for over 13 years, working at Dream a Dream since she graduated from the 10th standard. She attended Vidya College in the evening and completed both her pre-university degree and Bachelor of Commerce degree while working at Dream a Dream during the day. Her story reflects that of Dream a Dream graduates' in many ways.

Looking for a Job and Finding Evening College and Dream a Dream Instead

Around the time Pavi turned 15 years old in 2007, she realised there was "a lot of conflict within [my] family because we are three girls, and my dad always wanted a boy — at least one boy in the family. Fortunately, or unfortunately, we are three sisters. My parents had always thought their future was not secure because there was no boy in the family. Because we are girls, they assumed we would get married and there would be nobody who would take care of them. When my father became an alcoholic, many responsibilities that he used to carry fell on my mom. They started to fight a lot. I still remember, I don't think there was a month without a fight between my parents at that time." Because of the impact of her father's alcoholism on their economic stability, Pavi was the only person among her friends who could not afford to go to college. She had to work instead, starting from the 10th standard.

It was also at this time that one of her sisters and her mother started to have health issues. Pavi, as the middle child, was forced to take up some responsibilities within the family. Pavi recalled that she was pushed to learn a lot of things in a short amount of time, but she had a lot of confidence. At 15 years old, she found herself telling her mother to not worry, and that she would take care of the family. She had a big dream of working in the police department or being a lawyer.

Recalling that moment, Pavi says that she was able to be so confident because she had always heard, especially from her relatives, that going to school until the 10th standard was enough, that there was so much she could do with only that level of schooling. Now, when she looks back at what her relatives had told her, she believes they had said those things with good intentions. However, she also believes that it might have been true in their generation, but that it is not the case any longer. So much of the world has changed; she knows now there is much more that young people need to know before being able to get a job. But back then, she thought she could go out and look for a job quite easily.

Thus, Pavi took all her dreams of supporting her family with her when she went searching for a job. She learnt quickly, however, that there was a minimum age requirement for jobs. She also learnt that people were looking for her to have specific skills. At 15 years old, she did not know what they were asking about. She did not know how to get from one place to another. Pavi recalls, "I didn't even know how to navigate through the city by bus all alone." She found herself completely challenged by what she had thought to be a simple task of looking for and getting a job to support her family.

At the same time, Pavi had a friend at school with whom she used to go to sports and dance programmes. Pavi loved watching dance shows, to learn new steps and songs that she could use in her own dancing. When her friend invited her to watch a dance show, she agreed. It turned out to be Dream a Dream's show put on by its participants. That was when she first learnt about Dream a Dream and got to know some of the staff.

As Pavi continued to look for jobs, she thought perhaps having someone older with her might help her. Maybe it was his kind and approachable demeanour or his relative closeness in age to her, but she asked Vishal if he could come with her to help her find a job. Pavi, looking back, said she was now sure Vishal knew that she was too young, at 15 years old, to get a job. But instead of telling her that she should not be looking for jobs and should be going to school, Vishal just went with her. He walked with her from place to place as Pavi was repeatedly told to come back in three years when she was 18 years old.

Pavi and her friend then decided to approach Vishal for a job with Dream a Dream. Because Dream a Dream could not formally hire a minor, Vishal offered them the opportunity for an internship, with the task of designing and implementing a month-long summer camp for children. Because they had shared with Vishal their family's financial situation and their desperation for a paid opportunity, Vishal created a paid internship in response, the first of its kind to be offered by Dream a Dream.

Pavi showed leadership and took the initiative to design and run the camp. After the camp, Pavi voluntarily returned to Dream a Dream to ask for a longer internship. According to Vishal, "her family was in dire need, and Pavi was willing to commit to anything to earn an income for her family." So, he asked for an agreement from her that she would continue her education even as she worked as a paid intern for Dream a Dream.

Thus, Pavi was able to get a paid internship with Dream a Dream that allowed her to have some income for her family. If the internship had not been paid, Pavi would not have been able to take it, given her family's economic situation. The internship gave her more than an income, however. For example, she recalls, "It was only after I joined Dream a Dream that I learnt how to navigate the city via public transportation. I still remember the first trip that Vishal sent me on to collect an envelope from the Hippocampus Learning Centre in a suburb of Bangalore. I got lost. I didn't even know which side of the street to catch the bus from."

Completing those kinds of life skills tasks successfully helped her to consider taking on another challenge — continuing her education beyond the 10th standard. After learning about the possibility of going to evening college from Dream a Dream and after gathering stories of positive experiences from her friends, Pavi eventually decided to go to evening college.[39] Even though she was one of just three girls among 70 boys, even though going to evening college after Dream a Dream meant she had to return home alone after 9 p.m., and even though she wanted

---

[39] Evening colleges have emerged as an attractive option for those who want to use their days to work and their evenings to obtain a degree and/or upgrade their skills. While there might be a common notion that only low-scorers consider evening colleges, in reality, there is a minor difference between the cut-offs of day and evening colleges.
SOURCE: AISHE final Report 2018-19.pdf. (n.d.). All India Survey on Higher Education (AISHE) - Government of India, https://www.scribd.com/document/436745408/AISHE-Final-Report-2018-19-pdf

to quit many times, she wanted to show her family that she could do just as well as boys. With Dream a Dream's support and encouragement, Pavi committed to staying and finishing her degree.

Thus, for Pavi, one of the most influential staff members at Dream a Dream was Vishal. Not only did he accompany her on her trek to find a job when she was fifteen years old and refrained from giving her unsolicited advice, but he also continued to accompany her in her learning journey, which started by giving her very flexible hours in her internship so that she could go to her evening college. She recalls, "He gave first preference to education, telling me that I could leave the office at 4 p.m. so that I could go early to my evening college." These kinds of gestures helped her to value her education, even when she herself did not feel its value and wanted to give up formal education when things became difficult at school. She recalls that she would inevitably think, "What would Vishal think if I quit?" and then persist. Until she was able to internalise the motivation and persistence, he helped her to stay with her schooling, even through the rough patches.

Vishal also took her to her first Hindi movie. She described the experience as "a huge shock to go see Shilpa Shetty's movie, *Metro*, at the PVR theatre in the Garuda mall." She was very anxious and did not understand what was happening in the movie. When the credits rolled, she breathed a sigh of relief that it was over, thinking to herself, "Oh, thank God I completed watching the movie!" And then to her surprise, Vishal took her for coffee afterwards and asked her to reflect on the movie. She admits thinking, "Who would ask this?" No one had ever asked her to reflect on a movie and talk about it. After that first outing, she learnt to pay attention and reflect about the movies as they went to see more of them. Vishal would also give her books to read and ask her to write summaries to help her to think critically. She laughs as she remembers thinking to herself, "Noooo…" whenever he would ask her to do these tasks. However, she reflects that she "felt very lucky because at that time, the organisation was still small and [she] could get that kind of personal attention from not only Vishal but also from every staff member."

Pavi remembers that Vishal was always patient with her, always listening and responding, and modelling reflective thinking with her. She puts it this way, "Vishal is someone who would respond to calls at two in the morning, from even those who had graduated 12 years ago from Dream a Dream."

Vishal, in turn, remembers Pavi's drive, grit, resilience, hard work, commitment, and creativity. He recalls that Pavi did not know a word of English when she first came to Dream a Dream, but she faced the challenge of handling largely urban, educated, English-speaking volunteers. Pavi took the initiative to learn English on her own and learnt to use the computer on her own as well.

When Pavi turned 18 years old, she earned a full-time role at Dream a Dream, in charge of designing and managing Dream Fundays, which were day-long fun exposure activities for children and volunteers that had components of fun and engaging opportunities to develop life skills. In one year, she organised 54 Fundays, more than one per week, and she participated in all of them. That record of the highest number of Fundays organised still holds within Dream a Dream. Pavi shone in not just being able to execute a great number of Fundays, but also in creating what Vishal saw as "beautiful relationships with volunteers and children alike, for many of whom, a Funday was their first engagement with Dream a Dream."

Vishal also saw that when Pavi started earning an income, she supported her family. As her salary grew, Pavi ensured that her sisters got all the opportunities to study, learn, and explore that she did not get. Pavi also supported many girls in her neighbourhood with their school fees. She used to tutor younger girls after school in her neighbourhood post work and college. Vishal says the following about Pavi's growth at Dream of Dream and as a person: "Pavi has always been her own person with a strong, steadfast identity. Her experience at Dream a Dream was just the right nudge she needed to come into her own."

Starting the Career Connect Programme

After Pavi completed her internship and became part of the Dream a Dream staff, working with young people, the Dream a Dream team began to iterate the idea of starting a Career Connect Programme. By 2010, many graduates of Dream a Dream Creative Arts and Football After School Life Skills Programmes had turned sixteen years old and came back to Dream a Dream to ask, "Where can I go and apply for a job? What does it mean to wear formal clothing to an interview? I know that usually formal clothing is the sari, but I also heard that wearing shirts and trousers is also considered formal. What do I wear for a job interview?"

Because Dream a Dream staff had maintained strong and supportive relationships with the programme participants through the years, young people would feel comfortable coming to them with questions, even after they had graduated from the formal programmes. As they answered the questions one by one, the staff began to think that perhaps they could offer a programme about career preparedness to groups of young people.

What was becoming clear to Dream a Dream was that young people with adverse childhood experiences were making important life and career choices at 14 or 15 years old because either they needed to support their families or because they did not have the financial resources to pursue further education. Many also simply did not know what to do next with their life after completing their required formal schooling. With these emerging sets of common questions asked by their graduates, Dream a Dream began to see the gap between the desires of young people to have a way to support their families and the kinds of knowledge they needed to seek a meaningful career. There was also a gap between being 15 and wanting to work and being 18 and being age-qualified to work.

> **INFORMATION BOX 11A: THE NEED TO CLOSE THE WORKPLACE READINESS AND SKILLS GAP**
>
> According to the India Skills Report 2020 (Wheebox, 2020), more than 50% of Indian students actively seeking employment opportunities were deemed not ready for jobs by potential employers. The employers expected the following from prospective candidates, in addition to the technical know-how: (1) positive attitude (2) adaptability (3) learning agility (4) domain expertise (5) interpersonal skills.
>
> There is also an evident gap in terms of students being aware of the opportunities available to develop the above skills. This is highlighted by the fact that although 94% of the students understood the benefits of apprenticeship in their field, just 60% knew about the government's National Apprenticeship Scheme (NAPS).
>
> Skill gaps can be effectively addressed if the academicians, the government, and the businesses put joint efforts to focus on learning. About 45.9% of the students were identified as job-ready and there is a significant decrease by 0.1% from last year's employability score reported in Skill India Report 2021. A further deep dive into sectors' perspectives in the emerging areas suggests that there is still much work required to equip the talent pool of India's youth with skills of the 21st century. Especially when the industries have been put through challenges during the pandemic, the need for critical thinking, flexibility, resilience, and communication has been the top requirement. Some of the most preferred skills that employers were looking for were in life skills. The global demand for communication skills, problem solving capacity, and agile adaptability are high. These qualifications were

Contd…

given significant importance on par with domain knowledge in a given industry. There is an imminent need for carefully structured programmes that prepare students to deal with real-world problems (Wheebox, 2021).

Sources:
Wheebox, (2020). India Skills Report 2020: Reimagining India's Talent Landscape for a $5T Economy – People Strong. *https://www.peoplestrong.com/wp-content/ uploads/2020/02/India-Skills-Report-2020.pdf*
Wheebox, et al (2021). *India Skills Report 2021: Key Insights into the Post-COVID Landscape of Talent Demand and Supply in India.* https://indiaeducationforum. org/pdf/ISR-2021.pdf

Like Pavi at age 15, Dream a Dream's other 15-year-olds also had a lot of energy and dreams, and Dream a Dream staff felt that just giving them a stock answer that they needed to wait until they were 18 years old would be a loss of opportunity for the 15-year-olds to grow and learn in other ways. Dream a Dream staff knew that for some opportunities, like entrepreneurship, young people did not need to be 18 years old to begin to engage in earning money. They also knew that desperate young people would find other ways to get jobs in the informal sector, and that many or even most who begin in the informal sector never enter the formal workforce even when they become age-eligible, leading to a life of chronic underemployment. Thus, Dream a Dream created the Career Connect Centre as a way to help bridge this gap between young people and their desire to be professionally successful.

In addition, Dream a Dream's Career Connect Centre was started to create a physical space for young people to engage in authentic conversations, gain experiences, and develop the life skills needed to make healthy life and career choices. From the beginning, Dream a Dream envisioned the Centre as not a typical vocational skill development centre but a space for young people to explore, discover, try new things, fail, and try again, and develop life skills among caring, empathetic, and trustworthy adults. The programme had no formal curriculum and was designed to be flexible and personalised. The Centre was supported by Dell India Research and Development's Corporate Social Responsibility Initiative for over 10 years with funding, technology products, and employee volunteers.

In fact, the Centre has evolved continuously since it began in 2010. Currently, it reaches about 5,000 young people every year between the ages of 14 and 19, through two learning centres in Bengaluru. The focus is on developing life skills to help young people make meaningful transitions from adolescence to adulthood and learn to thrive. The design is youth centred with free, flexible space for young people to spend time together, sign up for programmes of their choice, seek mentorship and guidance, and be in a space they can call their own. Purposefully designed to be welcoming for young people, with rooms set aside for computer use or for sitting and chatting or for classroom use, the Centre is open for young people to walk in, anytime, even if it is at six o'clock in the morning. There are no restrictions saying young people have to be at the centre by 10 a.m. or that they close at 5 p.m. They are open all seven days, and there have been times when they have kept it open until late at night to meet young peoples' need.

The learning modules at Dream a Dream Career Connect Centre are highly personalised. They include English, communication skills, money management, dance workshops, design thinking, beautician studies, and general career guidance among others. The Career Connect Centre also offers career awareness workshops to help young people understand a broader range of opportunities and choices that are available to them. Guided by young peoples' interest, it also offers vocational skills courses such as a beautician training course. It also offers access to internships and jobs by maintaining relationships with the human resource departments of businesses and other organisations. The Career Connect Centre also provides scholarships through a selective guided application process. It offers participants to design and continue their education in ways not directly offered at the Centre, learn a new skill, or start a business.

A key innovation of the Career Connect Centre is peer learning. Many who attend courses at the Career Connect Centre also end up designing and facilitating courses for their peers and teach life skills through teaching the technical skill in which they have become proficient as a result of applying for and receiving a scholarship to pursue their own path of study. Thus, the Career Connect Centre has become the next programme to join after young people have completed the After School Life Skills Programme. The Centre enables Dream a Dream to continuously support young people between the ages of eight and 21.

Pavi and Dream a Dream firmly believe the Centre belongs to the young people, and that they are "just there to facilitate the process." The Career Connect Centre tracks young people for seven years after they have finished a module to see how they are progressing and if they need further support. The information about their graduates helps the staff to provide support to the young people currently in their programmes. Ultimately, they want to ensure that young people are better prepared to meet their future.

Pavi's own story resonates strongly with what the Career Connect Centre was attempting to offer to young people, whose backgrounds and needs she understood very well. She has worked at the Centre since its inception and is now its director.

Growing as a Leader with Dream a Dream

As the Career Connect Programme grew, so did Pavi. For example, Pavi learnt not just to navigate bus routes but also to embrace others and advocate for their needs. This included learning how to navigate the complexities of handling conflict with the police, for example, on behalf of some of the young people she works with. Growing up in neighbourhoods marked by poverty, violence, and crime also meant that sometimes young people are picked up by policemen merely on suspicion of committing a crime. This is a harrowing experience for many young people because they are beaten, abused, and put down by the officers, and they can sometimes languish in prison for months because their families cannot afford to pay bribes or post bail.

Pavi had experienced this first-hand in her own community and felt that young people needed to know that they have a trusted friend, guide, and supporter in Dream a Dream. Vishal notes that she has learnt "to navigate the vagaries of a weak legal system and while scared, anxious, and overwhelmed, she has not let her fears come in the way of helping young people." Pavi shares that she still carries the trauma of visiting young people in prison and has yet to come to terms with a legal system that was failing them. For many young people, being in prison, even for a few weeks, can be a life-altering experience, from which they can have difficulties recovering. Some young people then give in to a life of crime and violence. Pavi liaises with the police, lawyers, courts, hospitals, government, and the community to fight for the human rights of young people. It takes a toll on her emotional and mental well-being, Pavi admits. However, Pavi shares she does not feel alone anymore in her struggle to help young people in these dire situations because she has the supportive forces of love, compassion, and empathy that Vishal, Suchetha, and other Dream a Dream staff and young people bring to her life.

As the Associate Director of Innovation Labs, Pavi currently has 15 Career Connect Centre staff members and 49 After School Life Skills Programme staff members reporting to her. But at first, just being asked to be a leader at Dream a Dream felt like a "huge, huge challenge" to her because she had never led in an official capacity before. As she learnt how to be a leader, one of the first lessons she learnt was to practice integrity between her personal and professional lives. She would run into young people she was trying to teach and lead at the mall, the bank, and everywhere else. She learnt that if she cracked a joke during her personal time that she would not say at work and a young person happened to overhear it, it was easy to have them lose their faith and respect in her. To establish credibility with the people she was leading and create the kind of culture for her team to learn, she learnt how important it was to practice the same behaviours and values at work and in other spaces as it was easy to lose credibility with just one casual joke.

In other words, she began to understand that she could not behave one way at work and another in her personal life if she wanted to be a respected leader for young people. She felt that if she was facilitating a group with young people or staff members, the approach she took should be the same approach she would take with her husband, her parents, or her son. It had to be the same approach, she felt, so that people would not say that she wears a mask that comes on and off with a change in responsibilities. If she were consistent, others would trust her leadership more. With many people now asking her to mentor them, she has learnt to act with integrity.

She is also aware of her own role as a manager and leader. Because of her visibility, many of the girls want to have one-on-one conversations with her. Because she was unique in making a marriage based on love, for example, she knows that there are many young girls who want to talk to her when they themselves feel the pressure of getting into an early, arranged marriage. She knows that they ask her because they trust her. She does not take their trust in her lightly.

Pavi feels strongly about the kind of trust that is given to the staff and facilitators at Dream a Dream that makes young people want to come and talk to them. She knows that "it is the personal connection that we build at the centre" and that it is important that "it is not just a space where young people come for learning while the staff leaves and goes off somewhere else."

"Nothing is Cracked": Learning to Stay Humble and Flexible with Young People at the Centre

Pavi explains that what she has learnt over the past 10 years of working at Dream a Dream with young people is that each young person who comes through their doors is different. "They all come with different learning needs and different thoughts. They also challenge us because of this," she says. Thus, one of the challenges that Pavi addresses with her staff is to ensure that they actively seek the input of young people and listen to them, every year, and not say that a particular programme or module was "cracked" or "complete" or "figured out" because it happened to be successful once. This approach means that she and her staff continually try out new learning modules and new topics to ensure that they are meeting the changing needs and interests of young people.

For example, she shares that recently she has started to explore the possibility of offering a module on "ethical hacking" because a young person had come to her to say she wanted to learn about it. Pavi did not know what ethical hacking was, but she was determined to find out and find a way to provide a learning opportunity for young people to learn about it.

She also believes that validating young peoples' experiences is important. She notes, "To be honest, a lot of my insights come when I go into the session with young people. I need to be there so much because I feel they just throw themselves at us, saying that, you know, we are here. And I feel at the Career Connect Centre, we have so much power to shape many young peoples' lives." She underscores the idea that being and becoming a powerful leader of young people, even as a manager, means she needs to spend time with them and listen to them, while putting her own ideas and ego to the side.

Facilitating Young Peoples' Journeys

"It is very difficult to say that I have a single class module that is great for young people because we do not know what they want to do. Today, they might say they want to be a doctor; tomorrow, they will say they want to be a photographer. Between ages 15 and 24, young people are constantly looking for so many things because they are still trying to figure out what success means to them. The definition of success is different for different people," she observes. She notes that it is the young peoples' journey they are facilitating at the Career Connect Centre, even above and beyond providing a particular skill set or knowledge. Because of her experience, Pavi knows that it is important to give young people the same kind of open-ended freedom and space to explore what they are interested in exploring and become who they want to become.

Pavi gives an example of a young person who dropped out of a skill development programme into which Dream a Dream had placed her. When asked why she had dropped out, the young person told Pavi that while she went to work at the skills development centre every day, she was only learning to clean tables as her mother had done. "I don't want to do what my mother does because she has always told me, 'Don't do what I am doing.'" The young person wanted to do more than cleaning tables and was looking to experience dignity at work. The story shows that without having conversations and without listening to young people, even well-intentioned skill development programmes that were created to fill known, available jobs, would not lead to successful employment for young people.

Other programmes may have difficulty even attracting 250 people each year. They may also institute such stringent pre-entrance requirements that even with initial applications from 1,000 young people, the enrolment number drops to just 10 people. But the Career Connect Centre engages 5,000 young people, across two centres, each hosts 2,500 young people each year with retention rates at over 90% year-after-year.

Thus, Pavi learnt that the informal connections and relationships and the opportunities for talking, reflecting, and listening between young people and the Dream a Dream staff and facilitators are just as important, if not more important, than the formal classroom experience and programmatic content. Facilitators are selected for their passion and commitment towards young people as much as they are for their skills. With so many facilitators who are themselves graduates of the programme, their empathy is often natural. They are regarded as role models for students. Staff are actively encouraged not to stick to the curriculum if something more relevant to students' lives emerges from listening to them.

Pavi firmly believes that if the centre is not used by young people, "the blame should be on us because we are probably offering something young people find irrelevant to their lives." Pavi and Dream a Dream have spent 10 years in the community around the Centre, investing in forming relationships and learning to understand the families, schools, colleges, businesses, and other key stakeholders around them. They now know the community and the community knows them.

Pavi recalls that when she started her journey at Dream a Dream, no one had given her a road map, saying, "You know, Pavi, five years down the line, you will be leading a team of 15 people, and impacting 3,000 young people; and then 10 years down the line, you will lead a staff of 50 people and impacting 10,000 young people." She recalls the times when she had worked as a house maid and other odd jobs she picked up just to ensure that her family did not fall into the debt trap. Her journey was convoluted and organic, and it was taken step by step, with no set path. She remembers that Dream a Dream staff "responded to my situation, every time, even during those times when I felt too shy to express myself." When she felt she needed to find a job, at age 15, because of the pressure and sense of responsibility she felt at home, they did not criticise her nor try to "educate her." Instead, they listened, and walked with her — literally, in Vishal's case — until she came to the realisation that what she needed was to equip herself with further education and skills. For her, "most of the time it was not even financial support that I was seeking." She "just needed someone to listen…. to how [she] felt then."

Pavi has learnt what it means to "hold space" for young people and continually listen and adapt to young peoples' changing needs and interests. Suchetha Bhat, who is currently the CEO of Dream a Dream, helped her to grow in the skill of listening to young people. Pavi notes, "The kind of trust and guidance Suchetha gave me helped me to reach where I am today. She played a vital role in ensuring that I see myself in the bigger ecosystem of helping young people and how my journey can influence society."

Suchetha's primary support has been to help Pavi reconnect with her own story and learn to make meaning of the life experiences she has had that have shaped her values, beliefs, and identity. Suchetha has helped Pavi see herself as a woman in a largely patriarchal society and break out of the narratives that have kept her from living up to her true potential. Pavi shared that Suchetha has helped her to recognise herself as a leader and as a voice for young people growing up in adversity, calling out the systems, norms, and beliefs that "keep people poor and keep women down."

Dream a Dream's success with young people also stems from the long-term relationships they have built with them and the stakeholders in the local, regional, and global communities. When one of Pavi's students committed suicide, for example, Pavi went to talk to Suchetha because she knew that Suchetha would understand. Suchetha listened to her and assured her that she had done all she could. Pavi, in turn, offers similar support to her staff and young people, reaching out to them if she knows one of them is facing difficulties with a family member, suffering from an illness, or has just become a new parent. Pavi reflects, "We always try to ensure that we are there for each other; otherwise, this is not easy, because this work requires soul and heart." The testimonies of the graduates of the Career Connect Centre, which compose most of the chapters in this book, show the kind of difference that work done with knowledge, skill, soul, and heart that is centred on young people can make.

[Pavithra as lead facilitator at Dream a Dream's Change the Script Conference, Bangalore, 2018]

Waiting for Sunday – Leading the Career Connect Centre's Scholarship, Placement, and Entrepreneurship Programmes

Shiva Shekar

[Shiva Shekar at the Dream a Dream Career Connect Centre, 2019]

Another key staff member at the Career Connect Centre, in addition to Pavithra KL, is Shiva Shekar. When Shiva joined Dream a Dream's Career Connect Centre in 2013 as an 18-year-old participant, the classes for Dream a Dream took place on Sundays, allowing the students to work at their jobs from Monday to Friday. Shiva looked forward not just to the basic English and basic computer classes, but also talking to his cohort-mates and the facilitators before classes would begin. A very good mimic, he would make his classmates laugh with his caricatured imitations of people. He loved sharing his fun and friendly personality with others and the opportunity to fully be himself in the space that Dream a Dream created for their students. Every week, "I was literally waiting for Sunday," he recalls.

It was a dramatic contrast to his experience in school, where he usually sat on the first bench in the primary standards as he was short, and the students were organised to sit by height. The teachers "only focused on discipline," Shiva remembers. "They wanted short haircut, well-groomed uniforms, and polished shoes." They paid attention to those things and physically punished students with sticks, or by telling them to kneel or do sit-ups or push-ups if they did not follow the black and white rules of comportment. The physical punishments instilled fear of going to school in Shiva. When they focused on lessons, it was composed of writing the same thing repeatedly, so Shiva does not remember enjoying learning.

Teachers in the eighth standard and upwards did not focus as much on instilling discipline into students, and Shiva does remember enjoying his time with his friends. But for Shiva, learning remained basic even in the upper standards. For example, there would be a leader for each bench where students sat, and the leader would make notes of when different students spoke, but without paying attention to what was being said. "If I talked, they would write down my name and then make a plus mark even if I only said "hun" or "ah".

There were some opportunities for creative outlets when Shiva was recognised for having a good voice. One of his teachers in the ninth standard would ask him to sing occasionally, during lunch breaks, if he was in the mood to hear Shiva sing. Shiva would sing devotional songs and would be appreciated by the teacher and some of the 60 or 70 students in his class. But he remembers the rest of the classes being mostly about reading and taking dictations in Kannada or Hindi. Because Shiva was not very good at these subjects, he would try to create a delay to have enough time to complete his assignments. For example, he would tell the teacher that he had lost his pen. In addition to a lack of focus on creativity and creative expression, there was also little to no social interaction between boys and girls. Shiva was afraid to speak to girls and no girls would speak to the boys.

In contrast, he found Dream a Dream's Career Connect Centre to be an environment where there was a basic assumption that each person had something unique and positive to contribute. Girls and boys mingled comfortably with each other, and everyone treated each other as friends, regardless of gender. Even if Sundays meant classes at Dream a Dream, Shiva looked forward to each Sunday with excitement. He knew that not only would he develop his skills, including spoken English, but that he would also be meeting new people and making new friends. Like many other participants, he even looked forward to the variety of new snacks that Dream a Dream offered each Sunday. He knew that the staff would always be welcoming, and that every student would be celebrated.

Shiva had to fight his own insecurities, however, when he first began going to the Career Connect Centre. There was a time when he used to stay next to the wall, hardly speaking, because he thought he was not very good at learning and speaking English. The shyness was also in part because he had not had good experiences in other youth activities. For example, when he had been a participant as a younger student at another youth NGO, he had been selected to go to the national competition in Delhi for Tae Kwon Do. When he was the only one to return without a medal among the eight members from the NGO who went, he felt embarrassed. His shame at what felt like failure led him to do poorly in his school leaving examinations in the 10th standard. When he failed the exams, his family asked him to go to work, and he did so, working at a clothing shop on Commercial Street and an auto cleaning shop, where he ran errands like buying coffee and tea, cleaning the shop, and cleaning cars. But the work did not interest him, and he ended up quitting both jobs.

When the head of the youth NGO he had attended offered him a job after hearing his story about not doing well in his SSLC exams, he eagerly took it. He began in a data entry job, but after just a month, he became a facilitator, interacting with children and teaching them computer and other subjects. Shiva was very creative in his approach and the NGO rewarded him with public recognition and awards. But other colleagues who were older and more experienced were jealous and they put him down. They also complained to the head of the NGO that Shiva gossiped a lot, when Shiva felt that he did not even know what gossiping was. It made for an uncomfortable and toxic work environment and made him retreat further into himself.

Shiva was working at the NGO when he found Dream a Dream, and with the Career Connect Centre activities that encouraged him to speak even just a word or two at a time, he slowly became more and more comfortable in speaking English. Dream a Dream staff regularly encouraged the students to say just a little bit about themselves or share their thoughts casually during informal, icebreaker, or energiser activities. Even if his own spoken English was poor, Shiva knew that others would try to understand him and that they would use Kannada when they needed to, to make him feel comfortable as he learnt. No one scolded anyone and no one teased anyone else. Instead, young people were encouraged to tell their stories and talk about themselves and listen to each other without judgement and with welcome.

PRACTICE BOX 12A: DREAM A DREAM'S ENERGISER ACTIVITIES

Energisers are short activities that help move people away from a state of disengagement or lethargy or hyperactivity. Typically, the activities take the form of a game, song, or dance and almost always involve movement or voice. Energisers could be used to re-energise participants who have been sitting and listening for a while and to bring a more peaceful energy into a room after an intense, active session.

They can be particularly useful at the start of a session if a group is tired or is perhaps returning from their lunch break. They can be very useful to break the ice and help a group get to know each other. By leaning into silly or fun ways of doing something otherwise boring, such as introductions, energisers can help a group feel more at ease with each other.

An Example of an Energiser Activity from Dream a Dream: The Sun Shines On …
Participants sit or stand in a wide circle, with one person standing in the middle. The person in the middle calls out: "The sun shines on everyone who/with …" This phrase must be completed with a fact that has to be something true of them as well as potentially true for some of the other participants. Everyone that the statement includes runs around the outside of the circle as fast as they can to an empty space. The person who does not get a space then goes into the middle and repeats the process.

Examples of ways to complete the statement: The sun shines on everyone who …
- is wearing something blue
- is wearing socks
- plays football/cricket
- has a younger sister

Shiva felt that he wanted to spend more time in this kind of a welcoming environment. He applied to become a facilitator for Dream a Dream in 2013. He was a Creative Arts After School Life Skills Programme facilitator for three years, between July 2013 and 2016, before working in the Career Connect Centre. Shiva is currently an anchor at the Career Connect Centre for Dream a Dream, handling the scholarship, placement, and entrepreneurship programmes.

Now, as a staff person himself at Dream a Dream, he makes sure to give young people the appreciation and recognition he believes they deserve and need. Based on his experience, he knows that these warm showers of attention, accompanied with generous smiles, can motivate young people to continue to overcome the challenges they face in their learning and life journeys. He remembers getting calls from Dream a Dream staff if he missed a Sunday session because he had to work at parties as a costumed cartoon character or sell t-shirts for part-time jobs he had. The facilitators would say, "You should come; we missed you. Why don't you come to the session next week? I hope to see you." These kinds of one-on-one attention made him feel special and made him look forward to Sundays even more.

[Shiva Shekar facilitating a session at the Dream a Dream Career Connect Centre, Bangalore, 2019]

> **INFORMATION BOX 12B: DREAM A DREAM'S PRACTICE OF CALLING STUDENTS WHO MISS CLASS**
>
> Dream a Dream's Associate Director of Innovation Labs Pavithra KL describes why Dream a Dream calls students when they miss a class. Dream a Dream does it to understand why students were not able to make it and to ensure that they were doing okay. "If students miss a class, we make sure that we give them a call," she says. "We've done this from the beginning — it's a great way to build trust with them, and especially with the parents."
>
> Often, students might miss class because of other commitments and pressures. Some students might also be socially anxious and daunted by the thought of coming to a less familiar social environment. A call from a facilitator lets them know that they are important enough to be missed, that they are cared for, and that there is no shame in reaching out for support when they need it.

Creating Sundays to Look Forward to for Others

Shiva was the Creative Arts After School Life Skills Programme facilitator for students in the fourth through ninth standards when he first began working for Dream a Dream. As a facilitator, he found himself working on being flexible and adapting his facilitation to how different students behaved, so that he could provide the kind of warm and encouraging environment he experienced as a participant in the programmes.

With his strong singing voice, he learnt songs with movements and taught them to his students. With his gift for mimicry, he would also learn dialogues and characters from well-known movies and re-enact them for his students, delighting them in the process. With his efforts, he found himself "celebrated" by the students no matter which standard he taught. He remembers, "When I went to the fourth standard, they celebrated me; if I went to work with students in the fifth standard, they would welcome me. And I would welcome and celebrate them. Most of these students were only used to staring at the board and copying whatever the teacher wrote on the board."

In contrast to traditional schools, Dream a Dream programmes were designed to be fun-filled and energetic and conducted in a friendly atmosphere. To facilitate taking a more flexible view towards new experiences and to encourage the participants to develop new perspectives, the facilitators often changed how the students were grouped. Sometimes, they would sit in a big circle and listen to a presentation or share short insights; other times, they would sit in smaller groups and hold longer discussions.

Curricula for Dream a Dream was structured so that the fourth and fifth standards shared a curriculum; sixth and seventh standards shared another curriculum, and eighth, ninth, and 10th standards shared another curriculum. The differentiated curriculum made it easier for Shiva to further adjust these curricula to reflect the different interests and levels of the group of students that he was facilitating. Remembering how he shone after being recognised for his mimicry in Dream a Dream sessions, Shiva also made sure to find unique qualities of each child to celebrate and encouraged the rest of the group to see and validate those positive qualities in each other.

Shiva wistfully says he missed being with the students. He remembers that just a day before this interview, he ran into some students who had been part of his group when he was a facilitator for the After School Life Skills Programme at Christ University Centre for Social Action. While walking on the street, he heard voices call, "Shivu Bhayya! (Brother Shiva!)" The students had been in the fourth or fifth standard when he was a facilitator, and after five or six years, they were now in the 10th standard. There were about 10 students walking together to the church, and they asked whether he was married and how he was doing.

They chatted and Shiva felt they still remembered the life skills he had taught them. They even remembered a specific exercise that he did with them, called the "Airport Exercise", where he asked students to converse with each other, pretending they had run into each other at the airport in a few years, after achieving their dreams. They told him that they had achieved their goal of going to a good university and were pursuing their bachelor's degrees. "I felt very special yesterday," he reflects, "that they remembered and recognised me after so many years. They remembered my name, the Dream a Dream class, and life skills." He says it reinforced his belief that while after school programmes do not take up a lot of time (once a week, for two hours, for 25 weeks), they clearly play a big part in shaping students' experiences and memories.

Despite the pull of the students in the After School Life Skills Programme, Shiva decided to make a switch to becoming involved in the Career Connect Centre after some personal reflection. He felt that younger students have many opportunities to change and recover from mistakes made earlier in life; they also have time left to develop the skills they would need in life. Older students, in their later teens, however, have already seen and experienced more of life; their decisions have bigger consequences.

For example, when the students that he had worked with previously at another NGO came to him to share the challenges they faced, he noticed that older teens were much more aware of the challenges that their families or parents faced. They also faced bigger decisions about what to study, whether to continue studying after the 10th standard, and whether and how and where to work and how to support their families. They often navigate these questions without much support from other people. He remembers his own time as a participant in the Career Connect Centre in the 10th standard and how he felt he should go to college, but he did not do so because he thought his academic grades were too poor and because his family was pressuring him to go to work and earn money. He felt grateful to have ended up working with Dream a Dream and believed that with encouragement, recognition, appreciation, motivation, guidance, and opportunities provided at a critical time in their lives, the young adults had incredible potential to grow.

After these reflections, Shiva decided to switch to becoming involved as a staff member at the Career Connect Centre. He says that he believes he is preparing the young people for the reality of their lives. He himself is growing and learning from the books and learning that he is doing to find out how to better help them. He reflects that he has come to appreciate working with the age group of 14- to 21-year-olds very much.

Giving Wings and Winds to Young Peoples' Dreams: Leading the Scholarship, Placement, and Entrepreneurship Programmes at the Career Connect Centre

Shiva began working with the scholarship programme at Dream a Dream's Career Connect Centre in 2016. The scholarship programme was one of the programmes created at the Career Connect Centre around 2011, to help support young people to follow their dreams. Whether young people wanted to follow academic or non-academic paths, Dream a Dream decided to offer them financial support as well as guidance about how to follow their dreams. They give scholarships to those who want to attend traditional colleges or universities or postgraduate studies. They also give scholarships if a young person wants to take a flute, keyboard, or other skill- or training-related classes or start a business of their own.

The scholarships are awarded based on the young peoples' ability to make the case that the scholarship would allow them to pursue their passion. Performance on tests or academic ranks do not matter, but the application process assesses whether young people know how their decisions and choices will enable them to follow their dreams. For example, if a young person wants to become a doctor, in their scholarship applications, they describe the steps they will take to become a doctor, including the kinds of subjects they will study and any challenges and opportunities they foresee in following their dreams.

Dream a Dream staff help young people think through their steps, and once the application is complete, the young person prepares a presentation of about eight to 10 PowerPoint slides. They make the presentation to a group of about 20 people, composed of other young people, staff from Dream a Dream, and other relevant members of the community. The group will pose questions to the presenter such as "Why did you choose this passion? Why do you think this plan will work? What are some of the obstacles you think you will face? How will you overcome those barriers? If after 10 years, this job no longer exists, what will you do instead, with what you learnt?"

As of 2021, Dream a Dream provides about 200 scholarships each year to young people. Between 2013 to 2022, 2,292 young people received scholarship support. The amount given to a young person is on a sliding scale depending on the amount of fees required. Scholarships awarded range from Rs. 3,000 (or less, if the fee is less than Rs. 3,000) to Rs. 20,000 (if the fee is greater than Rs. 40,000); (Rs. 3,000 is about $39 USD; Rs. 20,000 is about $263 USD; Rs. 40,000 is about $526 USD). The aim is to encourage young people to reflect about their dreams and to teach them to make sound financial decisions.

The group decides whether to give the person a scholarship, weighing such factors as whether the young person has thought carefully about their passion. The Dream a Dream programme team then reaches out to donors to find sponsors who are willing to support a specific applicant and his or her aspirations. Sometimes, if the group feels that the young person is not ready, then they will not give the scholarship. But they always explain why and give specific recommendations on how to improve the presentation and the planning process, and there are opportunities to apply again. Young people who want to apply for a scholarship are given one-on-one help and guided through the process.

In addition to working with the scholarships programme, Shiva also leads the Placement Programme at the Career Connect Centre. He has found that young people come to the centre from a variety of backgrounds and with many different goals. There are some young people who are looking for work because they and/or their families are going through financial problems. Some are looking for jobs because they did not do well in school and either dropped out or decided not to pursue further education after graduating from the 10th standard. Some are looking for part-time jobs to enable them to have supplementary income while they are full-time university or graduate students.

Shiva takes all these situations into account as he visits human resource representatives of companies to learn about part-time and full-time opportunities. He looks to see what kinds of skills companies are looking for and he does his best to match them to young peoples' interests and skills. Once he feels he has a potential match between an organisation and a young person, Shiva connects the young person with staff from the organisation's human resources department for a preliminary phone call. After the initial introductory call of understanding what each person has to offer, the young person and the organisation hold a formal interview. Once the young person gets the job, Shiva follows up each month with a call to both the young person and the human resources staff member to understand how each of them are feeling about the match. If the young person is facing any difficulties that would be better addressed by Shiva, he speaks to the company's human resources department about them. If the company's human resources contact feels the young person could use further development of skills, Shiva brings that up with the young person and provides training at the Career Connect Centre, if appropriate. After a successful three months, the young people are invited back to the Career Connect Centre for a specific workshop about working and building their careers.

Shiva shared one example of how he uses his role to help young people in this role. Akash was one young person who found a part-time job near his house. On the first day of work, his manager asked him to observe the work he needed to do and to start working once he understood the process. Because it was a simple task, Akash understood what he had to do immediately. When he stepped forward to work, however, a colleague told him to just observe. Akash did so, but quickly got bored. When he tried again to pitch in and work, his colleague berated Akash. Akash left immediately without telling anyone. Shiva got a call from Akash, later that day, and Shiva went to meet him at a park.

As Shiva spoke with Akash, Akash made it clear that he would not work in an environment where he would be treated in such a way. Shiva found him another job in a more respectful environment, and Akash is now thriving in his new job. Shiva reflected that such experiences with young people taught him the importance of understanding young people and what they need to feel comfortable and safe in work environments.

With such care and individualised support in the follow-ups, the Career Connect Centre has grown exponentially. In 2018–2019, they successfully placed 50 young people out of 75 requests. In 2019–2020, they received 300 scholarship requests and approved 257 applications.

For those students who may not want to pursue a traditional career of working for a company or organisation, Shiva also oversees the Entrepreneurship Programme at the Career Connect Centre. It is a 30-day programme where they teach students life skills while also teaching them entrepreneurship. It is a very practical, hands-on class, where after the students learn the basics of entrepreneurship, the instructors send them out with Rs. 500 (about $6.50 USD) each. Students then use that money to start a business venture. "If a student brings back a bottle of soda they bought for Rs. 10 ($0.13 USD), for example, we will ask them, 'How many rupees can you sell this for, tomorrow?'" Shiva says. Then they work with the students to see how they could increase profit margins and reduce costs. Students reflect about their business ideas with each other and brainstorm ways to market what they sell.

During the programme, Dream a Dream staff also invites successful entrepreneurs and business leaders to speak to the students about their professional journeys, and why they decided to go into business. Young people then can ask questions. Shiva also leads the students on field trips to businesses. They recently visited a rabbit farming company where students learnt about everything from how they farm rabbits to how they market their products. Thus, through the entrepreneurship classes called "Nanna Payana" (My Journey), students are exposed to a range of innovative businesses from health and medicine to technology, to learn how entrepreneurs think creatively to address the needs of farmers, pharmacists, and cooks.

Shiva shares a story of another graduate of the Career Connect Centre, Asha[40]. She came from a family where her parents were quite protective of her, asking her about where she was going and who would be there, every time she wanted to step out of her home or even talk on the phone. But she wanted to be a dancer. Her parents did not want her to dance and were afraid it would encourage her to have a lot of contact with boys. She took a dance class at Dream a Dream, however, and applied for the scholarship programme to study dance, and she was selected. When she informed her parents, they were vehemently opposed to her plans. They said they were afraid that what they had seen in the movies and in the media about dancers being led astray and into leading difficult lives would be true for their daughter. Asha persisted in trying to persuade her parents. She told them, "You don't see my talent even though you are my parents, but someone else saw my talent, and they are supporting me with a scholarship." She also assured her parents that she would not do modern or popular dance but traditional Indian dance with more modest costumes. She ended up using the scholarship to enrol in dance classes at a dance studio, after

---

[40] Name changed for privacy.

continuing to advocate for herself to her parents, citing even the merits of being a dancer.

She also shared that she dreamt of starting an NGO to teach dance and drama to others. She told Shiva that she had a friend who was very good at hairstyling and another who is a good tattoo artist, and another who loved acting and was part of a theatre troupe. She said she wanted to start a business where they could offer lessons and services. Shiva was astounded that someone who was not very confident about herself and very shy when she had begun classes at Dream a Dream, and only knew dance, could grow to have a vision for a business that involved multiple people. "This is very, very special for me," Shiva says. He supported Asha by asking her questions that enabled her to reflect more deeply and affirmed her dreams and aspirations. "I was helping her become more confident and have further clarity in her vision," he says.

He also shared with Asha examples and told stories of other entrepreneurs who took risks to start their own businesses. He told her that taking a clearer, smoother road of following others at the beginning might lead nowhere, but that the more difficult, uncomfortable, and bumpy road to forging her own path might lead her to great adventures. Encouraged, Asha continued to convince her parents, and she was able to choose her own career path, where she could bring in income to her parents instead of staying home, as they wanted. Shiva reflects that as in the case with Asha, much can be accomplished with short conversations over time, listening to young people, forming a trusted relationship over time, and sharing knowledge, and connecting them with people who might know more about their areas of interest.

Maturing with Dream a Dream

Over the five years that he has been on the staff with Dream a Dream, Shiva has matured in many ways. He feels that not only has he grown his technical skills such as speaking to people or learning how to market the various programmes he anchors within the Career Connect Centre, but he has also become more empathetic and knowledgeable about how to best support young people in their journeys. He believes he now has a good understanding of how to speak to young people in a variety of ways.

He himself has grown in his ability to solve his own problems. He says, "I can balance my emotions and accept both negative and positive outcomes and receive feedback." He reflects, "It's learning for me every day; every day, something is changing, and I am learning something." Even though he had not known what an entrepreneur does when he started working at the Career Connect Centre, he has learnt a lot about entrepreneurship as well as a wide range of other topics related to finding jobs for young people. In other words, he grew, and Dream a Dream grew in its response to the needs of young people.

Shiva was 24 years old at the time of being interviewed for this chapter, and he was full of ideas for himself about what he wanted to do in the future. Pavi, head of the Career Connect Centre, shares about Shiva, "I have witnessed Shiva transition from being a graduate of the programme to being a role model for young people through his powerful story, which he owns and shares unapologetically. Today, Shiva is not just a facilitator but a visionary leader for the project that he heads. He is extremely creative and always brings a perspective that is applicable to the current context. I'm inspired and continue to learn from him to be an active learner every day."

Shiva has a million dreams for his future as befitting someone his age. He wants to be a published author. He wants to learn to play the flute, keyboard, and the violin. He wants to become an entrepreneur, a freelance facilitator, a storyteller, a counsellor, and travel through the state of Karnataka. He also wants to help homemakers find ways to earn money. With all these dreams, he knows his ability to develop life skills in young people is a special power he can use to build changemakers everywhere.

13 Walking Through Life's Challenges Together

Rashmi Kodihalli Shivakumar[41]

That Dream a Dream's Career Connect Centre is no simple programme merely dispensing career advice or classes on upgrading one's professional skills is illustrated further by Rashmi's story. Over the six years since she first enrolled in Dream a Dream's basic computer class in 2014 until 2020, when she was completing her final year of earning a Bachelor of Science degree in electronics and electrical engineering, Dream a Dream has been a part of her life. Rashmi took digital marketing and fashion design classes for about three months over the course of four years with Dream a Dream. Even though she is not officially enrolled in a class currently, she visits the Career Connect Centre to chat with the facilitators and talk about anything that is on her mind.

Her story illustrates the impact of "accompaniment," where Dream a Dream staff support participants through whatever life challenges that come their way. For young people who face multiple challenges, a single or even multiple programmes may not meet the unique needs they face. What makes Dream Dream's approach powerful may be that the programmes serve as means by which young people initially meet and build relationships with caring adults, who then walk with them through life's ups and downs. The

---

[41] No photos at the participant's request.

accompaniment is sometimes figurative and often literal as they walk with their participants to schools, workplaces, or even hospitals.

The Value of Accompanying Programme Participants through Life's Ups and Downs

When Rashmi was in her first year of university, her mother began suffering from skin problems. Rashmi and her mother would go to the hospital every day, and Rashmi stopped going to college to take care of her mother. Because they could not afford private hospitals, they could only go to government hospitals, where the staff gave them medicinal tablets but could not tell her what was wrong with her.

With the stresses and demands of taking care of her mother, Rashmi not only stopped going to college but also missed one session in the Basic Computers course that she was enrolled in at the Career Connect Centre. While many instructors in other organisations would not have paid much attention, thinking that students are disinterested, irresponsible, or deliberately choosing to not continue their studies, the centre's director, Pavithra KL ("Pavi" as students call her) called Rashmi and asked her why she was missing from class. Rashmi told Pavi about her mother's illness and how they had been visiting several government hospitals for over two years, without much impact. She confided in her that she felt her mother was being neglected at her current hospital. Pavi and Sheetal Lydia Prasad, another Dream a Dream staff member, made calls to people they knew and helped Rashmi identify a private hospital, with a good crowdfunding programme and a doctor who had a reputation of being trustworthy.

At the private hospital, they finally found out that her mother had liver disease and that it had progressed to such a degree that she had about 90% liver failure. The hospital recommended transferring her mother to a government hospital that could perform a liver transplant surgery, but no one in her family stepped forward to donate. The hospital then told Rashmi, "We unfortunately can't do anything else," because the disease had progressed so much. Her mother passed away as they were trying to find a way to raise the money for her operation.

Walking through Life Together, Helping Each Other

When Pavi and Sheetal accompanied Rashmi to the hospital to see her mother over the course of many visits over several months, Rashmi could not help but cry. Pavi and Sheetal would provide emotional support and cry with her. The empathy that Pavi and Sheetal showed for Rashmi's family's situation was a great comfort to Rashmi. Pavi and Sheetal also took care of Rashmi in other ways. For example, when they noticed that Rashmi was only eating once a day, with food she had packed to bring to the hospital from her home, they bought her lunch and encouraged her to eat more often.

Rashmi recalls that no one else stepped up to help her family during that difficult time. "When we were happy, everyone used to come and see and talk to us, but when we were in trouble, no one would come and see us," she says. But Rashmi felt that Dream a Dream was different. "When we were okay, they would be with us 50%, but when we were facing challenges, they would be with us 100%." This ethos of accompanying young people through life's vicissitudes, particularly during the difficult times, has been an implicit ethos of Dream a Dream's founding, when Vishal and other founding team members would first meet the wishes and needs of children with cancer and then try to meet whatever needs any child had.

It continued as more volunteers came on board, including Suchetha Bhat. It continued as Dream a Dream grew. Vikram Ghandeeswaran Narayanan, associate to Vishal Talreja, observes that given the staff are composed of a high percentage of graduates returning to work with Dream a Dream, most of the staff understand viscerally, from their own experience, the difficulties young people are going through. They have great empathy that drives them to help young people, not only in providing programmatic support but also emotional and other ad hoc support.

Learning to Solve Problems in Informed Ways, in Community, with Support

While reflecting on those days of caring for her mother during her illness, Rashmi feels that perhaps her mother would have had a better chance to live had she known earlier what she has learnt from Dream a Dream about trying to solve problems in informed ways. For example, Rashmi remembers going to temple every day with her mother, during her illness, with the hope that prayers alone would help heal her. They did not seek medical help at the time, and Rashmi wonders whether they would have been able to detect her mother's problem sooner had she confided in Dream a Dream staff earlier, who might have advised her to seek help from a hospital.

Her mother passed away during Rashmi's second year of college. Rashmi thought about discontinuing her education, and even told her principal that she would be discontinuing college, but Pavi and Sheetal supported and encouraged her, and she decided to continue her studies. When Rashmi needed access to a computer, Dream a Dream offered the use of the computers and laptops in their Career Connect Centre.

Dream a Dream even gave a scholarship to Rashmi, so that she could continue to pay for her university degree. Once Dream a Dream staff approve the application, they reach out to donors and find sponsors who match the specific application. Most donors make one-off payments to support a single young person, but some continue to be engaged over time. In Rashmi's case, Ashirvadam Trust, an NGO committed to supporting the underprivileged in education and healthcare among other initiatives, stepped in to sponsor Rashmi's education. They said they would support her for as long as she wants to study and expressed interest in sponsoring her professional aspirations as well.

Suchetha notes, "Most scholarship programmes in India only support those students who do well in their academics. This leaves out a large section of young people who might either want to pursue non-academic careers or are not able to study due to various compelling reasons like in Rashmi's case. That is why Dream a Dream started the unique scholarship programme in 2012. The only criteria to be eligible for this programme is the passion that the young people demonstrate during their presentation for their chosen career path."

After her mother passed away, Rashmi's younger sister ended up leaving college because she also came down with illness. Rashmi considered stopping her education again, but her father and sister insisted that she continue her studies. Her sister eventually got better and began to work at Mahindra, a large automobile company in India, as a tele caller.

Paying It Forward: Learning to Help Others

Even though the time she has spent in formal classes with Dream a Dream was not very long — just three months over the course of four years — Rashmi believes she has learnt about the importance of helping others through Dream a Dream's support during her family's health crisis with her mother. "Before then, I was not so good. I didn't help others, and I did not have a positive outlook towards life. I used to think mostly negatively," Rashmi admits. It was during her experience with her mother's illness and death and what Dream a Dream staff modelled for her that Rashmi emerged from the time more eager to help others and with a more resilient outlook.

Rashmi also learnt to withhold judgement about others and to avoid making assumptions. For example, she did not know much about talking with boys, and she would automatically assume that any boy and girl talking to each other were romantically interested in each other and involved. But as she got to know the young men in her Dream a Dream classes, and as she got to know their thoughts and feelings through facilitated discussions, she found herself with a more open mind and greater comfort about speaking with boys. She now regards them as friends and as brothers and finds herself jumping to conclusions less often and sees boys and girls as equals.

After her time with Dream a Dream, she did not get into arguments with friends and classmates as often and noticed she was less upset over silly things. For example, if she asked to borrow a pen and if her friend would not lend her one, she would stop talking to them. But after spending time with Dream a Dream Life Skills classes and facilitators, Rashmi learnt to not take such actions personally but to try to understand and have grace for other people.

She has also become more generous with people who need money. Instead of ignoring people who would ask her for money on the street and thinking to herself that they should get jobs, she now gives what she can, even if it is two rupees out of five rupees ($0.03 out of $0.07 USD) that she has. She believes that going through her own difficulties has made her more generous, as has receiving financial help and grace from the hospital when her family needed it. Rashmi reflects, "I realised this after my mother's death. This understanding came from my own self-reflection. It was a very difficult phase when nobody, not even our family members came to help. But when help came in the form of unknown people, my mindset completely shifted. I'll never forget Pavi and Sheetal's help during this tough time."

Dreaming and Renewing Dreams

Even though Rashmi is studying engineering, her childhood dream was to become a doctor. Her mother had been sick most of Rashmi's life, so Rashmi studied hard to prepare for exams to earn a medical degree, the MBBS (Bachelor of Medicine, Bachelor of Surgery). She did well in the exam, but when she went to a medical college to ask about the fee structure, she learnt it was Rs. 6,00,000 (approximately $7,885 USD) per year. Rashmi gave up on her dream because she thought she would never be able to afford the tuition. Thus, she chose engineering instead.

Reflecting about that time, she wonders had she been with Dream a Dream earlier, she might have found a way to earn her medical degree. "Not might," Rashmi corrects herself. "*Surely,* I would have been doing my MBBS degree." She knows now that Dream a Dream provides scholarships to students and that the staff would have brainstormed solutions and given her information to help her make her dreams come true.

Now that she is in her final year of earning her engineering degree, Rashmi is grateful for the support she has received from Dream a Dream and their staff. "They are like pillars for me," Rashmi says. "Without them, I am not."

INFORMATION BOX 13A: SUPPORTING FIRST-GENERATION UNIVERSITY STUDENTS

First-generation college students are those who are the first person in their immediate families to attend college. These students face many barriers, from the process of application through to graduating. Lack of familiarity with processes and scarcity of resources lead many to refrain from applying in the first place. In India, language is often a barrier as well. In addition, it is also likely that they will face financial barriers in paying for college.

Suchetha notes "While the application process itself can be daunting, the lack of guidance and support from parents can also dissuade young people from getting a formal college degree. Along with helping young people with choosing and applying to the colleges and classes of their choice, Dream a Dream also helps young people to negotiate with their families on which career option they would like to pursue and the long-term benefits of obtaining a college degree."

Here are some ways to help first-generation college students:
1. Help them in the application process — read through the necessary materials and processes and ensure that they can source all the required documentation.
2. Assist with out-of-pocket costs such as textbooks and event costs, if possible.
3. Help them find resources within the college that they can turn to, e.g., academic advisors and social groups for other first-generation students.
4. Understand that things that are routine to people who are familiar with college might be intimidating and alien to those who are new to the space of higher education.

With her father having finished the fifth standard and her mother having finished the seventh standard, the family is very proud of Rashmi, who will be the first in her family to graduate from college. It is a significant feat, not the least because fewer than 15% of college-age Indians go to college[42]. Because there is no one in her family who has attended college, Rashmi has found the practical support provided by Dream a Dream staff who have attended university to be very helpful. She looks to her future with positivity, knowing that with support, she has overcome some of the toughest challenges in life.

---

[42] Sengupta, Somini (2016). *The end of karma: Hope and fury among India's young.* W. W. Norton & Company.

14

Learning Entrepreneurship to Forge Her Own Path to a Beautiful Life

Rajeshwari Aladiyan

[Rajeshwari Aladiyan at the Dream a Dream office, 2022]

The Career Connect Centre's formation in 2010 filled in a big need in Bangalore, if not in India. In 2012, the median age in India was 26, while comparably, in China, the median age was 35 and in the United States, 37[43]. With a population that is young, India needs to create at least 10 million jobs annually, as every month between 2011 and 2030, nearly 1 million Indians will turn 18 and join the labour force[44].

---

[43] Sengupta, Somini (2016). *The end of karma: Hope and fury among India's young.* W. W. Norton & Company.

[44] ibid.

Rajeshwari Aladiyan is one of those young people, born in 1998, and thus, born after broad economic reforms began in India in 1991[45]. After generations of having their dreams be bound by their class, caste, or gender, children of both the rich and the poor, regardless of their background or gender, can now dream of new possibilities and brighter futures. At 21 years of age, Rajeshwari is one of them. She has been working as a beautician for two years at Veda Earth Spa Salon, and she has recently started her own business, with skills she learnt from Dream a Dream's Career Connect Centre. She takes a holistic approach to her profession. People want to improve their outer appearance, but she believes that paying attention to beauty is also about knowing how to take care of one's basic health and thinking about how one's physical health impacts the condition of one's skin, nails, hair, hands, and feet.

Given her thoughtful approach, one would think that she is a classically trained dermatologist, but she is a self-taught, passionate life-long learner, always reading, watching videos, and seeking to learn from other beauticians. Her journey to becoming a beautician and business owner was not smooth, however.

> ### *i* INFORMATION BOX 14A: THE NEED FOR ENTREPRENEURSHIP EDUCATION
>
> Individual attributes such as risk-taking, creativity, need for achievement, and managerial competence can be enabling qualities for entrepreneurship. In India, age and family background can also influence an entrepreneur's journey. For instance, researchers Gadgil and Singers found that having family property helps entrepreneurs (Kazmi, 1999). Researchers Sharma and Singh observe that capital formation and the confidence to administer business are essential for the development of industrial entrepreneurship; they note that people who already have a business or industrial background are more able to possess them (ibid).
>
> Though India is a country with the third largest number of start-ups in the world and with the current government supporting start-ups, Dream a Dream has found

---

[45] ibid.

that many young people are not confident in exploring non-traditional career paths. The education system and society still favour academic study to broadening the range of subjects to include the cultivation of creativity, for example. With the job market becoming more demanding and fewer positions opening, young people are finding it difficult to find a job; coming from vulnerable background makes them more susceptible to remaining unemployed or move into the unorganised sector, where abuse is high.

In such a context, Dream a Dream's Fund My Project provides mentoring and encourages young people to try their hand at starting a small business. It pairs young people with a mentor who has been an entrepreneur and who has an inspiring story to share about starting their own business. The goal is to expose young people to original business ideas and to inspire them to think of self-sustaining business ideas that also promise the dignity of labour to those who are working. As young people meet with experienced entrepreneurs, they also work on coming up with a business plan. Dream a Dream supports them with a small seed capital.

Source:

Kazmi, A. (1999). *What Young Entrepreneurs Think and Do: A Study of Second-Generation Business Entrepreneurs. The Journal of Entrepreneurship, 8(1)*, 67–77. doi:10.1177/097135579900800104

A Challenging Beginning

Rajeshwari learnt about Dream a Dream's free and fun computer education classes from friends when she was in her second year of pre-university education in 2014. While she was attending her pre-university classes, she also took and enjoyed Dream a Dream's spoken English class and a course that taught her to use the accounting software Tally, in addition to the basic computer classes that Dream a Dream offered. She thought Dream a Dream offered the freedom to not only be herself but also explore to learn more about herself and the society and world around her. Dream a Dream was a world different from her experiences of growing up labelled "dumb" and a "waste" by her family, even though she had been working as a maid along with her mother since she was seven years old[46].

After she finished her second year of pre-university education, however, she stopped her formal education as her father suffered from the ill effects of alcoholism and was too sick to work. With four girls in her family, they did not have the financial means to support Rajeshwari's continuing education through formal schooling. She shares, "We lived everyday with uncertainty; we didn't know where our income would come from for the next day. We completely depended on my mother; it hurt me to see my mother work so hard every day. This forced me to look for jobs at a very early age. I used to help my mother with work and at the same time look for jobs for myself."

Given her family's circumstances, Rajeshwari went to work at a call centre once she turned 18 years old for a salary of Rs. 5,000 ($66 USD) per month. But she continued taking classes at Dream a Dream because their weekend classes and flexible schedule allowed her to take more classes with them. The classes were also free, an attribute that meant much to someone working to support her family. She took a jewellery designing class and a class about the basics of becoming a beautician. She discovered through these classes that she had a lot of interest in becoming a beautician and that she also had some talent in the area. After attending classes in a safe and encouraging space like Dream a Dream, her self-perception as a learner changed from disengaged to curious. "I have been basically waiting to learn," she realised.

---

46 Talreja, Vishal (2019, 5 November). Silent no more: How two young women found their voice [Blog Post]. https://thriveglobal.in/stories/silent-no-more-how-two-brave-young-women-found-their-voice/

Vishal observes, leveraging 20 years of experience working with young people and developing the programmes at Dream a Dream:

Young people during their adolescent years have many ideas and dreams for their future but are not certain of the career path they will finally choose. What they need at this crucial age before they enter adulthood is access to authentic information, supportive adults, and opportunities to explore and try out their various interests.

In the case of young people growing up in adversity, they are hardly ever given opportunities to explore. The world decides for them, usually a vocational programme or college degree, and then they are stuck in that field for the rest of their life. What young people need is access to short-term experiences to explore various interests, try out different vocations and fields, and have the option to decide that a particular field is not for them. This exploration gives them confidence and does not make them feel like failures.

If they choose to move from computers to tally to beautician like Rajeshwari did, we at Dream a Dream see our role to support them. When young people join the Career Connect Programme between the ages of 14 to 21, they are given an opportunity to sign up for as many programmes as they wish to try. If they drop out of a programme or decide they don't want to pursue a programme after completing it, there is just acceptance and no judgement from us.

This is what has helped many young people like Rajeshwari explore their passions and discover their talents and dreams. We believe that when young people find their passion and the pathways to pursue it, they will commit to their own learning, become lifelong learners, and will succeed.

She described herself as someone who used to be a "very quiet and silent girl," who did not know much about herself or her talents. Rajeshwari blossomed, however, as the staff at Dream a Dream helped her become more confident and helped her improve her communication skills, including learning to speak in English. As she spoke in English during the interview to tell her story, she observes, "I basically did not know English because I learnt only in the Kannada medium at school." Her spoken English skills that enabled her to participate in an interview to tell her story, solely came from the classes she took with Dream a Dream and from practising at Dream a Dream while taking classes.

As she gained more competence in her language skills, she also learnt to be curious about other people; she would say, "When I'm talking with you, I want to know about you." Before, she would not even go outside her home alone, and she would not speak with anyone when she did step out. She would stay only with her friends and people she knew. But as she attended the Dream a Dream workshops on Saturdays and Sundays, she had the opportunity to meet many new people and practise her communication and social skills. The skills enabled her to open up and eventually become a beautician who relies on communicating well with her customers and making them feel cared for with her conversational and social skills.

She says she felt a similar kind of safety and trust in the Dream a Dream facilitators and staff during the process of exploring the new idea of becoming a beautician. She was "scared to go alone" through the process of doing something that not many people she knew did. She knew she was taking a different route than most of the beauticians who get recruited to work in beauty salons after being trained at large Indian beauty conglomerates like Lakme and VLCC.

Her family was not supportive at first when she told them she was training to become a beautician. However, the staff at Dream a Dream felt like supportive brothers, sisters, and family members to Rajeshwari as she took the first exploratory steps towards what she knew she wanted to do. She says the Dream a Dream staff not only guided her but held her hand and "pushed" her while also acting as bedrocks of support. When she told them about her fears one by one, they assured her, "Don't be scared. I will be there." They said, "We are helping you; you can do anything." They encouraged her and gave her confidence when she felt insecure.

Dream a Dream not only provided her with knowledge and support but also gave her Rs. 20,000 ($263 USD) in a seed grant, for which she had applied through the scholarship programme. Along with other programme participants, she filled out an application and gave a presentation on why she needed the money and how she would use it to pursue her dream of starting a beauty business. The facilitators offered to speak with her parents on her behalf; they even encouraged her to bring her family to her final presentation, so that they could see that Rajeshwari was not the only one pursuing her dreams, and that there was a structured process for supporting her desire to become a beautician. Her mother was impressed by her daughter's confidence, sparkle, and clear love for her desired profession. Her family was much more supportive after they began to see how Dream a Dream had helped Rajeshwari. Consequently, Rajeshwari grew more determined about pursuing her dreams.

According to Rajeshwari, her story is different from the story of many young people, whose families tell them to work in a high-status profession, such as becoming a bank manager or a doctor, without consideration for what the young people themselves might want. She feels that even though young people might have dreams of their own, they may be pushed to live the dreams of their parents. Even if young people decide they know what they want to do, there may be no one to support them or teach or guide them on how to make their dreams a reality.

By contrast, Rajeshwari found that Dream a Dream did not tell her what to do or what they felt she needed but only asked her what she wanted and what she needed. They told her, "Don't live other peoples' dreams. Decide what you want to do and achieve those things. We will help you." They treated her and her classmates like "kings and queens," Rajeshwari recalls, helping them towards their dreams, whether it was to become an engineer, a football player, a fashion designer, a photographer, or a beautician.

A Different Path to a Beautician's Life

When Dream a Dream chose her, along with a handful of other young people to whom to give a grant, Rajeshwari was able to use that money to purchase the beauty products she needed to provide spa services to her clients. She started by providing services at the homes of her clients, and as she listened and learnt about her clients' struggles with beauty and skin care, she would pursue solutions by seeking information from diverse sources. She devoured books, YouTube videos, and websites about skin care and passionately sought to learn from other beauticians.

She feels proud of being able to "stand on my own" and support herself and her family. "I'm very happy now," she shares, in having the ability and the opportunity to work at some of the best spa salons in Bangalore and soon starting her own business. She says that when her father became too ill to work, she and her sisters decided to support their family by learning and using their knowledge to earn a good income.

She has also taught three classes of students at Dream a Dream about becoming a beautician. She was frightened to teach her first class, but Dream a Dream staff, once again, reassured her and helped her, reminding her that she only needed to share what she knew. She studied to prepare to teach her classes and took copious notes. Her classes were very successful, and she ended up deciding to donate her fees from teaching one of the classes to Dream a Dream, so they can continue to support dreamers like her.

In fact, after she taught her first class, Rajeshwari, with the guidance and support of Dream a Dream facilitator Sheetal, discussed and designed an evening event where her students would showcase the skills they had learnt in their beautician class with her. She organised an event where her students provided beauty services to those who attended, at a fixed price, for two days. They invited the Career Connect Centre school and college partners and parents of the young people as well. They raised Rs. 11,000 ($145 USD) from those two evenings. Rajeshwari says it was an experience that enabled her to learn new skills and took her confidence to a new level. She says it was something she considers a highlight of her life, a wow moment and a turning point.

Thus, she experienced a transformation — the whole of the Arc of Transformation — with the help of Dream a Dream's Career Connect Centre. With trust and engagement from her facilitators, she was able to challenge her limiting beliefs about herself as someone who was not good at learning into believing that she was. The safe space in which to explore new interests with increased confidence and courage led her to embracing the possibility of becoming an excellent beautician. She was not only able to make changes for herself but also lead other students into exploring a new career path by teaching them. In connecting with parts of herself that brought her joy, she was able to connect with others and with the world in making contributions that enabled others to dream.

All that she had learnt in Dream a Dream — about how to talk to people, to be friendly, to take an interest in others, to ask questions, and to listen carefully to their answers — serves her well in her current profession. "It's mainly about balancing the skills of how to talk with the customer, how to explain [the products and processes] during the consultation, and how to provide good care." She confides that one can lose a client just because of a little thing.

She worked as a skin specialist at the time of her interview; she was also working to become a hair specialist and a make-up specialist. By 2022, three years after the interview, she was promoted to working as a manager at Waves Family Salon, maintaining supplies and accounts. "It is one of my biggest achievements," Rajeshwari says. She believes that the field of beauty and skin care is like "an ocean." She has learnt to navigate through the wide, open waters towards her future and has caught the wind for her sails through Dream a Dream.

[Rajeshwari demonstrating her skills as a beautician at the
Dream a Dream Career Connect Centre, 2018]

15

Changing the Script to Write His Own Script

Shahid Afrid

[Shahid Afrid at the Dream a Dream office, 2022]

Shahid Afrid, at 20 years old at the time of our interview in 2019, bursts with energy and his eyes glistens with excitement at being able to share about his experience with Dream a Dream. He has been involved with the organisation since the fifth standard, when he was just 11 years old. He tells me he is earning a Bachelor of Engineering degree from Bangalore Technological Institute, which is affiliated with the Visvesvaraya Technological University (VTU).

He wants to study at the University of Pennsylvania to fulfil his dream of becoming a robotics scientist. He explains how this journey would not have been possible without the tangible, practical, and financial help and encouragement from Dream a Dream and the many people he encountered through the non-profit. Shahid admits, "Without Dream a Dream, I would have dropped my studies after the 10th standard, and like my father or my uncle, I would be working somewhere right now, instead of going to university." Dream a Dream enabled him to not only change his script but also write his own script.

A Taste of Learning about the World through Dream a Dream

Shahid got to know about Dream a Dream when he was in the fifth standard, when a Dream a Dream staff member came to offer the Creative Arts After School Life Skills Programme at his school, the Excellent English School in Mangammanapalya. He appreciated the fact that Dream a Dream taught the students "how the world is [and] how to explore it." It seemed to him a dramatic contrast from regular schooling that focused on rote learning and teaching the set syllabus and not deviating from it.

When he was in the 10th standard, Dream a Dream revisited the school and spoke to the students about the free classes they were offering at the Career Connect Centre, such as basic computer training and spoken English classes. Shahid appreciated that these classes were free, in contrast to other similar classes that charged around Rs. 5,000 to over Rs. 10,000 ($66 to $132 USD) per course. His father worked as a carpenter, so Shahid's family did not have any disposable income to afford the classes that Shahid wanted to take. Remembering how much he had enjoyed the After School Life Skills Programme, Shahid signed up and started attending classes, taking advantage of the free course Dream a Dream offered as part of the Career Connect Programme, thanks to the donations from individuals, corporations, and foundations.

Shahid also signed up for a Photoshop class, offered by Melvin, a facilitator Shahid remembers as being remarkable. Melvin was well versed in technology; seeing Shahid's happy curiosity and eagerness to learn, he stayed after classes to allow Shahid to explore different technology platforms with him. Melvin shared with Shahid resources that helped him explore Photoshop and graphic design beyond what was taught in class. He made himself available over phone whenever Shahid got stuck exploring new features. Shahid says that his "career started" when he took the class.

It was then a logical next step to get his first part-time job earning about Rs. 3,000 ($40 USD) a month at Artflute, an online marketplace for artists, whose CEO, Padmaja Nagarur was on the board of Dream a Dream. Using the knowledge and skills he had gained through Dream a Dream, Shahid was responsible for designing creative content for social media platforms and for weblogs and for virtually placing a painting in customers' homes using graphics.

In the 12th standard, Shahid began attending Sri Sai Ram Vidya Mandiram College and opted to study PCMB (physics, chemistry, mathematics, and biology), which is regarded as the most competitive and academically challenging of the streams that students choose after the 10th standard[47]. The tuition fee was high, but Shahid was passionate about learning science. Others discouraged him, telling him that it would be very tough, but Shahid persisted. Dream a Dream helped him believe that he could pursue the challenging

---

[47] Other streams include the arts and commerce.

course of study; one-on-one conversations with his facilitator and the goal-setting activities in his life skill development sessions helped him make the decision.

Dream a Dream facilitators also helped him and other students to identify their dreams, in ways that most other organisations and most others his age are not able to do. Facilitators encouraged participants to identify their strengths and skills and guided them in making long-term career choices that aligned with their passions. "This is markedly different from career options offered by traditional education systems that focus only on helping [young people] get a job," observes Suchetha Bhat, Dream a Dream's CEO. Shahid echoes her assessment from a student's perspective: "When you go to most students to ask about their goals, they will say that they do not yet know and have not yet planned them. But most of the students at Dream a Dream know their passions, and they are already working towards them."

Receiving Scholarships to Pursue His Dreams

After the first year of pre-university classes, Shahid realised that he could not afford to pay the fees to continue his studies. When he went to Dream a Dream staff members for advice, they gave him a scholarship, based on his passion about the subject. This opportunity enabled him to continue his studies and begin his studies to get a Bachelor of Engineering from Bangalore Institute of Technology. Dream a Dream also provided him with a scholarship to help him earn his degree, including covering the cost for his books.

Shahid credits the Dream a Dream facilitators' approachability as the reason he could reach out to them with his challenges and ask for help, without hesitation. Shahid recalls, "The facilitators maintained a friendly environment with students. They spoke to us like close friends and understood students well. They understood our problems, and when I asked for help, they told me, 'Yes, we will help you.'" He notes that when other students' parents opposed to their coming to Dream a Dream to learn, the facilitators would call and speak to the parents to advocate on the students' behalf.

Recently, Shahid has been taking python programming through Michigan University's online classes, and he has earned a Digital Marketing certificate from Google. He is also working on a project to train machines to identify images. He is also working with the VK Academy to learn robotics and build bionic limbs to help those who are paralysed and cannot walk or those who cannot use their arms. He is pursuing his desire to become a robotics engineer by learning software engineering in college, and then learning hardware skills through the Skill Development Initiative of the Indian Government (Pradhan Mantri Kaushal Vikas Yojana). He further plans to take a mechatronics (intersection of mechanical engineering, electronic engineering, and software engineering) course with the scholarship from Dream a Dream. He has also earned a scholarship spot at University of Pennsylvania as a part of their Community College Initiative offered in partnership with the US Consulate in India, but due to the COVID-19 pandemic, he could not join.

Thus, Shahid is pursuing his passion by using a variety of different sources. He says that he has learnt it all from his facilitator, Melvin, at Dream a Dream and from others he looked up to, such as APJ Abdul Kalam, former President of India and former aerospace scientist. They taught him that schools and colleges are not the only places to learn, but that he could learn from many different places. Dream a Dream has a regular practice of referring their students and graduates to other organisations that offer advanced training and even offering scholarships to take those courses. The staff actively encourages students to pursue their interests and continue their studies, even after they have graduated from Dream a Dream.

[Shahid Afrid with his friend at his pre-university graduation, Sri Sai Ram College, 2018]

Developing Fully through Dream a Dream

Dream a Dream helped him in more ways than just providing him with scholarships and encouragement to pursue his dreams despite the difficulties. Their wide variety of classes enabled him to learn about a broad array of topics such as yoga, painting, and money management. Shahid, for example, enrolled in the Vocational Training programme that allows students to explore the different aspects of the retail sector, and in which Shahid chose to explore more deeply the role of the cashier. He also joined other students to paint the walls of the Career Connect Centre.

In addition to learning the skills he needed to pursue his dreams, he credits Dream a Dream with teaching him how to make friends, how to speak without fear to anyone, and how to control his anger. When Shahid was younger, he would get very angry if someone teased him or was rude to him. He says that Sajjad Ahmed, who was his principal and runs the Noori Foundation, acted as a role model and taught him many things, such as learning to control his anger.

Melvin, one of the Dream a Dream facilitators, also helped. For example, when Shahid quarrelled with his friends for two days during a computer class, Shahid was so angry that he could not sleep, thinking only about how to respond to his friends for the wrong he believed he had suffered. Melvin, noticing that Shahid was visibly distracted, asked him if he was okay. After he listened to what had transpired, Melvin just asked, "Did you gain something from that?" The simple question caused Shahid to reflect and made him realise that he had gained nothing out of staying angry for two days. Melvin went on to explain that he could have used that time to do something else. "Your time is very precious," Melvin told

Shahid. Shahid says that the insight helps him maintain a different attitude whenever he feels he is wronged.

Shahid's family also noticed all that he had gained from Dream a Dream. His father is proud of him for pursuing an engineering degree and tells anyone who will listen that his son is earning a BE. His younger brother noticed that they no longer fought. He was surprised to see that Shahid did not fight back, even when he deliberately provoked Shahid. It was a big change from before, when his parents would tell the brothers to go outside and fight because they fought so much. Now, Shahid shares his problems with his brother and his brother does the same. When his brother asked him why he did not fight back and how he was able to change, Shahid credited Dream a Dream with giving him the skills and the perspective to not engage with every disagreement.

Until the sixth or seventh standard, whenever his parents asked him what he had learnt that day, he would never say much. But after being with Dream a Dream for a while, his parents noticed that he would describe his experiences elaborately. They would say to him, "Stop! I know you have learnt a lot." Shahid laughs and says that the change came from being at Dream a Dream, after having many opportunities to listen to other students and share his own thoughts. He has learnt the value of listening, talking, and learning from Dream a Dream.

Paying it Forward through Dream a Dream

Shahid appreciates the fact that at Dream a Dream, there is no partiality with regards to gender, caste, or religion. "If someone is a Christian, we speak to him; if one is a Muslim, we speak to him as well. Everyone is equal, and we sit and have food together and play together. But when we go out into the world, people have stereotypes about others and say, 'Oh, you belong to this caste, so you must be like this; you hate this religion, so you must be like that.'" In contrast, in Dream a Dream, he has found that "we are the same here. Even if we are outside, we are the same as we are here. We are all human." What Shahid is learning about equality and equity in Dream a Dream, according to him, is reinforcing the values that his parents taught him. His father had told him, "Whatever is good, you take. Whatever is bad, just leave."

Shahid also appreciates that at the beginning of each class with Dream a Dream, the facilitator explicitly says, "I am not your teacher; we will be learning from each other. I will learn from you; you will learn from me." He appreciates the egalitarian environment of mutual respect and mutual learning that is set up by Dream a Dream staff. He recently had the opportunity to pay forward what he had gained from Dream a Dream when he was asked to offer Photoshop lessons to other students as a facilitator, after he had earned a mastery certificate on the topic. Shahid says that it was "a really big opportunity to be a student and also teach others." After that, he has continued to offer a digital marketing class to other students too.

Shahid loves teaching, and he believes "the way that Dream a Dream teaches is awesome." It offers a remarkable contrast to many of his other classes, where information is delivered through lectures by teachers. There are not many opportunities to discuss the ideas with other students or even check if they understood what had been taught. He appreciates that he is given the chance to implement, apply, and use what he has learnt in Dream a Dream classes, so that there is a greater chance of remembering what he has learnt. "Anyone can write exams and earn degrees," he says. "But even if you have a degree but you do not know how to use what you have learnt, it will not be impactful."

He has passed on his enthusiasm about Dream a Dream to his younger brother. His brother noticed that Shahid had learnt new skills, and when he asked him how he knew those things, Shahid told him that he had learnt them from Dream a Dream. He also told him, "If you need any support or need very good friends, ask for Dream a Dream."

16

Rewriting the Script of an Early Marriage and Family Conflicts with Nurturing Support and Life Skills Development

Kashvi[48]

Since Dream a Dream focuses on meeting and supporting young people where they are, one of their strengths is that the staff can successfully serve young people with a broad range of adversities and life circumstances. One of these young people is Kashvi, who encountered Dream a Dream for the first time as a young, 18-year-old bride, recently separated from her husband after just two months of marriage. She had also miscarried and was in deep depression, unable to confide in family nor friends, who were more prone to judging rather than understanding her.

A chance encounter and then a year-long engagement with Dream a Dream's Career Connect Centre, however, led her to make several big changes in herself and her family. Now, at the age of 21, she is studying for a bachelor's degree in business administration and working as a facilitator at the Udhyam Learning Foundation, where she helps young people and others start businesses. At the time of our interview, Kashvi was seriously considering reconciling with her husband.

She still stays connected to Dream a Dream by going to events and activities when she can. The life skills she gained through

---

[48] Name changed at the request of the participant.

Dream a Dream, such as how to understand and follow instructions, interact with others, manage conflict, overcome difficulties, solve problems, and take initiative, led her on a journey of building her personal and social capabilities. Her story demonstrates that the nurturing environment and the social and emotional support provided by Dream a Dream facilitators is powerfully healing, no matter what the age or background of the participant at their first encounter.

A Sheltered and Confined Life

Unbearable conflicts in her marriage and an unsupportive environment in which to suffer through a miscarriage was not the life that Kashvi had seen herself living when she was younger. As the eldest of six sisters growing up at a farm in K. Channasandra in Bangalore, Kashvi saw her parents as both demanding and overprotective. "Since you are the oldest child, you represent the house," they used to say. They would direct her, "You should act this way; you should stay within these limits."

In many ways, her early childhood echoed that of Sita', the wife of Rama in the epic tale Ramayana. It is one of the two major Sanskrit epics of ancient India, along with the Mahabharata (which includes the well-known Bhagavad Gita). The Ramayana is popularly told in comic books and in dances that children learn[49]. In the story, Rama, the protagonist, is a prince who is banished to a forest. His wife Sita, depicted as the paragon of female purity and virtue, joins him. Sita is left at home alone and told not to stray from it, with a literal circle drawn around the hut that she was not to cross. When

---

[49] ibid. p.170-171.

she encounters a hungry Brahmin, however, she crosses the circle to feed him; the Brahmin turns out to be Ravana, a demon king, in disguise. Sita is abducted, a battle ensues, and she is rescued by Rama. But her purity is doubted, and she is forced to endure a trial by fire. Though she passes the test, she is banished by her husband back into the forest. She is reunited with Rama later, but when her purity is challenged again, she becomes distraught and with deep sadness, says, "If I am pure, this earth will open and swallow me whole." The earth then opens and swallows Sita.

Like Sita, Kashvi, because she wanted to be a "good" daughter, stayed obediently within the confines of the farm and school. With the added pressure of setting a "good" example for her younger sisters, she did not know what the outside world and people were like. She was 18 years old when she finally saw K. R. Puram (Krishnarajapuram), a neighbourhood just outside of Bangalore, for the first time. With limited experiences in public places, she felt she did not know how to act in these spaces outside of her home. When she was just 18 years old, she was married off to a 32-year-old man by her parents, without her knowledge. When she conceived and suffered a miscarriage, her in-laws blamed her for it. This cruelty, coupled with emotional neglect from her husband, led her to separate from him just two months after the wedding. Relatives and friends did not understand how she could leave her husband. They told her, "Your life is over now."

Kashvi says that all the criticism from relatives and acquaintances and disappointment with her marriage led her into a kind of depression, where she felt like she was a child again. She felt that people did not accept nor understand the amount of physical and emotional pain and distress she had been through. She remembers that at the time, she did not feel like doing anything; she did not want to leave her room, nor speak to anyone else. Like Sita at the end of the Ramayana, Kashvi became despondent. "I was depressed. I spent one year like that," she said.

Kashvi says, in the context of where she comes from, "We never used to share and talk about the mistakes that we make normally in life. We used to have a fear of what problems would come from sharing these things. At home or at my village, if people shared what was in their heart, or about some problem in their lives, other people would put them down. So that is why we never used to share what was happening. [The Dream a Dream class] was the first time I was comfortable with sharing what was happening in my life."

INFORMATION BOX 16A: DEPRESSION AMONG ADOLESCENTS IN INDIA

According to Moses (2010), the factors for depression among adolescents in India include relationship issues with parents or at home, not being allowed to go for higher education, poor financial condition, and other family-related issues among others. The common symptoms include a decreased inclination towards participating in recreational activities, short attention spans, behavioural problems in the form of anger and aggression, decreased appetite, and poor sleep among others.

Stigma directed at adolescents diagnosed with emotional and behavioural disorders by individuals in their interpersonal network likely also undermines their well-being. Sahoo and Khess (2010), in their study on male college attending population, found that about 18.5% had depressive symptoms, 24.4% had anxiety and about 20% were stressed, with 12.1% and 19% having clinical depression and generalised anxiety disorder, respectively. Depression and comorbid anxiety were high and 87% of the population with depression also suffered from anxiety disorder. The authors note that detecting such symptoms in the college-attending population is a critical need to prevent disruption in learning process, which also requires health policies directed at young men's depression, anxiety and stress.

Sources:

Moses, T. (2010). Being treated differently: Stigma experiences with family, peers, and school staff among adolescents with mental health disorders. *Social science & medicine, 70*(7), 985-993.

Sahoo, S., & Khess, C. R. (2010). Prevalence of depression, anxiety, and stress among young male adults in India: a dimensional and categorical diagnoses-based study. *The Journal of nervous and mental disease, 198*(12), 901-904.

An Unexpected Encounter with Dream a Dream

But unlike Sita, Kashvi's story did not end with her being unable to break out of the challenges in her marriage and her depression. It was just after she had separated from her husband that Kashvi began taking classes with Dream a Dream. She found them while looking for a job to support her family. Many of the jobs she wanted to apply for required that she complete a basic course in computers, which usually cost Rs. 10,000 to Rs. 12,000 ($131 to $158 USD). She could not afford them. As she shared her burden with instructors at her college, one lecturer told her about the basic computer class that Dream a Dream offered that was free, thanks to donations from individuals, corporations, and foundations.

Eagerly, Kashvi joined the class, expecting to learn about basic computer skills so she could have a job. She was surprised to find, however, that the Dream a Dream class was different from the ones she was used to at school. The facilitators who were teaching at Dream a Dream expressed interest in what was happening in her life and taught students life skills along with basic computer skills. The classes and the internship, for example, also taught her about how she might misunderstand other people and how she might face everyday problems well, with confidence.

She took the basic computer and life skills class, and later, a photography class, over seven months. She then worked as a paid intern for three months with Dream a Dream. Through these experiences, Kashvi found that she could explore different questions she had about the challenges she had encountered thus far in her life. She realised she had rushed through big life events — marriage, pregnancy, and a miscarriage — before she was even equipped with the skills to navigate them. It was through the opportunities for reflection that Dream a Dream provided that her thoughts had time to catch up to her experiences and even mistakes she felt she had made.

Opening Up in a Safe and Caring Environment

She was able to find the space for reflection in part because the Dream a Dream facilitators created an emotionally warm and safe environment. The facilitators explicitly told the participants that if there was something they did not understand, the facilitators would teach them, even after class was officially over. The facilitators were also humble and open to feedback from students about the class, including listening to what the students did not like.

Kashvi says that she felt she had "never met any people like the facilitators in [her] whole life." She felt that the facilitators paid careful attention to how students were impacted by how the facilitators were running the classes. Kashvi had never seen adults pay such careful attention to how students were experiencing adult decisions at school or at home. Dream a Dream facilitators' care signalled a sensitivity to and respect for the students' thoughts and feelings. Moreover, the facilitators acknowledged and made space for students to contribute to and shape how the classes were planned and conducted.

Being in such a welcoming and encouraging environment made it easier for Kashvi to share about her life, even when she felt overwhelmed and confused. Kashvi was not close to her mother nor any other adults in her home. Even with so much happening with her marriage and miscarrying a baby, she did not feel that she could talk to them about anything. She also did not feel she could share easily with her friends. "Whatever was happening in my life, whatever problems I was facing, it stayed with me unexpressed," she recalls. Kashvi did not know what to do nor even how to face those situations. She wanted to talk to someone about it, but she felt that if she spoke, there would be more problems.

She was scared to even speak about it with Dream a Dream facilitators. But when she did share, they said, "We are with you." It was the first time Kashvi had heard that kind of positive and supportive response, rather than being told that it was her fault, or that she faced a terrible future. Dream a Dream staff instead told her such things as, "You can do something," "You have the power to act," "You can move towards the achievements you want," "Your life is not over," and "There's so much still ahead of you; you've only seen one step of your life. You've been put down in that moment of your life, but you can think about how to get out of that." She says that Dream a Dream facilitators were like friends who gave help and suggestions whenever she needed them, and that the centre was a unique place in her life where she could go for such help.

Dream a Dream facilitators not only explicitly discussed issues with the students in their classes, but they also shared with the participants the observations they made about them, to help them reflect. For example, they noted that at the beginning, Kashvi did not mingle much with the other participants during activities such as games. She would participate in the basic computer class activities, but when it came to the life skills portion of the class, where the facilitators encouraged active engagement in games and interaction and reflection with others, she would not participate; she would just observe. When curious facilitators asked Kashvi about her non-participation, shyness, and hesitation, she shared that even though she was only a year older than most of the participants, she was married, while most others were not. She shared that she was afraid that others would look at her as being different. In the back of her mind also lingered memories of the times in the past when people criticised her when she spoke at home and at school about the challenges she faced.

The facilitators encouraged her to share, nonetheless. They specifically encouraged her to share with just one person with whom she felt comfortable, saying that the other person might be able to give her suggestions, guidance, or encouragement. With their support and understanding about her fears, Kashvi was able to take the small initial step of sharing with just one other person, which was Ameera, a Dream a Dream facilitator. Ameera came and sat next to Kashvi and held her hand and said, "If you're feeling scared to say anything to us, don't say it. But if you share, the fear and that feeling in your heart will go away." Even though Ameera did not directly ask her to share, Kashvi recalls that before she knew what she was doing, she was telling her stories to Ameera. Kashvi felt that she wanted to be vulnerable with Ameera and no one else. She said, "I felt so much relief at the time," when Ameera spoke to her in a loving and friendly way.

Kashvi says her fears about speaking to others were not found to be true in Dream a Dream classes, and she learnt that sharing stories in thoughtful ways could be helpful, rather than harmful. In one of the class sessions with Ameera, Ameera shared her life story, which encouraged other students in the class to also share their stories. Kashvi recalls that when heard other students' stories, "that's when I understood that there was no one who did not have problems."

She learnt that it was important to learn how to face her challenges. "Normally, we just stay still, feeling like there is no way to face our problems, and we feel put down. But if we keep solving them, we will learn something from that journey. And if we keep moving, we will experience success from trying and moving forward," she observes. Kashvi says that after she shared everything on her mind in a nurturing and safe place, she felt at ease and calm. She felt like she could move on. She started to mingle with more people and felt like everyone was equal and "unified in a friendly community." Other students would come and speak to her, and she would find it was easy to share as many activities in this space encouraged interaction.

Ameera also encouraged Kashvi to speak to someone new every day and to listen to other peoples' stories. Ameera told her, "There will be something to learn from each person, and you will find some stories will help you. None of the students have had easy paths; they have also faced many problems." Kashvi finds it difficult to describe the role that Ameera played in her life because Ameera's role went beyond what she thinks of in terms of a teacher or facilitator. Ameera accompanied her on her first trip to Dream a Dream's office in Jayanagar, "like a sister," so that Kashvi could go to her first photography class. Kashvi says that Ameera reassured her the entire time, telling her not to be afraid and to just attend the class and observe. Ameera, like other Dream a Dream staff, also combined challenge and support, telling her that while she would accompany her on her first trip, she would expect her to go on her own on subsequent trips, so that she would become more independent. Kashvi says that because of those kinds of actions, she now goes to the office in Jayanagar by herself, feeling free and without anxiety.

Using Life Skills to Positively Influence the Dynamics in Her Family

As a result of how she was transformed through Dream a Dream, Kashvi says that her relationship with her parents also changed. Before, whenever her parents said something to their daughters, such as "stop going to college," they would stop going to college; or when her parents told Kashvi, "You should get married," she got married. Her parents did not ask how their children felt. Kashvi and her sisters never asked why or how decisions were made and never disagreed with their parents. Kashvi felt that she could never share her feelings or anything that was on her mind. She felt that her parents would only be upset or shout at her if she did speak what she felt. She worried what her parents would think about her.

As Kashvi opened up with others at Dream a Dream, her relationships with her family members also changed. Before, when she was depressed, she did not feel she could talk to her family as they did not speak with her openly about their thoughts and feelings. But as Kashvi treated her younger sisters the way that Ameera and other Dream a Dream facilitators treated her — with patience, kindness, and sensitivity — she and her sisters began to talk more about what happened at school and about different things that are happening in their lives. Now, her sisters confide in her, and Kashvi feels she can speak to her sisters about things in her life too.

With her parents, Kashvi now speaks up if she disagrees. For example, when her parents said that it would be the same for her younger sister as it had been for Kashvi — an early marriage before she had the chance to complete college — Kashvi spoke up and told them what happened to her should not happen to her sister. She advocated that her sister should continue her education and finish her degree before she marries. Kashvi explained to her parents that she felt that someone who was 22 years old was more likely to have better judgement about what to do in life; she shared her thoughts with her parents that someone who was 18 years old was not yet mature enough to make big decisions such as whom to marry. Her sister also came to Kashvi to ask her to speak to their parents on her behalf.

At first, her parents did not agree with her, but Kashvi explained how she felt after going through with an early marriage. She spoke about how unprepared her sister was for marriage, and how her sister did not want to be married yet. Kashvi explained that if her sister had a chance to complete her studies, she would be able to know what kind of life she wanted to lead, including what kind of job she might want. The additional time would enable her to experience and practice overcoming everyday challenges as well. Her younger sisters agreed with Kashvi, and eventually, her parents relented.

---

i INFORMATION BOX 16B: EARLY MARRIAGE IN INDIA

The Prohibition of Child Marriage Act of 2006 makes marriage of women under 18 years of age and men under 21 years of age a punishable offence. Yet, about 30% of 20- to 24-year-old women are married before they attain the legal age. The Indian Census, 2011, estimated that 17 million 10- to19-year-old children were married. Seth et al. (2018) mention a UNICEF study that partially attributes domestic violence and infant, child, and maternal mortality to child marriage. Godha, Hotchkiss, and Gage (2013) highlight that maternal child marriage is significantly associated with a) higher likelihood of being underweight and stunting in children born in the past five years, b) having a miscarriage or stillbirth, c) multiple unwanted pregnancies at frequent intervals due to low contraceptive use, leading to pregnancy termination and sterilization of many young women by the time they are 25 years old, d) depression, and e) maternal mortality.

According to several studies, social, cultural, and patriarchal mindsets discourage girls aged 10–12 years from attending schools and get married at the onset of menarche. This mindset is the driving factor behind low levels of knowledge

Contd…

in female about negative health outcomes such as miscarriages, anaemia, and infections, which in turn affect their physical and mental well-being (Seth, R. et al., 2018).

Sources:

Seth, R., Bose, V., Qaiyum, Y., Chandrashekhar, R., Kansal, S., Taneja, I., & Seth, T. (2018). Social Determinants of Child Marriage in Rural India. *Ochsner Journal, 18*(4), 390-394.

Godha, D., Hotchkiss, D. R., & Gage, A. J. (2013). Association between child marriage and reproductive health outcomes and service utilization: a multi-country study from South Asia. *Journal of Adolescent Health, 52*(5), 552-558.

Kashvi now speaks to her parents about many other decisions as well, although she never speaks to them in anger or argues with them. Instead, she waits until she can speak calmly, and her parents are able to listen to her. She presents her case, as she was taught in the life skills classes at Dream a Dream. She says the results were much different than when she would speak to them in anger and they would speak back to her in anger, without being able to listen to each other. "Many problems arose from that way of discussing," she says.

Before learning at Dream a Dream about how to best speak to others about contentious issues, Kashvi says that she would start by challenging her parents furiously, "Why not? How come?" Her parents would then respond with irritation, "Why are you speaking to us like this? Is this the way to talk to us? Your sister is our daughter. We can do whatever we feel is right. You just focus on your life." They would then hit an impasse, speaking heatedly and defending their positions. But once Kashvi learnt to wait, until neither she nor her parents were agitated, to explain to them what she was thinking and why she was thinking that way, her parents responded to her calmly as well. Once she saw the dramatically different results from speaking with composure, she saw the benefits.

After many such conversations, now, if there are any big decisions to be made, her parents and her sisters approach her to ask her thoughts. For example, she has been able to advise her family about their business of selling vegetables, applying what she has learnt from her observations as an intern for Dream a Dream's entrepreneurship class. Her father worked on a farm and would sell vegetables at the market, but he would often lose money.

Kashvi noted that in places where vegetables were scarce, vegetables could be sold for more money, especially if they looked clean and fresh. Kashvi explained to her parents the concepts of profit and loss that she had learnt at from the Dream a Dream entrepreneurship classes that she was able to observe. Her parents and Kashvi discussed a plan for how they could make money from what they sold. When they agreed on a plan, they put it into practice, resulting in her father making more money. Before that, her father would just make the decisions and they would be final; he did not ask anyone for input. Now, he asks the family for ideas and opinions; when he has an idea, he asks for feedback and suggestions on that idea from Kashvi and the rest of the family.

A Lifelong Journey of Learning

Kashvi learnt from Dream a Dream to focus on changing herself first before trying to change other people. Kashvi used to ask staff members about their work, their lives, and their journeys in making changes in their lives, and the mistakes they made along the way. Dream a Dream staff told her and other participants that it would be difficult to convince others to change if they are wrong themselves. She reflects, "First, I have to make sure that I am doing things the right way. Next, my family should try to do things the right way. Only after that, I can make suggestions to other people. If my life is not right, if I don't even understand what's going on in my own life... and then go and tell my sister how to live, she's not going to listen to me. So that's why these steps exist — first, I have to try and change myself."

Dream a Dream staff also encouraged her when she felt that she was failing. For example, as an intern, she had the job of calling and inviting young people to come to Dream a Dream events. She felt bad when fewer than expected people came. But Dream a Dream staff reassured her when she felt afraid that she had failed. They encouraged her to continue calling and gave her suggestions about different ways to invite people and told her not to feel so tense and anxious about her task. Those kinds of specific and supportive feedback helped her and encouraged her to continue learning.

Kashvi found Dream a Dream helpful in other practical ways as well. When her family faced financial difficulties and Kashvi needed to find a job quickly, while studying in college, Dream a Dream staff connected her with the current job that she holds. Kashvi reflects that before joining Dream a Dream, she did not speak to people because she was scared, and she did not know how to speak to different kinds of people. She did not have much practice about putting herself in other peoples' shoes. She also did not go anywhere alone. She felt confused about the challenges that she faced and could not tell what she had done wrong and what she could do differently. She says that she would look to others for their opinions and thoughts and did not ask herself first about what to do. She did not know what she wanted. She was not able to help other people nor give suggestions. She would leave her challenges unaddressed.

Now, she can speak to anyone and knows how to listen to others and give good suggestions. She knows what she wants and needs in her life. She feels she can make good decisions and judgments about her life. She is also able to take on challenges as they come. For example, she has seen many positive changes with her parents and sisters. Even though she has been separated from her husband now for three years and her father is afraid to have her reunite with her husband, Kashvi feels like trying to impact her husband, too, in positive ways.

She reflects that she could see that there is both good and bad in people. She feels that she can try to understand even people who might be hurtful towards others. She knows that, often, they themselves are hurting. She also wants to finish her education and help her sisters finish their studies. She says that her family, friends, and relatives would all agree that she has changed for the positive. Learning to open herself to others in appropriate ways in an environment where she felt safe led her to learn the life skills she needed to create an unexpectedly better life for herself and for her family.

Sita's story, as it was passed down through generations of Indians, echoes Kashvi's story of her childhood. But Kashvi's story of thriving after encountering Dream a Dream's Life Skills Programme at the Career Connect Centre's computer and other classes also needs to be told and shared with others, so that generations following Kashvi, including her sisters, could mirror how she was able to navigate her life on her own terms.

17

Learning to Lead Her Community

Pallavi Shyamsunder

[Pallavi Shyamsunder with young people in Bangalore, 2018]

Kashvi's story and the stories of other Dream a Dream graduates in the previous chapters show how developing life skills is central to Dream a Dream's programmes. A focus on life skills development gradually evolved over time for Dream a Dream since its inception. The focus began to receive national and global attention when Dr. Fiona Kennedy and Dr. David Pearson worked with Dream a Dream to develop the Life Skills Assessment Scale (LSAS) between 2008 and 2013.

The development of the LSAS began as a broader conversation about how Dream a Dream could measure the impact of their programmes. Fiona recalls, "We kept saying we can't measure it if we don't know what the problem is — we talked about whether the measure of success should be happiness, becoming middle class, better mental health, among other outcomes. Finally, we landed on life skills." Dave adds, "We spent hundreds of hours sitting under the coconut grove at Ananya Trust, talking round and round until we landed on this. The life skills concept avoided judgement. We did not want a framework that centred on judgement. Our bottom line was that we must take something massively complex and make it simple — if we can't do that, we can't do the programme."[50]

What Vishal, Fiona, and Dave landed on after these discussions was to use the 1997 World Health Organisation's publication on life skills education. The report discussed life skills as promoting psychosocial competence, "a person's ability to deal effectively with the demands and challenges of everyday life... [including the] ability to maintain a state of mental well-being and to demonstrate this in adaptive and positive behaviour while interacting with others, his/her culture, and environment."[51] For the purposes of developing the LSAS for Dream a Dream's programmes, Vishal, Fiona, and Dave determined that they would assess the following skills: 1) understanding and following instructions 2) taking initiative

---

[50] Quotations taken from "Dream a Dream: Case Study with IIMB." Unpublished manuscript provided by Dream a Dream.

[51] World Health Organization (1997). Life skills education for children and adolescents in schools: Introduction and guidelines to facilitate the development and implementation of life skills programmes. Geneva, Switzerland. As cited in Kennedy, F., Pearson, D., Brett-Taylor, L. & Talreja, V. (2014). The life skills assessment scale: Measuring life skills of disadvantaged children in the developing world. *Social Behavior and Personality*. 42 (2), 197-210.

3) overcoming difficulties/solving problems 4) interacting with others 5) managing conflict[52].

Vishal clarifies that these skills "were not chosen because they were the most important life skills. They were chosen for the purposes of measurement; these were the life skills where their behavioural manifestations were easily visible and observable across multiple contexts and multiple programmes run by Dream a Dream." Vishal, Fiona and Dave also recognised that life skills are inter-connected so when programmes assess a set of life skills, they know that other life skills have also been developed. Dave explains this best with a metaphor. He says, "If I want to know whether you can drive a car, I just need to observe if you can drive a car. I do not need to measure if you can open the car door, sit in the driver's seat, know how to start a car, change gears, apply brakes, etc. When you know how to drive a car, you can do all the functions that support the driving of the car. Hence, in the case of life skills too, I do not need to measure every life skill and observe every behaviour."

Life Skills Assessment Scale Gains National and Global Attention for Dream a Dream

The Life Skills Assessment Scale (LSAS) is the first of its kind; it is a standardised, validated, and published scale to measure life skills in children from disadvantaged backgrounds in India. In 2019 and 2020, Dream a Dream's Life Skills Assessment Scale was recognised as one of hundred innovations in K-12 education

---

[52] Kennedy, F., Pearson, D., Brett-Taylor, L., & Talreja, V. (2014). The Life Skills Assessment Scale: Measuring life skills of disadvantaged children in the developing world. *Social Behavior and Personality*, 42 (2), 197-210.

globally by HundrED, an organisation that looks to identify and recognise 100 innovations in K-12 education from all around the world. The LSAS has been downloaded over 1,06,000 times by people around the world. Within Dream a Dream, LSAS has been administered with over 42,970 young people since 2013–14. Twelve organisations were using the scale within India and four organisations were using the scale outside the country as of 2022.

Pallavi Shyamsunder learnt these life skills during her eight years[53] at Dream a Dream both as a participant and as a staff member for five years. Twenty-two years old at the time of her interview with me, she started with Dream a Dream as a programme participant when she was 14 years old, in the eighth standard. Dream a Dream facilitators came to her school, the Round Table School, and gave information about their offerings: a computer skills class or rugby. She took the basic computer skills programme along with 15 to 20 of her classmates. Later, she also took spoken English classes at the Career Connect Centre when she was 16. Of the 15 to 20 of her classmates who took the first class with her, 10 to 12 of them continued to take other classes with Dream a Dream. About eight of them are currently working as facilitators for Dream a Dream, she reports, noting that she was not the only one receptive to Dream a Dream's approach. In 2020–21, 49% of young people re-engaged with the Career Connect Programme.

Because of Pallavi's positive experience, both of her younger sisters have been Dream a Dream participants in the Football After School Life Skills Programme. Pallavi says that the life skills they

---

[53] At the time of the interview, in 2019.

learnt — how to lead, how to interact with others, and how to understand other people and other perspectives — have helped each of her sisters to make their own paths. One of her sisters decided to pursue studying business in a pre-university course after exploring what she wanted to do through Dream a Dream. Another sister was very quiet and sensitive. After joining Dream a Dream, however, she searched for a job on her own, saw an advertisement for an opening, and went to the interview by herself and got the job. One sister started to take more responsibility at home by cooking and doing other chores, which she loathed to do before joining Dream a Dream.

Facilitator Created Safe Spaces as Vital Environments in Which Life Skills Can Be Learnt

Like other former programme participants interviewed, Pallavi believes that her sisters and many of her fellow classmates continued with Dream a Dream because of the safe space that Revanna and other Dream a Dream facilitators created that was different from what she and her classmates had experienced in other learning spaces. These safe spaces are the necessary environments in which growth takes place, enabling participants to take creative risks, try new activities, or skills, fail, try again, and learn.[54]

In contrast, spaces in schools and homes had rules and restrictions that did not allow them the freedom to explore their

---

[54] For research that associates success with organisations and cultures that cultivate psychological safety, see, for example, work by Edmondson, Amy C. *The Fearless Organization: Creating Psychological Safety in the Workplace for Learning, Innovation, and Growth*. Hoboken, NJ: John Wiley & Sons, 2018.

interests and ideas, Pallavi notes. She says that when she or others hear about a new idea and then share it with the Dream a Dream facilitators, the facilitators encourage them to explore that new idea, whether it is a job or an event. "They are very helpful in doing new things," Pallavi notes. The feeling of safety also encouraged Dream a Dream participants to share about other aspects of their lives that were not perfect.

Thus, when Pallavi's mother passed away about two years ago, after a 15-year-long battle with kidney disease, Pallavi could share her troubles with Dream a Dream staff. They showed invaluable support, giving her encouragement and love during her time of mourning. They asked after her, enabling her to share her needs and emotions while grieving and working to support the rest of her family.

In fact, Pallavi calls Dream a Dream her second family. When one of her sisters suffered serious illness and had to go to the hospital, fellow Dream a Dream staff members understood the additional set of responsibilities that Pallavi had to take on during that time. They made sure to ask after her and her sister, two or three times a day. Others knew about her situation because Dream a Dream facilitators are encouraged to share not only their work experiences, successes, innovations, and challenges, but also their troubles or problems during their monthly meetings. While not everyone may choose to share everything, every single facilitator is encouraged to speak up so that there is good understanding among the facilitators about what each person is going through, both professionally and personally. For many of these young people, and not just for Pallavi, Dream a Dream acts as an extended family and plays the role that a caring extended family member would play. Pallavi contrasts this organisational culture with that of her church, where she goes to find solace in God, but where there is not much personal contact with other members of the church nor opportunities to seek support.

Expanding Her Horizons through Dream a Dream, through Travel

Dream a Dream not only provided Pallavi care and comfort, but also encouraged her to push past her comfort zones to experience and learn new things. This included learning new life skills. Travel enables young people to naturally practice and learn the skills of planning, budgeting, time management, problem solving, adaptability, and learning cultural openness and humility[55]. For example, Pallavi was able to travel to Brazil for two weeks with Dream a Dream, to play football, when she was 18 years old. She and five others were part of a "Football for Hope" festival organised by a Dream a Dream partner, StreetFootballWorld Network under the aegis of the Football World Cup in 2014. She was the first young person in her community to travel outside of India.

Vishal remembers meeting Pallavi for the first time when he heard that she would be representing Dream a Dream at the festival. He remembers that Pallavi hardly spoke when Vishal asked her a few questions. She was quiet and nervous. Vishal wondered then if Pallavi was the right young person for this global event. However, Revanna had observed Pallavi in different situations and knew she had immense potential. He felt she needed to build her confidence

---

[55] See, for example: Stone MJ, Petrick JF. The Educational Benefits of Travel Experiences: A Literature Review. *Journal of Travel Research*. 2013;52(6):731-744. doi:*10.1177/0047287513500588*

and believe in herself. The trip to Brazil became that important nudge that Pallavi needed.

On the trip, she met young people from all over the world, including from Zambia, she remembers. In addition to playing in mixed gender football matches, they learnt how they could influence their community positively through football. They learnt leadership skills and how they could address gender equity to ensure that girls would also have equal opportunities and respect in society. They had the opportunity to travel within Brazil and meet young people from all over the world. They exchanged information about their cultures while they participated in activities that addressed community issues within Brazil.

Pallavi's experience is not unique. Dream a Dream sends many of its programme participants and staff on trips within and outside of India. This is in part because Vishal's journey of awareness started when he travelled to Finland for a three-month exchange programme when he was 21 years old. Living in another country and experiencing their culture, values, and traditions and how society was designed in ways different from what he had seen in India transformed his understanding of the world and his place in it. He says, "The experience helped me question some of my beliefs, become curious about other possibilities of how we can live as a society, and gave me a sense of purpose that I didn't have before."

Since then, Vishal has brought this idea to Dream a Dream. When young people have new experiences, it can encourage them to become curious, question, and challenge some of what they had believed until then. Thus, Dream a Dream has consistently made efforts to bring opportunities for travel and exposure to young people through its network of international partners and relationships. In Pallavi's case, it was the partnership with StreetFootballWorld that helped young people in Dream a Dream's football programme get an opportunity to travel to Brazil, France, Russia, and Qatar. A partnership with the US Consulate in India provided the means by which every year one to two students get a chance to get a fully paid scholarship to study in a community college in the US for a year. Dream a Dream's Creative Arts Programme students and staff have travelled to Wales; other youth leaders have had opportunities for leadership development and travel through Eisenhower Fellowships, WISE, Dubai Cares, and the OECD.

Each of these experiences has been life-changing for young people and their families. It has helped them broaden their understanding of the world and helped them break out of some of their own limiting beliefs. It has also helped them find new pathways to their career and life. For example, Rajesh, who after a one-year community college stay in the United States, returned to India and started his own NGO helping youth in his neighbourhood. Pallavi became active in her own community after her international travel. Another Dream a Dream participant, Manjunath (profiled later this book), started his own Football Club after spending a few months with a football club in Germany; other participants Arshita and Lekha came back from their travels, inspired by the idea of a girls' football team — they started one in their own community to encourage more girls to play football; Vishnu (profiled later in this book) started a Rugby Community Club as part of his youth leadership programme with Eisenhower Fellowships; another participant, Chinnappadas, started Change The Narrative, a platform for young people to learn about their own issues and work together to find solutions, after he made a pitch for this idea during his travel to Dubai.

For Pallavi, travelling with her football team "changed her world view and her view of herself, bringing about the possibility of viewing herself in a larger context. Keeping up relationships with people in countries like Russia, Brazil, Zambia, and Qatar has extended her sense of self beyond her neighbourhood and the football fields. It has opened an expanding horizon of possibilities."[56]

[Pallavi with young people during the 'Play for Change' event organised by Dream a Dream, 2018]

Leading in Her Family and Community with Skills Learnt from Dream a Dream

In learning life skills in a supportive environment and having the opportunity to have new experiences like global travel, Pallavi

---

[56] From Quantum Consumer Solutions (2018). Project thrive: A research study by Quantum Consumer Solutions PVT LTD for Dream a Dream to explore the nuances of thriving among young people from adverse backgrounds. https://staging.dreamadream.org/wp-content/uploads/2021/04/Project_Thrive_-_A_research_study_by_Quantum_Consumer_Solutions-compressed.pdf

strengthened her confidence, a key factor in her development as a leader in her family and in her community. Pallavi says that before Dream a Dream, she was shy and without a lot of confidence. For example, growing up in an all-girl household, she was not used to speaking to boys. Dream a Dream's mixed-gender programmes gave her the opportunity to become more comfortable about interacting with all kinds of people, young and old, men and women. She also became more confident about her own ability to manage difficult situations.

For example, one of the first events she organised for Dream a Dream was at Annaswamy School. It was a "Life Skills through Sports and Arts" event with students, teachers, and parents from 10 different schools and a myriad of different backgrounds participating. It was the first event she organised, and like anyone organising their first event who lacks experience, she did not quite communicate nor manage time as well as she could have. She also made some mistakes in creating documents needed for the event. When she made the mistakes, however, staff from Dream a Dream helped her to see them. They pointed to the different stakeholders who needed to be included in her communication and supported her in making a more complete plan and executing it well and on time. Instead of dwelling on what had gone wrong or berating herself for her failures, she learnt to correct her mistakes.

It was an experience that enabled her to move forward to take on other responsibilities with Dream a Dream's support. In coaching Pallavi to put on the event, Dream a Dream staff were practising the activities that research shows is helpful in positive youth development: 1) express care 2) challenge growth 3) provide support 4) share power 5) expand possibilities.[57] They were not micromanaging Pallavi's decisions and did not prioritise a perfectly planned and executed event over Pallavi's growth, which included making mistakes. In the words of youth development researcher, Thomas Nikundiwe, "Young people feeling their power is more important than guiding them through a successful action."[58]

At home, too, Pallavi has increasingly taken responsibility to support others, including her sisters, father, and grandmother. It is a role that traditionally boys play in families, her manager Revanna notes, but one that Pallavi has taken with great success. She is the only one among her family of five who is working. She is supporting her younger sisters to finish their studies, and she helps her father with his responsibilities. When a decision must be made within her family, her voice is the final one to speak, she says.

Given all that she and her sisters have gained from their time with Dream a Dream, Pallavi wishes there were more people in her community who were learning life skills, including parents and teachers. Particularly in her community, the Roopena Agrahara, NGR Layout, Gulbarga Colony, which is a slum community. She feels that more awareness and infusion of knowledge about the importance of life skills would be helpful. Because everyone within the Colony have come from Gulbarga, a district outside Bangalore, and they know each other well. The men usually work as day labourers in construction sites and the women work in the garment district, for about Rs. 350 to Rs. 400 ($4.50 to $5.25 USD) per day. Most of the adults have not received much formal schooling.

---

[57] https://www.search-institute.org/developmental-relationships/developmental-relationships-framework/

[58] Nikundiwe, T. (2020). Flipping the script: Leaving room for youth to grow in their power. In Brion-Meisels, G., Fei, J.F., & Vasudevan, D. S., At our best: Building youth-adult partnerships in out-of-school time settings. Information Age Publishing: Charlotte.

Only the elderly and the young children stay at home. While many children attend school, some, especially girls, do not attend as they cannot afford to pay the school fees or purchase school supplies. Parents are not used to sending their children out to play sports or participate in enrichment activities. Thus, there are many obstacles for someone like Pallavi, trying to encourage more children to participate in Dream a Dream programmes.

However, Pallavi has had some success. As an example of the kind of children who inspire her to continue to work hard for her community, Pallavi tells the story of a boy, Shanidevan, who is in the seventh standard. His family lives in poverty and his older brother was put into jail recently. But Shanidevan wakes up early, at 5 a.m. and cooks, and washes dishes and clothes for everyone. He then brings the children in the neighbourhood to the football sessions that Pallavi runs in the morning, from 6:30 a.m. to 7:30 a.m., before school. During their time together, she has seen him grow in his responsibilities and in his ability to talk, make decisions, and play the role of a leader. She noted how he works hard, helping with tasks such as distributing snacks and staying after the session is over to help with any planning or tasks that are left.

As those experiences accumulated over the days, weeks, and months, Pallavi built her skills and confidence as a facilitator and leader. In her more recent work with a nearby school, the Sri Sadguru Sai Baba school, she noticed that people would put a lot of garbage near the open space around the school. In addition to the constant stench, the space had become a breeding ground of disease and a place for people to drink and smoke. It was impacting the quality of learning for all children in the school. Pallavi and her fellow facilitators spent the next eight months bringing together young people, parents, community leaders, school leaders and volunteers to request the government to clean up the space and convert it to a playground for children in their community. She went to talk to the local member of the Legislative Assembly and the corporator (elected official responsible for solving problems within the community) for her area, and after considerable pressure from her and the group, they gave her permission to clean the area. She got a local philanthropist to support the expenses of cleaning and clearing the space, organised parents and volunteers to help with the cleaning and turned the space into a thriving playground.

Vishal remembers getting a call on a Sunday morning from Pallavi requesting and almost insisting that he visit the community that morning. When he visited, he saw a beautifully clean, fenced open ground brimming with over 1,000 young people and parents. It was the formal inauguration of the playground that Pallavi had worked so hard to get for the young people in her community. Vishal saw that there were a dozen or more men on the podium, and each one of them was praising this 22-year-old woman who had convinced them to invest in the future of their community. From Vishal's first impression of Pallavi, she had come a long way today to become a community leader and an inspiration in her community.

Now, students from nearly 30 schools use the space daily and for special events, such as a recently hosted "Community Cup" by Dream a Dream for 250 students, 50 teachers, and 50 parents from 15 schools to learn life skills and play football. After experiencing the life skill sessions, some of the schools have become eager to participate in the Dream a Dream After School Life Skills Programmes. For the past year and a half, the ground has been open for access to every person living in the area. Children and teenagers play cricket and football in the space and adults and the elderly use it for walking in the early mornings and evenings. The entire Bommanahalli community now uses this open space for a variety of events. Pallavi today has a special place in the hearts of the community members; they reach out to her for solving many other community issues such as fixing open drains, supporting young girls with education, supporting dialysis for poor patients in memory of the suffering faced by her mom.

Like other participants interviewed, Pallavi's story highlights how Dream a Dream participants can grow to learn to support and lead not only themselves and their families but also their communities, with increased confidence and skill. With resilience and empathy that stem from walking through challenging life circumstances such as the early death of a parent and shouldering the responsibilities of heading a family as a young woman, Pallavi has grown as a trusted leader within her community that needs more young women and men like her to be role models and inspire the next generation of changemakers.

18

Extending the Life Skills Assessment Test for 17- to 22-year-olds

Naavya[59]

Naavya is a vibrant, curious 23-year-old woman (at the time of our interview), eager to learn and serve her country. She has completed her master's degree in biotechnology. She currently works at Pharmaceutical Product Development (PPD)[60] as a clinical trials coordinator in Bangalore. She also volunteers with an NGO called Abhyudaya that provides free schooling for children.

She is studying to take government examinations known as the UPSC (Union Public Service Commission) examinations, to join the Indian Administrative Services (IAS). Examinations to enter the Indian civil services are difficult and competitive. It is not uncommon for applicants to take years off just to prepare for them. It has been her childhood dream to "serve my nation," Naavya says. Because she grew up poor, she saw many UPSC and Indian Administrative Service (IAS) officers. "To serve our nation, only a good thought is not enough. We need some power. These exams help us get that power to do something good for the nation. Taking the exams is the way to fulfil my dream of becoming an IAS officer," she says.

---

[59] Name changed and no photographs included at the participant's request.

[60] PPD is a global contract research organisation providing comprehensive, integrated drug development, laboratory and lifecycle management services.

Although she had her childhood dreams, for most of her childhood and as a teen, she had followed what others around had told her to do, rather than acting to make her own dreams come true. In fact, as she was growing up, others advised her to go into nursing or business. But her encounter with and development through Dream a Dream when she was in pre-university classes instilled a confidence in her to determine and chart her own path. The life skills she learnt at Dream a Dream, including interacting with others, managing conflict, overcoming difficulties and solving problems, and taking initiative, in addition to understanding and following instructions, helped her to grow in her agency to choose and follow her dreams.

The development of these life skills constitutes the core of Dream a Dream's programmes. When Dream a Dream's Life Skills Assessment Scale (LSAS) was found to be successful in providing an effective measure of programme impact for children between eight and 16 years old, Dr. Fiona Kennedy, Dr. David Pearson and Dream a Dream, who had developed the initial measurement, worked to ensure that the instrument also worked for providing effective feedback on life skills to young people aged 17 to 22. This chapter tells the story of Naavya's experiences with Dream a Dream and the effort to extend the LSAS age norms to the age groups of 17–19 years and 20–22 years.

Learning confidence, gaining self-esteem, and helping others through Dream a Dream

Dream a Dream facilitators came to her college when she was 17 years old, to talk about the basic computer and spoken English classes they were offering through the Career Connect Centre.

After learning that the classes would combine theoretical and practical knowledge and that the Centre was located close to where she lived, Naavya joined the computer class with her younger sister. She appreciated that she would be able to obtain a certificate of completion after she finished the classes to use when applying to other programmes or jobs in the formal labour market.

When she took the classes, like many other Dream a Dream graduates interviewed for this book, she was struck by how interactive they were. She also noted how the facilitators seemed to "support each and every student," taking note of students, and getting to know them individually. She noticed that most of the students were either very silent or had some challenges that they did not want to talk much about at first. However, many of them started speaking and started to express exactly what they really needed in their lives and what kinds of issues they were facing. She says, "The main idea is to explore ourselves through Dream a Dream. Even if some of the students did not pass their exams in school, most of us did something better and meaningful with our lives because of the support from Dream a Dream."[61]

After completing the required basic computer and spoken English classes, Naavya then took Dream a Dream's business, money management, drawing, entrepreneurship, and handmade jewellery-making classes and continued to learn life skills in the process. She reflects, "It's my nature. I want to learn everything I need to learn." She notes that the classes she took were not necessarily related to her chosen field of study, life sciences.

---

[61] For more profiles of Dream a Dream graduates who are following their chosen paths and thriving, please see: KL, Pavithra, Lydia, S., Das, A., & Ravindranath, S. (2017). Thriving: Stories of success redefined. Dream a Dream.

But Dream a Dream's range of classes gave her the opportunity to explore new areas of interest, such as entrepreneurship and cashier courses.

One of her memorable experiences from Dream a Dream was the process of developing and then giving an oral presentation for her entrepreneurship class on the kind of business she wanted to start. She says the facilitators encouraged the students, guided, supported, and gave feedback at each step. They did so in such a way that students were able to realise what they were doing wrong and could then help others. They were also able to relax and feel safe in the process. Naavya ended up presenting a business plan based on the handmade jewellery class that she took, proposing how she would make a special kind of terracotta and silk-threaded jewellery and how she would gather supplies and market her products. With practice, she was able to give a presentation about her business plan. She says that the guided process she had gone through gave her the confidence she needed for the presentation.

According to Naavya, one of the main differences between giving presentations in college and at Dream a Dream was that in college, they gave presentations based on the topics they were studying. At Dream a Dream, however, the presentations included solutions to problems the students saw around them. She says that through the learning process with Dream a Dream, she gained confidence, self-esteem, and learnt how much she was able to do. She also learnt to help others. "Everyone at Dream a Dream is helping in some way or another," Naavya observes. They help people find jobs, provide scholarships, teach classes, and help others to teach classes. The payment they receive for teaching classes, Naavya notes, helps students to further their studies.

She herself was able to teach a class on jewellery making at the Bommanahalli Career Connect Centre with Dream a Dream. In the process, she learnt how Dream a Dream develops facilitators to be more than just deliverers of knowledge. Facilitators intentionally incorporate fun into how they interact with students, creating a warm, safe, and engaging environment so students develop not only knowledge but confidence.

Students also experienced support and encouragement from each other as well as the facilitators. She learnt that students in her classes were different — some might be hyperactive while others more subdued, some might be aggressive, some arrogant, and some submissive. Naavya learnt to adjust how she spoke with each student and how to guide each person differently based on their personalities, strengths, and challenges. But the key, she also picked up, was to be friendly, so that students felt comfortable approaching her to talk and explore with her. The life skills she gained from Dream a Dream about how to interact well with others, including communicating effectively and showing sensitivity to others' needs and feelings, served her well.

She remembers assuring her students that jewellery making was simple and that it would teach them life skills such as patience. She told them that it would also help them relieve stress in that jewellery making is a kind of meditation. She also told them it would help them study as jewellery making is a way to practice focusing their attention on a task. She was gratified when students gave her the feedback that what she had told them was true, and that they had less anxiety because of learning jewellery making. Moreover, her students were able to sell what they had made in the class. So, Naavya felt that the experience was a success not only for her, but for her students as well.

Learning to Say No to Find Her Own Path

One of the key things that Naavya says she learnt to do at Dream a Dream was how and when to say no. "Most of the time, I'm kind of a passive person," she admits. But how could one be considered passive when one has earned a postgraduate degree and has taken so many classes with Dream a Dream? To that question, she says it was a relatively new thing for her to pursue her passions. In the past, even if someone made a difficult request when she was already overloaded with work, she was not able to say, "I can't." Instead, she would say, "Okay, fine. I will do it." Until she was in pre-university classes, she says that she would do whatever came to her, without consideration about her own thoughts, feelings, desires, or even health.

For example, because she had migrated from Tamil Nadu to Bangalore during the ninth standard, she struggled with the new local language Kannada and faced other struggles at school. She ended up failing ninth standard. She did the best that she could, following whatever others told her to do with her studies and her career.

But after joining Dream a Dream, she decided to stick with what she wanted to do. The practice she had in Dream a Dream classes to talk about herself and express her feelings and listen to others do the same enabled her to tune into her own voice and be confident in her decisions. For example, after secondary school, her mother pressured her to study medicine to become a nurse. But Naavya knew her passion was working for government services, so she selected to pursue a science degree at the Maharani Science College for Women in Bangalore. She had such a passion for the subject that she ended up completing a master's degree in science. She also identified working with young people and children to be one of her dreams, so she found her current volunteering opportunity to satisfy that desire. She is continuing to prepare for the UPSC exams in pursuit of her long-term dream, even as she works to support her family in other ways.

Now, she makes decisions "based on the things that I want to do, not on compulsion from others or on the kind of situation I am facing. I am doing what I want to do, what Naavya wants to do in her life," she says. Having the common shared space of the Career Connect Centre, in which she experienced the empathy of caring and compassionate adults who trusted and accepted her as she was and who believed in co-creating learning with participants, gave Naavya the courage and internal compass with which to chart her path confidently.

Brainstorming solutions to challenges and acting to solve them developed her confidence even further. She realised that she could not juggle so much and that "the word 'no' is actually a powerful thing which I was not using much." She noticed that once she started to say no, most of her burdens were lifted. Now, this is the kind of advice that she passes on to people who are doing multiple tasks or doing something that they are not comfortable doing. She found that she and her peers shared similar challenges and that she was not alone. The knowledge, confidence, and strength she gained to make decisions for her own life enabled her to not only thrive but also help others do the same.

Expanding the Life Skills Assessment Scale to 17- to 22-year-olds

One of the ways that Dream a Dream went about making sure to document and show the evidence of their success in working with young adults like Naavya, was to extend the LSAS age norms (previously with age norms of eight to 16 years old) to the age group of 17–19 years and 20–22 years so that they had a simple, valid, and reliable assessment tool for children and young people from the age of eight to 22. As Naavya's story demonstrates, young people aged 17–22 years can make important gains in life skills, and they need and deserve support to do so.

In 2018, Dr. Fiona Kennedy and Dr. David Pearson began to work again with Vishal Talreja, Suchetha Bhat, and the Dream a Dream staff to recruit 656 young people between the ages of 17 and 22 years for their study. The group had an equal number of boys and girls and participants were recruited to reflect the general population of disadvantaged young people in India. They were drawn from urban and rural families, and in formal education, in shelter care, and not in a system (young people who are not registered as being in education or formal employment, including young people who are street sellers, married, or informal labourers)[62].

Trained observers assessed young people in the five life skills that the LSAS was designed to assess: interacting with others, overcoming difficulties and solving problems, taking initiative, managing conflict, and understanding and following instructions. The skills were determined based on the World

---

[62] Pearson, D., Kennedy, F., Talreja, V., Bhat. S., & Newman-Taylor, K. (2020). The Life Skills Assessment Scale: Norms for young people aged 17-19 and 20-22 years. *Social Behavior and Personality: An international journal*, 48 *4), e8938.

Health Organization's (1997) definition of life skills: "Psychosocial competence is a person's ability to deal effectively with the demands and challenges of everyday life. It is a person's ability to maintain a state of mental well-being and to demonstrate this in adaptive positive behaviour while interacting with others, his/her culture and environment."[63]

The follow-up study of 17- to 22-year-olds found that the LSAS can be used seamlessly for practical everyday use with children and young people aged from eight to 22 years, with reliability and validity. The results were published in the journal, Social Behaviour and Personality (SBP) in 2020. Someone like Naavya would have scored lower on the scale when she first enrolled in Dream a Dream's programme, but with continued support from Dream a Dream facilitators, now she would score higher on such skills as interacting with others, overcoming difficulties and solving problems, taking initiative, managing conflict, and understanding and following instructions. Dream a Dream's tracking of its participants' LSAS scores show that across the After School Life Skills Programmes, in 2019–2020, 91.6% of participants showed a positive change in their life skills; 96.1% of young people were scoring 2.5 points or above the norm by the end of the programme. There was a 95% retention rate in the programme. The After School Life Skills Programme grew from 824 participants in 2018 to 1,024 in 2019.

---

[63] World Health Organization. (1997). Life skills education for children and adolescents in schools: Introduction and guidelines to facilitate the development and implementation of life skills programmes. Geneva, Switzerland. As cited in Kennedy, F., Pearson, D., Brett-Taylor, L., Talreja, V. (2014). The Life Skills Assessment Scale: Measuring the life skills of disadvantaged children in the developing world. *Social Behaviour and Personality*, 42 (2), 197-210.

With the LSAS for eight- to 16-year-olds being used by not-for-profit organisations in other parts of the world,[64] LSAS for 17- to 22-year-olds is likely to be used by other organisations as well, ensuring that Naavya's story does not become an isolated case of success but one that can be told by thousands, if not millions of others around the world.

---

[64] Pearson, D., Kennedy, F., Talreja, V., Bhat. S., & Newman-Taylor, K. (2020). The Life Skills Assessment Scale: Norms for young people aged 17-19 and 20-22 years. *Social Behavior and Personality: An international journal*, 48 *4), e8938.

19 Reaching Teachers and Increasing Impact with Dream a Dream's Teacher Development Programme

Manjunath Anand

[Manjunath Anand, 2022]

ven as Dream a Dream's work with Dr. Fiona Kennedy and Dr. David Pearson on the Life Skills Assessment Scale helped Dream a Dream show evidence of its success in working with young people from backgrounds of adversity and earned it national and global attention, the organisation grew in other ways. Manjunath (called "Manju" by his colleagues and friends) Anand's journey with Dream a Dream demonstrates how the organisation grew with its participants. This chapter discusses Manju's time with Dream a Dream and how the organisation was able to scale its impact and influence the environment that surrounds young people by starting the Teacher Development Programme in 2013.

Growing with Dream a Dream

While Manju was growing up, his parents fought often and eventually, they separated. Without his father, his family had financial difficulties, and his mother could not afford to pay rent, even with the support she received from her parents. She also fell ill. With such challenges at home, Manju went to live at BOSCO[65], a youth hostel for children from disadvantaged backgrounds, in 1998, when he was about eight or nine years old[66]. He entered the formal school system in the fourth standard, even though he was two years older than the average student in the standard. From the eighth standard onwards, he attended an English medium school, St. Joseph's High School in Briand Square.

His mother continued to be ill while he was at BOSCO. She was hospitalised and eventually passed away when Manju was about 11 or 12 years old. He never regained contact with his father. Manju remembers that it was a challenging time, as it was difficult to lose his mother at such a young age. As a child, he needed the warmth of maternal and paternal care and love. He would isolate himself in his grief and would cry by himself. He needed someone to speak with, to make decisions, but he found himself alone.

However, in the middle of his grief, sports, particularly cricket, appeared as a bright light. Sports helped him to calm down and released good feelings that helped him fight some of his sadness.

He was able to play sports through Dream a Dream's partnership with BOSCO. By the time Manju came to know Dream a Dream,

---

[65] BOSCO is a Non-Governmental Organisation working with street and working children in the city of Bangalore since 1980. https://boscoban.org/

[66] For many children from backgrounds of adversity, birth dates are difficult to know. The director of the Ananya Trust, an organisation that works with children from such backgrounds, notes that she tries to turn the lack of a known birth date into a positive, encouraging children to choose their own birth dates, as a special privilege that they have.

around 2004, when he was 14 years old, Dream a Dream was starting to offer various long-term programmes and events, such as Dream Fundays, where they played sports, and outdoor overnight camps for two to three nights. Vishal remembers that during his first few encounters with Manju, he showed tremendous grace, generosity of spirit, and leadership qualities. Younger children at BOSCO would follow him around and be in awe of him. Vishal saw that Manju was a natural leader and a great big-brother presence for younger kids feeling abandoned and alone. Vishal relied on Manju taking charge of things during the many Dream Fundays and outdoor camps organised by Dream a Dream.

INFORMATION BOX 19A: THE CHALLENGES OF LOSING PARENT(S) AT A YOUNG AGE

According to studies, a parent's death "usually worsens the family's economic status, creates pressures to take on responsibilities of the dead parent, and may isolate the child from friends" (*Stokes et al. 2009*; *Tremblay and Israel 1998*; *Worden and Silverman 1996*; as cited in Cas, Frankenberg, Suriastini, & Thomas, 2014).

A 2011 literature review of studies about the impact of death of parents on the survival and well-being of their children found that the death of a mother significantly increases the risk of her children's death, especially in the younger years (Atrash, 2011). While the effects of fathers' death had lesser impact in comparison, it too had negative consequences for how and whether the child survived (ibid). A mother's education, health, socioeconomic status along with other factors play an important role in the level of death risk of the children.

Earlier, when maternal deaths used to be more common, 'parent loss' discussions focused on the consequences to children of mother's death during childbirth. In recent years, the main cause of young, dependent children has changed and injuries and other critical conditions make up for the majority of leading causes of death in young adults. Health leaders around the world call for attention to the impact of maternal death on children, the families, and their communities.

In India, children with the most educated parents usually experienced substantially lower levels of mortality. Maternal education is an important factor that independently reduces the risk of childhood mortality. The influence of father's education is assumed to be largely of socioeconomic nature. Father's occupation and working status are also major factors contributing to childhood mortality. (Simmons & Bernstein)

Contd...

In a study about the impact of losing one or both parents during the December 2004 Indian Ocean tsunami, researchers found that the death of both parents had a negative impact on human capital accumulation of 15- to 17-year-olds of both genders and of females 9 to 14 years old (Cas, Frankenberg, Suriastini, & Thomas, 2014). The impact of parental death of one or both parents is also associated with lesser education for the children.

Death of a parent or parents and identifying the impact of the loss is complicated as it is likely to be correlated with other, unobserved factors affecting child well-being. It potentially affects psychosocial health and future aspirations. A grim reality after the onset of the COVID-19 pandemic is that more children have been orphaned who face adverse consequences of poverty, abuse, and institutionalisation.

Sources:

Atrash, H. K. (2011). Parents' death and its implications for child survival. *Revista brasileira de crescimento e desenvolvimento humano, 21*(3), 759. *https://www.ncbi.nlm.nih.gov/pmc/articles/PMC4501914/*

Cas, A. G., Frankenberg, E., Suriastini, W., & Thomas, D. (2014). The impact of parental death on child well-being: evidence from the Indian Ocean tsunami. *Demography, 51*(2), 437-457. *https://www.ncbi.nlm.nih.gov/pmc/articles/PMC4229656/*

Simmons, GB, Bernstein, S (1982). The educational status of parents, and infant and child mortality in rural North India. Health Policy Educ. 1982;2(3-4):349–67. [PubMed]

Manju remembers a particular moment with Dream a Dream in the eighth standard when he attended the Dream a Dream Outdoor Experiential camp organised by Dream a Dream. One of the activities was to take a boat from one island to another. They were in groups of four to five people accompanied by a facilitator and volunteer, and he was one of the older kids. Manju's boat happened to have a hole in the bottom and began to fill slowly with water. He panicked, shouting and asking for help. It was a big learning process to become calm enough and solve the problem by directing other boys in his boat; he told some of the boys to use whatever they had in the boat to dump overboard the water in the boat, while he and other boys rowed the boat to safety as quickly as possible. With teamwork and problem solving, they were able to arrive at their destination safely. Though the hole in the boat was an accident and not a planned activity, Manju recalls that it was the first of many times he overcame challenges with support from staff at Dream a Dream.

After his pre-university education, in the 12th standard, Manju was looking for a job. Though he was working as an assistant for the finance team at a furniture maker's at the time, Manju realised that because he had had a difficult time in his childhood, he wanted to help children who were in similar situations. One of the priests at BOSCO, Father Cyriac, suggested that there was an opening as a field coordinator for Dream a Dream. Dream a Dream had just revamped the After School Life Skills Programme in 2007. Manju remembered the happiness, positive energy, and smiling faces of Dream a Dream volunteers and staff. He recalled the love he had felt as a participant, and he decided to apply to become a part-time field coordinator.

"A Pretty Fantastic Journey with Dream a Dream"

Manju still remembers the day he came to the Dream a Dream office for his interview. It was a warm day in June 2009. It was his first formal job interview, so he was a mixture of emotions — excited and anxious. As he sat in a corner, people who came by greeted him, "Hi." Manju was so nervous, all he could stammer out was, "Yeah." He did not think to bring a resume but went into a meeting room for the interview. The interviewer, Boobymon George, Manager of the After School Life Skills Programme, was understanding about his not having a resume and told him, "No problem. Let's have the conversation anyway." The conversation was unusual in that they did not ask him about his grades or where he came from. Instead, they talked about the programme, which he knew well, having been a part of Dream a Dream activities as a participant at BOSCO. The way everyone made him feel comfortable despite his nervousness made him realise that he really wanted to work at Dream a Dream.

It was important that Manju had such a supportive first experience with a job interview. Dr. Rao, the head of Ananya Trust, mentions in her interview for the book that she made a special effort to place her graduates in an understanding environment like Dream a Dream for their first jobs. Young people growing up in adversity may not have all the hard and soft skills needed to perform consistently well with their first professional responsibilities. Over the years of helping hundreds of young people obtain and maintain their first jobs, Dr. Rao notes that if their first placement is with an organisation that is patient and understanding with them (i.e., trauma-informed), through young peoples' ups and downs, then the first-time employees are more likely to be successful[67].

Manju was able to join Dream a Dream as an After School Life Skills Programme field coordinator for football, taking care of logistics such as making sure that all the students were coming for the sessions and that equipment and playgrounds were available among other things. Manju had always loved sports, and he came to appreciate how life skills can be woven into sports. He says the following about his first day as a facilitator: "I had about 120 young people sitting in front of me. And I could see myself in them. All kids had that excitement, a light in their eyes; they wanted to

---

67

do something in their lives. And I was able to connect instantly with them." Even as a coordinator, Manju could interact with the participants in the same positive, warm, and kind ways that he remembered being treated as a child by Dream a Dream volunteers.

He considers joining Dream a Dream as a staff member in 2009 as a turning point in his life. He found among the other staff members the kind of familial support that had been missing when he was growing up without parents. He became good friends with his colleagues, and he had many conversations with Vishal about his future. "Those supportive relationships were very helpful in terms of moulding my thoughts and moulding my intention of what I needed to be," Manju reflects. "I grew because I received a lot of support from people around me."

He worked as a coordinator for two and a half years, and then, he became a life skills facilitator for three and a half years. Because he had been a cricketer for 10 years, he knew "something could happen in sports" for young people, including learning about teamwork, managing problems and conflicts with tact, and learning leadership skills such as motivating other team members. They were skills he acquired while playing cricket.

But he says he was confused at first about how to weave life skills into coaching sports as a facilitator and why Dream a Dream did certain activities. He knew he was very happy while playing sports as sports allowed him to let out his anger and frustrations in positive ways. But as a participant, he was not as aware about how intentionally life skills can be woven into activities that he thought of as pure fun.

Every time he came back to the Dream a Dream office, after his sessions, with questions to his manager, his manager answered him patiently. For example, his manager took time to explain how learning to balance with a ball would give children the opportunity to practice focus and concentration. "I never thought of it from that angle," Manju admits. He began to see almost everything from the perspective of connecting an increase in specific life skills with whatever sports activities they did. For example, even the simple activity of speaking to 10 people while reflecting about a drill they practised, if done intentionally, can teach young people courage and communication skills, such as making eye contact while speaking with others. As a master facilitator now, he continues to connect everyday activities with the life skills that are being developed, to allow others to see what he now sees easily.

Manju continued to learn as a facilitator, but when a new position opened in 2011 or 2012, that would allow him to supervise and mentor facilitators, he applied and was accepted. Then he became an anchor, managing facilitators while also handling school partnerships with about 25 schools, managing equipment, budgets, and relationships and communications with vendors and school leaders. He learnt to build and manage new partnerships while overseeing programmes and managing logistics.

Training Teachers through the Teacher Development Programme with Dream a Dream

Just as Manju was realising that he wanted to continue working with children and people more directly, Dream a Dream began the Teacher Development Programme in early 2013. Dream a Dream had realised that training adults who work with youth using the Arc of Transformation framework and methods to create safe, nurturing spaces to enable growth would help in reaching more children. It was a key strategy in achieving scale. Dream a

Dream invited PYE senior trainer Nadia Chaney to return to build the capacity of Dream a Dream staff to design and deliver such training.

Current CEO Suchetha Bhat recalls, "Over the course of three years, Dream a Dream along with Nadia from PYE developed an eight-day module for teachers, using the same principles in the Arc of Transformation framework that was used for designing programmes for young people. The trainings helped teachers unlock their creativity, develop listening and validation skills, learn facilitation skills, and re-imagine their role as a facilitator instead of only a teacher."

Manju realised that working with the Teacher Development Programme would enable him to work with teachers. He knew that he could reach more children if he was able to train and equip the people working with young people and share his knowledge and experience with them. His thoughts aligned with Dream a Dream's desire to reach more children and young people.

While unfamiliar with Urie Bronfenbrenner's ecological systems theory describing the micro-, meso-, exo-, macro-, and chrono-systems that impact children's growth and development, Dream a Dream's strategic approach targets the different systems that surround the child.[68] For example, with the establishment of the Career Connect Centre in 2010, they had targeted the chronosystem, focusing on extending their support into the young adulthood (16–22 years) of their participants. With the Teacher Development Programme, they wanted to target the micro-, meso-, exo-, and macro-systems, by influencing teachers, school

---

[68] Bronfenbrenner, U. (1974). *Developmental research, public policy, and the ecology of childhood. Child development*, 45(1), 1-5.

environments, education systems, and the attitudes and ideologies of the culture at large.

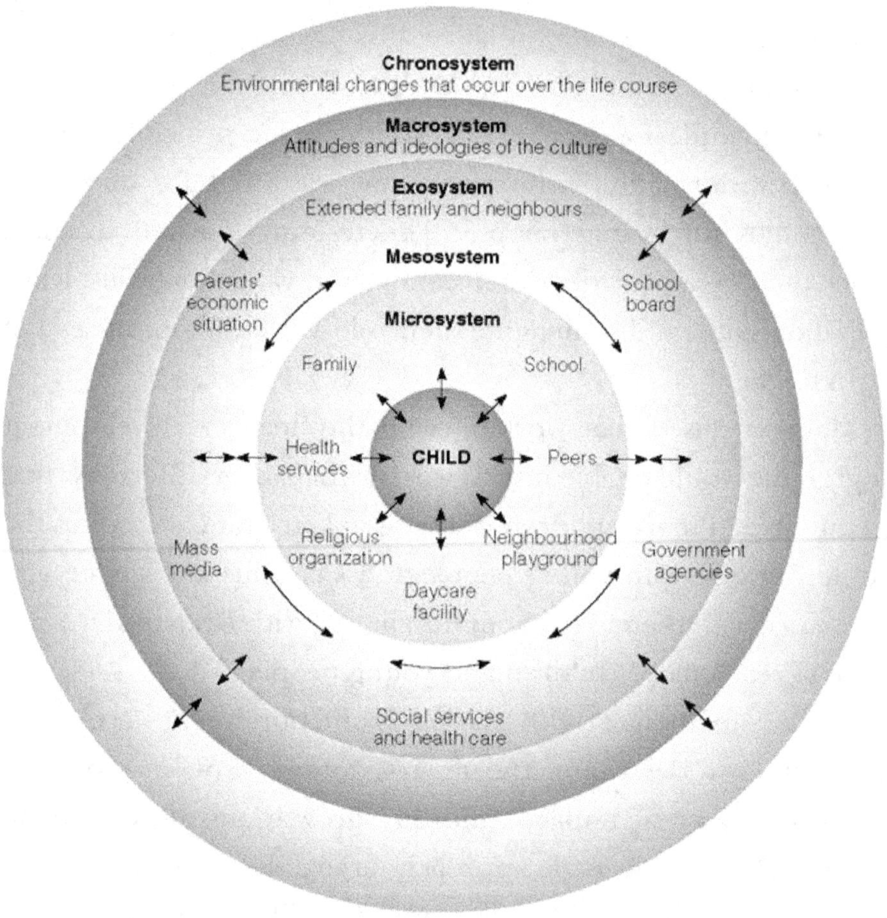

[From: Bronfenbrenner's Ecological Systems Theory from https://
www.simplypsychology.org/Bronfenbrenner.html]

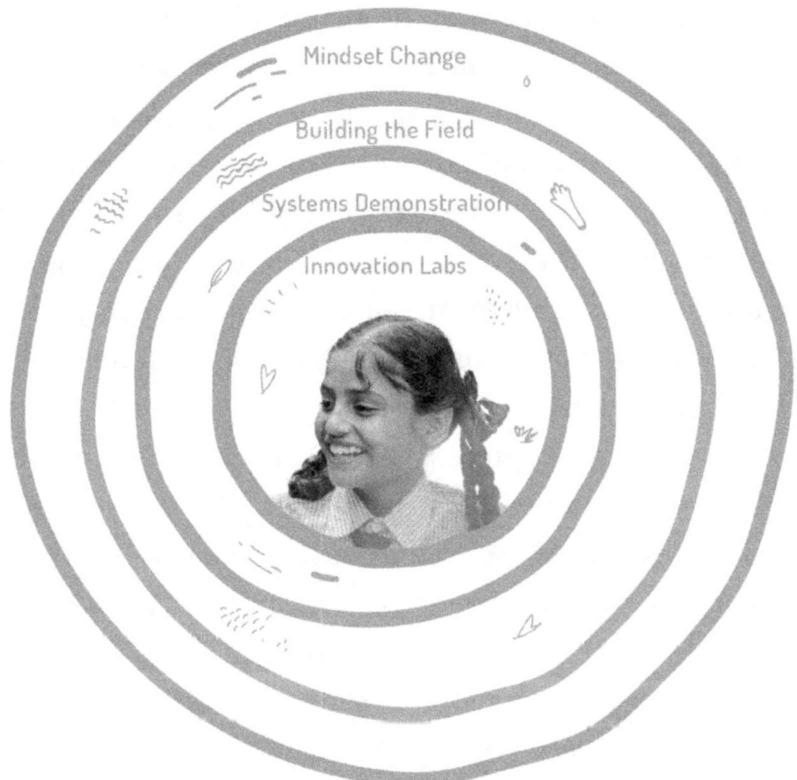

[Dream a Dream's Strategic Approach, n.d.]

After working directly with children and learning how to do so well in what they considered their Innovation Labs — the After School Life Skills Programmes and the Career Connect Centre — Dream a Dream wanted to equip more adults, especially teachers, not only with the skills but also with the attitudes and values that would enable them to have caring and supportive relationships with their students. For Manju, joining the Teacher Development Programme would enable him to channel his desire for new learning and experiences. It would also help him grow and test his new skills.

Again, similar to when he first applied to be an after-school coordinator, he was bubbling with nervousness and excitement when he applied for the position for training teachers. As part of his application process, he had to give a demonstration of his facilitation skills. But just as he had experienced with his first job application, and what he had experienced on the boat during the adventure camp with Dream a Dream as a student in the eighth standard, he knew it was part of the process of his personal development to face challenges and grow in his responsibilities.

Manju was accepted as a teacher trainer. He has been able to successfully train thousands of teachers across Karnataka. While most "teachers and school principals in India reflect a hierarchical and authoritarian mindset"[69], depending on a banking model of education,[70] Dream a Dream sought to help teachers to look inward. Dream a Dream staff encouraged teachers to reflect critically on their thoughts and behaviour in a safe and nurturing environment and consider how to best support students to develop life skills and become creators and designers of their own lives.

The programme consists of four two-day workshops offered over the course of eight months. In between workshops, participants are encouraged to continue to reflect about what they had learnt and put to practice some of the skills they had learnt.

---

[69] Natraj, A. & Jayaram, M. (2018). Developing life skills in children: A study of India's Dream a Dream Program. In Reimers, F. & Chung, C. (Eds). *Preparing teachers to educate whole students: An international comparative study*. Harvard Education Press.
[70] Freire, P. (1974). The banking concept in education. *Set: Research Information for Teachers*, (1). doi:10.18296/set.1476

[Manjunath at one of the Dream a Dream's camps at Banjara, Bangalore, no date]

> ### INFORMATION BOX 19B: TEACHER DEVELOPMENT PROGRAMME'S WORKSHOPS
>
> The four workshops of Dream a Dream's Teacher Development Programme consist of the following content:
>
> **Workshop 1: Discovering the participant's own creative potential with the following key outcomes:**
> a) Increased self-awareness and increased confidence about the ability to be creative
> b) Understanding of the definition of life skills and how to develop the participant's own life skills
> c) Ability to conduct easy-to-lead experiential activities to develop life skills in young people
> d) Familiarity with a few tools to facilitate experiential learning
>
> **Workshop 2: Becoming more empathetic with the following key outcomes:**
> a) Increased understanding of early childhood development, adverse childhood experiences, and the impact of adversity on development and learning for young people
> b) Increased awareness of the impact and importance of effective mentoring in a young person's life

Contd...

c) Increased familiarity with a few deep listening and validation practices to engage young people more effectively

Workshop 3: Learning to facilitate young people's learning with the following key outcomes:
a) Increased understanding of the role of effective strength-based facilitation in developing life skills in young people
b) Increased familiarity with tools to practice strength-based facilitation
c) Increased confidence to facilitate learning through experiential learning techniques and tools
d) Increased understanding of how to develop supportive communities within their networks, including the importance of doing so

Workshop 4: Celebrating one's role in a young person's life with the following key outcomes:
a) Appreciate and celebrate one's role as a teacher, community worker, and facilitator
b) Increased confidence to integrate life skills within current curriculum and pedagogy
c) Increased understanding of how to design life skills sessions or programs for young people

Source:
Natraj, A. & Jayaram, M. (2018). Developing life skills in children: A study of India's Dream a Dream Program. In Reimers, F. & Chung, C. (Eds). *Preparing teachers to educate whole students: An international comparative study*. Harvard Education Press

Facilitators created opportunities in which teachers could experience music, dance, theatre, play, and simple exercises in a non-threatening, reflective, and supportive environment. There were opportunities to work collaboratively with others, ask questions, take initiative, make friends, and learn from others' perspectives[71]. After experiencing such a learning environment themselves, teachers are asked to reflect on what they think about the experience, the impact of such experiences on them, how a similar environment might impact students, and how to bridge the

---

[71] Natraj, A. & Jayaram, M. (2018).

gap between the positive aspects of what they experienced and how they currently teach in their own classrooms. A few of the shifts that were documented to occur in teachers are the following[72]:

1) They shifted from an authoritarian and didactic approach to a more facilitative and collaborative behaviour towards young people. Teachers mentioned that they realised that they had been operating in authoritarian ways before participating in the Teacher Development Programme. After the workshops, they limited the approach of passing on a set amount of knowledge to young people, and instead, developed the approach of facilitating learning that young people wanted.

2) They shifted from asking "what" questions to "why" questions. Teachers reflected that they had developed a habit of asking "why" questions from students and that they themselves became more curious. They also reported that they were more likely to encourage students to ask exploratory questions and learn more rather than limit themselves to delivering set answers.

3) They reported an increased sense of agency. Instead of settling for an unhappy status quo, they realised that they could change their situations, trying out new ideas and solving problems.

Manju acknowledges how his journey with Dream a Dream has come to impact others. He was in north Karnataka, for example, holding a teacher development session. One of the teachers he was working with was someone who easily jumps to conclusions and judgments and rejects others' viewpoints. As a result, she did not have great relationships with her relatives, including her aunt and uncle. But the Dream a Dream training session that Manju had

---

[72] adapted from ibid.

held helped her to become more non-judgmental about others' appearances or behaviour; instead of jumping to conclusions, she learnt to practise validation and to try to understand where others are coming from. After implementing the learning from the session, she proudly reported to Manju that she could react less often to her relatives with antagonistic behaviour and more with empathy and understanding. Manju also noticed that earlier she used to yell at children or physically punish them, but now she is calmer, more peaceful, and able to understand why children are behaving the way they are behaving. As a teacher, she can see that perhaps children are excited and are full of energy, and that perhaps she could find more positive ways to direct that energy. Manju felt that it was "powerful" to see these changes happen in people and relationships because of the training that he leads. Even if the transformation rate of those attending the training is not 100 percent, the impact is nevertheless powerful as each teacher works with so many children.

He also reflects that teachers may have a passion to help children. Often, however, they can be "confused or muddled" as "there are endless things that fall on them." He sees his role as a facilitator to help teachers experience and see the power of creating safe, compassionate, and warm spaces where they can discover who they are as people and who they are as teachers. Then teachers, with that kind of clear vision, can create a similar warm space for their students.

He also believes that role modelling is key to the effectiveness of the training that Dream a Dream conducts. He notes that throughout India's history, particularly with colonialism, there have been people who tell people what to do and how to do things, with a focus on rote learning. Manju believes that much of what is taught lives inside people's heads only, never becoming part of their value systems. But when someone models what he or she is telling them, people tend to believe, "This person is not only saying it, but he is living it, and is able to practice it."

He shares an example of a training session he conducted. The hosting school wanted to make sure that the trainers received good treatment. They put the trainers into a separate room for lunch, with different food from the teachers and the students. But Manju declined the special food and said that he wanted to sit with the teachers and the children. "Children are our loved ones," he told them. The teachers could then see how he practised what he taught about equality and respect for children. He says that when he now goes to private companies to train employees, he receives an extravagant welcome, often receiving special food and/or special places to sit. For him, "it is really hard to accept" the special treatment, so he usually declines and sits with the people he coaches.

Manju reflects that part of why he makes those kinds of decisions is because he has grown up with many challenges, and he has a particular sensitivity to unequal conditions. He also knows that there are millions of children who are still facing the same challenges today. He feels that in those difficult situations, one caring, compassionate adult can make a difference for that child.

But he also understands that there are not many adults, yet, who have the skills to communicate that level of compassion to young people. "That's when I realised you need people who are passionate, people who are committed, people who can listen to people and understand their emotions and feelings." He knows that a group of these kinds of people can positively shift their environment, and he sees the Teacher Development Programme at Dream a Dream playing a major role in increasing the number of people equipped to interact with others in empathetic and compassionate ways. He is implementing his learnings and values not only in the Teacher Development Programme but also in creating a non-profit football club for young people from vulnerable backgrounds. He is hoping that this club supports young people to play sports and build careers in the sports sector.

"I Started to Find Happiness"

Manju is reflective as he says that he himself has changed through his engagement with Dream a Dream. Instead of expecting the community to give to him, he is looking to give to the community. "From my childhood, BOSCO and Dream a Dream communities have invested in me. Now, I am at a point where I can give back to the community. When I started as a field coordinator, I could not directly interact much with children. When I became an After School Life Skills facilitator, however, I was able to work with young people directly and give back. I felt the natural progression to give more to the community would be by training the teachers, who, in turn, will have a deep impact on children. This transition meant taking on a bigger responsibility with more challenges."

He had always been competitive and hardworking as an athlete, but he says he believes his approach has shifted over the years of being with Dream a Dream. He now focuses more on how to contribute by building up and strengthening others. Sports, for him, has become more about how to create a space for his team and how to build that team to be stronger, rather than about purely winning for himself.

With the skills and the strengths he found and developed through these professional opportunities, he continues to work as a trainer and facilitator on a consulting basis for several organisations, including Dream a Dream. In the more than 10 years he has worked as a facilitator, he has been able to train hundreds of teachers across Karnataka with Dream a Dream. He calls it "a pretty fantastic journey with Dream a Dream."

Manju says he thinks he himself has become stronger as a person in that he has become more peaceful. He used to be very anxious, but now, he is calmer. "I started finding happiness," he says. "At one point in time I believed that happiness comes from the outside, but I realised it comes from within you as you start doing things that you like and start doing things that you love to do. And that's where you find your happiness. I think that's where I started building those qualities of being happy and stronger. Whatever I do, I do with passion and love." Dream a Dream helped him to understand and transform who he was as a person by providing not only support but time, space, and empathy for his journey. It is that kind of space that he wants to create and share with others.

20 — "Everyone is a Changemaker at Dream a Dream"

Manja Devendra

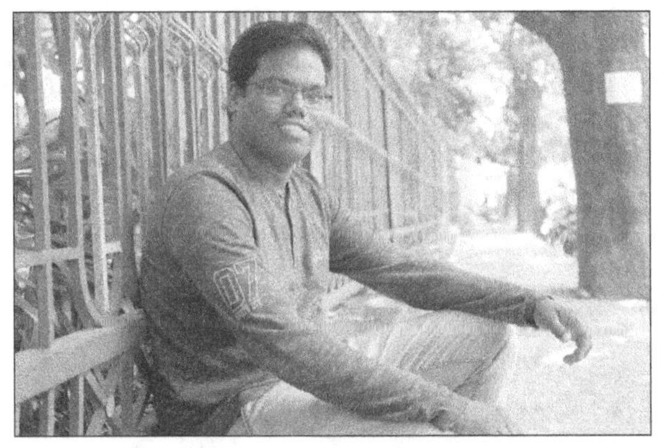

[Manja Devendra, Bangalore, 2022]

Manja Devendra is a 24-year-old young man with glasses and a quiet and thoughtful bearing. At the time of our interview in 2019, he was working at Dream a Dream as the Teacher Development Programme Data Manager. He was gathering data for research using Dream a Dream's Life Skills Assessment Scale for children by going out to visit programmes and conduct observations. He had received a bachelor's degree in business. He was working on earning a master's degree in business as well, with the goal of teaching business students at college. He was teaching accounting and business studies during his weekends, offering his services for free to students.

He has a vision for teaching differently than how he was taught and wanted to incorporate stories and practical and experiential learning into his teaching. This vision came from his experience as a participant and as a staff member at Dream a Dream. Dream a Dream, in turn, grew in its scope and vision in part, from its openness to learn from others, including partners around the world, such as PYE (Partners for Youth Empowerment) and Dr. Fiona Kennedy and Dr. David Pearson, as detailed in previous chapters. This chapter builds on those ideas and explains how Dream a Dream nurtures an environment where positive change takes place not just in people but in its own culture, in part by inviting experts — whether a professional rugby player from England or gender reconciliation trainers from South Africa — to introduce new ideas and skills to its participants and staff.

Manja was able to earn his degrees because of Dream a Dream's financial and other support — Dream a Dream funded his higher education for three years with Rs. 10,000 ($131 USD) per year. He contrasts his experience with that of his older and younger sisters, who both graduated from the 10th standard but did not further their education due to a lack of support. His older sister is married, and his younger sister works at a local food chain store.

Manja has been with Dream a Dream for 10 years, since he was 14 years old, playing rugby with the After School Life Skills Programme in the eighth standard. He was a programme participant for four years, including two years in the Career Connect Centre, when he was 17 and 18 years old. He took the basic English and computer classes at the Centre. He joined the staff of Dream a Dream when he was 18 years old, first as a life skills facilitator for the Football After School Life Skills Programme. The part-time job suited him well as he attended college for four years. In 2016, when he completed college, he transitioned to a full-time job with the Teacher Development Programme at Dream a Dream.

He enjoyed playing rugby with Dream a Dream, particularly, as it gave him the opportunity to travel and play outside Karnataka. Furthermore, he says Dream a Dream changed him by making him more social and open to experiences. Before becoming a Dream a Dream participant, he would go straight home after school; he did not talk to anyone, much less play with them. He did not listen to anyone, and he said that he did not respect anyone, including his mother. "My family did not create the space to interact with others, make friends, or learn new things," Manja recalls. His father, a flower seller, had been a heavy drinker and passed away when Manja was five years old. With only a limited formal education like her husband who only studied until the fourth standard in Tamil Nadu, his mother worked in the garment industry to support herself and her children from then on, leaving little time and energy for her children. But she treated her children the best she could, even if they could only afford just three daily meals of rice most of the time. Manja is the first in his family to graduate not only from secondary school but also go to university and obtain a graduate degree.

He did not interact with many peers, including girls, before joining Dream a Dream's rugby programme; his normal routine would include going to school, returning immediately home, and playing games at home. At the beginning, he did not mingle with other rugby team members and would step back from interacting with them. However, he warmed up to others as he experienced Dream a Dream's accepting environment. Like others interviewed, Manja remembers that while he would be scolded for making mistakes at school, with the rugby programme, the coaches and others would continue to encourage him and be positive, even when he kept on making mistakes for the first two months. "That changed a lot in me," Manja says. He continued his efforts as his coaches and teammates encouraged him to play and learn. As he started to learn new skills, with the opportunity to play outside and learn more about himself during the reflection sessions that accompanied the rugby After School Life Skills Programme, he gained more confidence. He began to open up to others, learning to communicate better, including how to have meaningful conversations.

Rugby also presented him and his classmates with several opportunities to foster collaboration and manage conflict with each other. For example, he remembers an incident that happened when he was cycling back from a game with Dream a Dream participants. He tripped over into a ditch, full of dirty water. Manja felt embarrassed when he fell, but his friends just joked about it and supported him by telling him about similar incidents that had happened to them and the injuries they had received. Instead of being embarrassed by his fall, he felt encouraged. Manja and his friends got through all the injuries and difficulties they faced in rugby with a similar attitude of good-natured support for each other.

He received recognition not only from his teammates but from others. In the eighth standard, he was selected to represent Karnataka in the national youth rugby team and travelled to Delhi to play. It was a big honour as he was just one of three young people selected from a hundred. Manja was featured on TV and newspaper articles. When he returned to school, his principal called him and two other students to speak about their experience in front of their 600 schoolmates. Manja did so despite his fear and nerves, and he was rewarded with applause and congratulations from his peers. "It was a proud moment in my life," he says, recalling the positive way he was recognised.

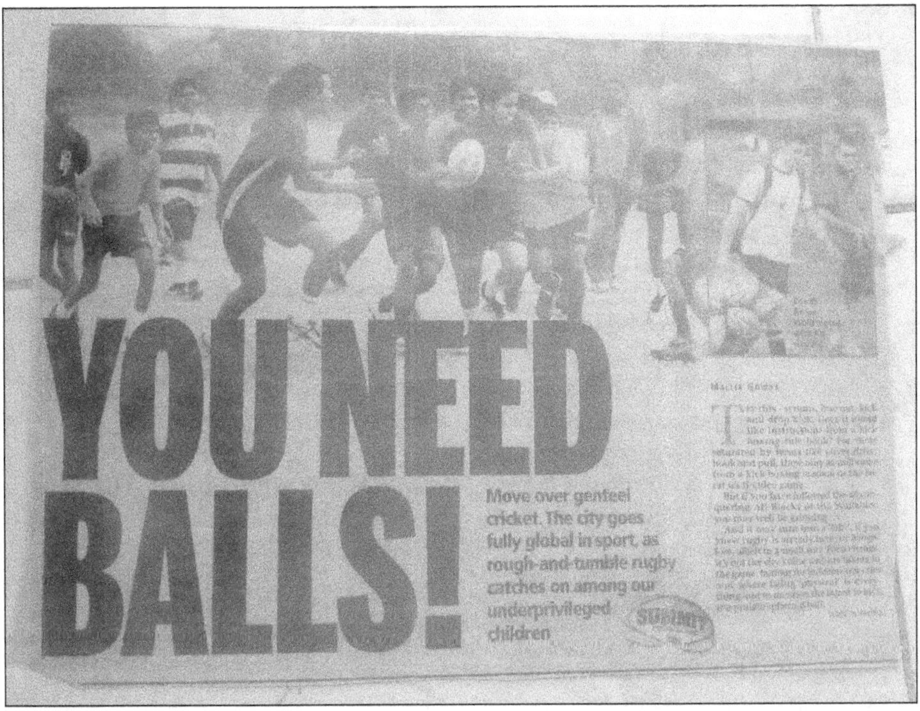

YOU NEED BALLS!

Move over genteel cricket. The city goes fully global in sport, as rough-and-tumble rugby catches on among our underprivileged children

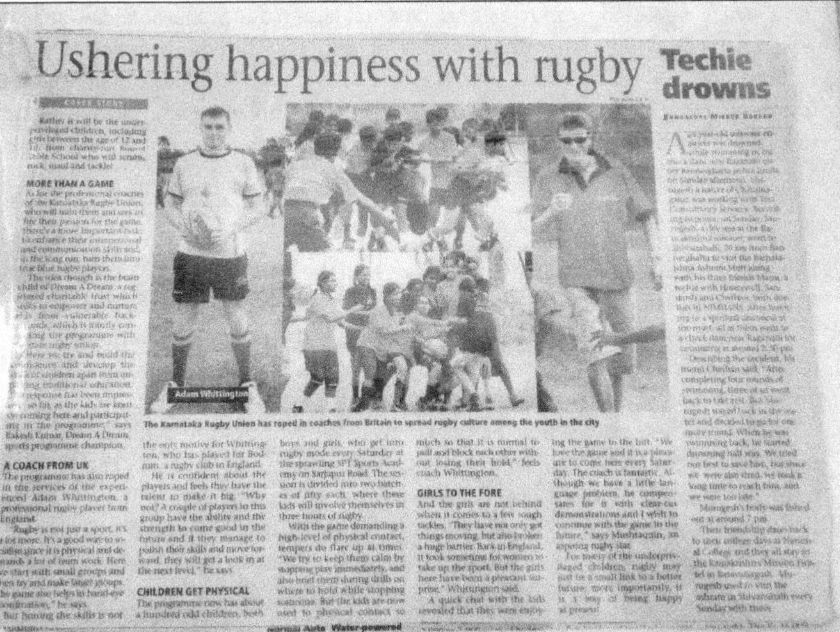

Ushering happiness with rugby

Techie drowns

The Karnataka Rugby Union has roped in coaches from Britain to spread rugby culture among the youth in the city

MORE THAN A GAME

A COACH FROM UK

CHILDREN GET PHYSICAL

GIRLS TO THE FORE

You Need Balls!

Move over genteel cricket. The city goes fully global in sports, as rough-and-tumble rugby catches on among our underprivileged children

Ushering Happiness with Rugby (a transcript of the photo of the article above)

[Mallik Gowda, Bangalore Mirror, 20 July 2009]

Try this — scrums, line out, kick and drop kick. Does it sound like instructions from a kick boxing rule book? For those saturated by terms like cover drive, hook and pull, these may as well come from a kick boxing manual or the latest sci-fi video game.

But if you have followed the all-conquering All Blacks or the Wallabies, you may well be grinning. And it may turn into a 'Oh!', if you knew rugby is already here, in Bangalore, albeit in a small way. For a change, it's not the city's elite who are taking to the game, famous for its Maori war cries and where being 'physical' is everything, not to mention the talent to kick the prolate spheroid ball.

[Cover Story] Rather it will be the underprivileged children, including girls between the age of 12 and 16, from charity-run Round Table School who will scrum, ruck, maul and tackle!

More Than a Game

As for the professional coaches of the Karnataka Rugby Union, who will train them and seek to fire their passion for the game, there's a more important task to enhance their interpersonal and communication skills and, in the long run, turn them into true blue rugby players.

The idea, though, is the brainchild of Dream a Dream, a registered charitable trust which seeks to empower and nurture kids from vulnerable backgrounds, which is jointly coordinating the programme with the state rugby union.

"Here we try and build the confidence and develop the skills of children apart from imparting traditional education. Their response has been impressive, so far, as kids are keen on coming here and participating in the programme," says Rakesh Kumar, Dream a Dream, sports programme champion.

A Coach from UK

The programme has also roped in the services of the experienced Adam Whittington, a professional rugby player from England. "Rugby is not just a sport, it's a lot more. It's a good way to socialise since it is physical, and it demands a lot of teamwork. Here we start with small groups and then try and make larger groups. The game also helps in hand-eye coordination," he says.

But honing the skills is not the only motive for Whittington, who has played for Bodmin, a rugby club in England. He is confident about the players and feels they have the talent to make it big. "Why not? A couple of players in this group have the ability and the strength to become good in the future and if they manage to polish their skills and move forward, they will get a look in at the next level," he says.

Children Get Physical

The programme now has about a hundred odd children, both boys and girls, who get into rugby mode every Saturday at the sprawling SPT Sports Academy on Sarjapur Road. The session is divided into two batches of fifty each, where these kids will involve themselves in three hours of rugby.

With the game demanding a high level of physical contact, tempers do flare up at times. "We try to keep them calm by stopping play immediately, and also brief them during drills on where to hold while stopping someone. But the kids are now used to physical contact so much so that it is normal to pull and block each other without losing their hold," feels coach Whittington.

Girls to the Fore

And the girls are not behind when it comes to a few rough tackles. "They have not only got things moving, but also broken a huge barrier. Back in England, it took some time for women to take up the sport. But the girls here have been a pleasant surprise," said Whittington. A quick chat with the kids revealed that they were enjoying the game to the hilt. "We love the game, and it is a pleasure to come here every Saturday. The coach is fantastic. Although we have a little language problem, he compensates for it with clear-cut demonstrations and I wish to continue with the game in the future," says Mushtaquin, an aspiring rugby star.

For many of the underprivileged children, rugby may just be a small link to a better future; more importantly, it is a way of being happy at present.

The Karnataka Rugby Union has roped in coaches from Britain to spread rugby culture among the youth in the city

Manja reflects that Dream a Dream programmes taught him about positive and professional behaviours, creativity, and career awareness. He also learnt to understand people better, including understanding children's behaviour, including what are often understood by adults as "misbehaviours." He learnt to manage stress and not shout at others in anger in ways that his sisters, who were not part of Dream a Dream, did not. His coach, Adam Whittington, a professional rugby player from England, helped him look back at incidents of anger that took place on the field. As Manja reflected on what triggered his anger, he would practice thinking before acting and talking. "Whatever I learnt during the game, I learnt to use it in my life," Manja notes. He says that now, when he works with programme participants, others appreciate him for his empathy, his listening skills, and his supportive efforts. These were all skills that he says he did not possess before his participation with Dream a Dream.

Dream a Dream's Rugby Programme was offered in partnership with the Karnataka Rugby Union (KRU) which in 2008–2009 was in its early years and mostly consisted of volunteer players. These players (Indian and from other countries) typically worked in multi-national corporations based in Bangalore and were looking for avenues to continue to play Rugby in Bangalore. Adam was one such person. Players like Adam played Rugby with the KRU to stay engaged with the sport. They also volunteered for the Rugby programme that the Karnataka Rugby Union was running for youth at Dream a Dream.

Rugby also helped Manja earn a scholarship for college. When he went to his college and showed them his national certificate in rugby and told them that he had represented Karnataka as a sportsperson at the national level, the college rewarded him with a 50% scholarship. With Dream a Dream's Rs. 10,000 ($131 USD) scholarship, along with the scholarship for rugby, he was able to pay for college, something he would otherwise have not been able to afford, given his family's financial situation.

[Manja (sitting, first from right) at a rugby tournament in Odisha, 2014]

Dream a Dream also supported him financially in paying for his master's degree in business, with Rs. 10,000 ($131 USD) for each year, without many strings attached. Because Manja had selected a correspondence/online course, the fees were more inexpensive; the Rs. 10,000 Dream a Dream covered paid for his annual fee. Manja was able to save money for his sister's wedding and says he supported his other sister in paying for her beautician courses.

Learning and Practising Gender Equality

Manja also learnt about gender equality from Dream a Dream, when they brought in South African facilitators from the Gender Equity and Reconciliation International (GERI)[73] to offer training on a voluntary basis to staff who wanted to receive it, in 2016. GERI's founders Will and Cynthia were introduced to Vishal by PYE Global's co-founder, Charlie Murphy, during one of Vishal's trips to the United States. Vishal was aware that Dream a Dream was looking to practise gender equity in all their programmes and wanted to deepen their practice. GERI was already working in India through other partners and had a good understanding of the context of the efforts to increase gender equity in India. As a first step, all the staff at Dream a Dream took the GERI training and explored their own gendered lenses and blind spots. Subsequently, any employees who were interested in becoming Master Trainers through GERI's approach went through advanced training. Some of them used these trainings to review, inform, and redesign Dream a Dream's curriculum and pedagogical approaches to be better focused on promoting gender equity.

For Manja, this was all very new. He had never explored his own gendered perspective and the biases he grew up with. He knew from his experiences in school and other places the opportunities for men and women were not equal. "I would hear in conversations all the time that 'girls can't do, boys can do.' Men are sometimes given preference, workwise and study-wise," Manja says. "I observed in my community and in other places, including college and at home, women are not treated equally, and not given equal opportunity. But when I joined Dream a Dream, I observed

---

[73] Gender Equity and Reconciliation International. *https://www.genderreconciliationinternational.org/*

that they gave equal opportunities to boys and girls. For example, in rugby, when making selections for participating in a tournament, they select both girls and boys. But in schools, they don't select girls for tournaments." Even in the cases when the school and/or parents did not allow both girls and boys to participate in sports, Dream a Dream worked with the school staff and the community to open the opportunity for girls, when possible. They cited physical, social, and other benefits for all participants, regardless of gender.

When he worked as a facilitator in a traditional Muslim community, at the Raza Education Society's Excellent English School in Tilak Nagar, for example, Manja found that girl children were not allowed to play sports. This was in part because they were not allowed to wear shorts. Instead, all the boys were in the sports programme and all the girls were in the creative arts programme. The principal was a woman, and she was supportive of his efforts to bring more girls to play sports.

With her help and support, Manja spoke to parents and teachers about the benefits of life skills learnt through football and through creative arts, for both boys and girls. He offered gender equity workshops, with trainers from Gender Equity and Reconciliation International. About 30 parents came to a first meeting with parents organised with help from the principal. Manja offered a voluntary gender-related workshop for an hour every Saturday morning, for three Saturdays. About 20 parents came, with some of them who were also teachers who had their own children in the school.

The following year, girls were allowed to play football and about 10 girls joined, with two to three of them receiving an opportunity to play in a district-level football tournament that gave them a chance to see other neighbourhoods. When additional girls got the opportunity to play in state-level football matches, word began to spread in the community about the Football After School Life Skills Programme for girls. "A mindset shift happened in the community," Manja recalls. After those successes, more parents and teachers started encouraging girls to participate. In fact, parents were persuading other parents to send their girls for football, with a change in belief that girls could also be successful in playing football.

With three years of conversations with teachers and parents, through voluntary workshops offered on Saturday mornings, Manja worked to convince the community with determination. By Manja's third year at the school, there was greater gender balance in both programmes, with 70 girls and 80 boys participating in football. More boys also joined the Creative Arts Life Skills Programme, with numbers of boys and girls eventually evening out at 70 boys and 70 girls. Manja shared his strategies with other facilitators at Dream a Dream. When he left the school to take on facilitation at other schools, they gave him an award and spoke well about him. Even when another facilitator took over the school, the gender parity remained[74].

Manja reflects that he was not interested in making changes in the community when he was younger. But as he spent more time with Dream a Dream, where he was encouraged to make observations and become more aware of social challenges facing communities, he grew to want to do something about the issues he saw. He learnt

---

[74] The following are the number of participants for Dream a Dream After School Life Skills Programme:
2018-2019: 2906 Boys & 2752 Girls
2019-2020: 2694 Boys & 2694 Girls
For Career Connect Centre:
2018-2019: 704 Boys & 932 Girls
2019-2020: 946 Boys & 1048 Girls

to take initiative through facilitating after school programmes, noting what he saw, and making changes with support from other staff at Dream a Dream. "I wanted to do something for my society, in my community," he says. The success at Raza "motivated me and gave me more energy and confidence to face challenges," Manja says. So recently, when he noticed that sanitation workers were not coming regularly to his neighbourhood, he informed his local BBMP councillor[75]. The problem was quickly rectified.

> **ℹ INFORMATION BOX 20A: GENDER EQUALITY**
>
> Gender equality is the disparity between men and women in various economic, cultural, social, political and legal aspects (Jha & Nagar, 2015). Many national and international organisations, and policy makers strongly believe that gender equality and equity will strengthen all areas of action to reduce poverty as women bring in new energy and insights.
>
> According to the United Nations Development Programme's Human Development Report (2013), India ranks 132 out of 187 countries on the gender inequality Index. The report states that all countries in South Asia, with the exception of Afghanistan, were a better place for women than India, with Sri Lanka (75) topping them all (ibid).
>
> **Sources:**
> Jha, P., & Nagar, N. (2015). A study of gender inequality in India. *The International Journal of Indian Psychology, 2*(3), 46-53.

Learning to Teach Differently

Manja also tried to practice other things he learnt through Dream a Dream. Manja remembers being in college where professors would pass on information to students and then test them. Most of their work was to memorise books. He started a master's degree in business management so that he could teach his students differently

---

[75] The BBMP (Bruhat Bengaluru Mahanagara Palike) is the administrative body responsible for civic amenities and some infrastructural assets of the Greater Bangalore metropolitan area.

than how he was taught. He wanted to move beyond memorisation and instead, teach for understanding by asking his students to collect information.

He recognises that part of learning skills is putting them to practice and applying them in life. He wants his students' education to be more experience-based, and he wants to use the life skills he learnt at Dream a Dream to do something positive in his community. He currently teaches business and accounting on weekends in a college, something he began to do after telling his lecturers that he wanted to try teaching. He tells stories from real-life examples of how products are sold and bought and encourages his students to ask questions. He has noticed that his students better understand the concepts he is trying to teach when he weaves storytelling into his classes.

Manja reflects, "All children need life skills to live their lives confidently and lead their lives positively. I learnt those things, and that is the reason I am working with Dream a Dream." He counts among those skills the ability to take initiative, exercise empathy and have respect for everyone, communicate well, and the ability to assess and respond to life's challenges and opportunities. He says, "Dream a Dream gives support to vulnerable children; they do not give money, food, shelter, but they give life skills; life skills [includes the ability] to make inner changes, changes for good. [For example,] if I change myself [to have good manners, then I can reach a goal, and if I [continue] to go in the [right] direction, I will meet the right people. Everyone is a changemaker at Dream a Dream."

Serving His Country by Serving Young People

Vishnu Reji

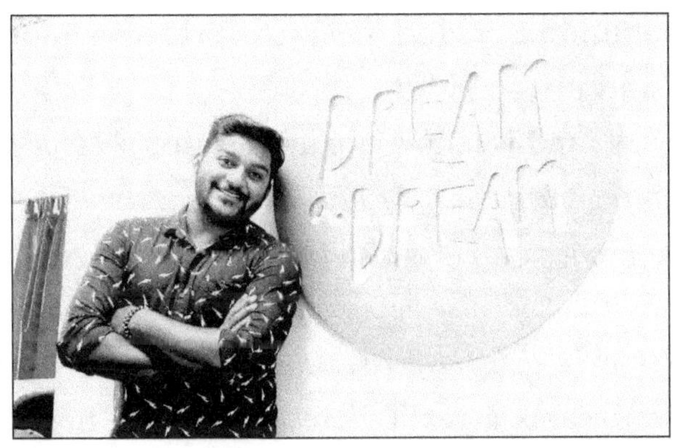

[Vishnu Reiji at the Dream a Dream office, 2017]

Young people, regardless of background, are full of dreams. Those from backgrounds of adversity learn to navigate towards those dreams, however, through more obstacles than their peers. As circumstances change, dreams, goals, and purposes change. As young people learn to know themselves better through new opportunities and challenges and digest new information about the world they live in, their dreams can change too. Organisations, too, evolve and change, as they grow. As leaders and staff respond to new opportunities and challenges, and as those who steer the organisation develop, so too, does the organisation. This chapter discusses the journeys of Vishnu Reji and Dream a Dream as they navigated challenges and obstacles that ultimately shaped their dreams.

In 2017, Vishnu Reji was selected as one of 32 Eisenhower Youth Leaders by the Eisenhower Fellowship in the inaugural cohort, when he was just 22 years old. Selected from the countries and regions in the Eisenhower Fellowship network, the Eisenhower Youth Leaders are young women and men with demonstrated leadership qualities who want to serve and lead their communities and peers to create a more peaceful, prosperous, and just world.

Vishnu wrote in his fellowship application, *"I love playing rugby and dream of using the game to bring about social change. I would like to use the sport to bring awareness about our surroundings and… empower the youth coming from adverse backgrounds with skills that will help them overcome problems in their own community."* In 2019, he worked on making these dreams a reality. He launched a non-profit called Change the Game that intends to teach rugby and other sports to youth from disadvantaged backgrounds and equip them with life and leadership skills. In co-founding this non-profit, Vishnu was bringing to fruition a dream that was almost never birthed because of challenges he faced. Dream a Dream helped to birth that dream by helping him navigate those obstacles and helped him experience concretely what it means to bring about social change, not only in society but also within its own organisation. This chapter discusses Vishnu's journey and Dream a Dream's journey to recalibrate its culture, from 2010 until Suchetha Bhat was named CEO in 2018.

Excelling in Academics but Wanting to Follow His Dream and Play Rugby

Vishnu grew up in a small village in Kerala and moved to Bangalore in Karnataka, an eight-hour train ride away, when he was about eight years old, in the third standard. His family moved to improve their economic circumstances and start a business in the big city. His new school was a metropolitan school[76], and one of the Round Table Schools[77] that was private, until the seventh standard, and then a government-aided school from eighth standard onwards. It was in Bommanahalli, just a stone's throw from Bangalore's 800-acre IT hub, Electronic City.

In his new school, Vishnu excelled in his classes and was at the top of his class academically. He was so well-known for his academic performance that when Dream a Dream came to his school in the eighth standard in 2008 to offer life skills development through computer ("Learn IT"), spoken English, and rugby classes, his principal pushed him into taking the computer and spoken English classes, even though what Vishnu really wanted to do was to play rugby.

There was a reason he wanted to play rugby that was beyond the desire to spend more time with his friends. When he was growing up, Vishnu's big dream was to be an officer for the Indian Navy or Army. Going through the Indian army's website, Vishnu found that people who have a national-level certificate in sports have a higher likelihood of being able to join the army, as they would be

---

[76] **METROPOLITAN SCHOOL** is an English medium co-educational **school** in metro cities like Bangalore, Pune, Mumbai, Chennai, Kolkata, and Delhi.

[77] The Round Table is a social and philanthropic organisation that has chapters in cities and towns across India. Through their Freedom Through Education Program, they identify existing schools (private) that cater to the underserved and build up infrastructure and help to maintain the operations of the school.

selected under a separate sports quota during recruitment. The army had a professional rugby team, which was one of the top rugby teams in India. "I started playing sports, because I thought that if I could get the national-level certificate, it would be helpful." Rugby was one way he knew he could have a chance at joining the Indian military, his dream.

But his principal insisted that Vishnu not play rugby, so during the eighth and ninth standards, Vishnu took English and computer classes and watched his friends Ranjith and Nandish play rugby. In the 10th standard, however, he managed to play rugby, but not with Dream a Dream. Dream a Dream had ended the rugby class in 2009 as it was expensive, and the organisation was struggling to find committed coaches and playgrounds that were safe. Rugby required grass fields, but those were rare to find near most schools in Bangalore and were expensive to rent. Dream a Dream thus switched to offering life skills through football, which could be played on any open surface, including dirt, to their programme participants. For the approximately 150 students who were playing rugby through the Dream a Dream programme, it was a big disappointment.

Vishnu, however, continued to learn rugby from his friends who had taken Dream a Dream's class, during the physical education period or during his free time. His knowledge that succeeding in rugby could help him gain entrance into the Indian Army gave him added focus and drive. In 2010, he started playing with five other friends who were also graduates of the Dream a Dream after school programmes in the Bangalore Bombers Rugby Club. They biked 12 to 13 kilometres weekly to practice and train with the clubs. When the time for tournaments came, however, they found that time after time, out of the six of them, the clubs would only select one or two to play, creating a big disappointment not only for the players who were not selected but also for those who were selected but could not share the experience of travelling to and playing in tournaments with their friends. When the same instance occurred in three to four tournaments, the six of them thought that it was time to start their own club.

Vishnu reflects about that time, "I used to get opportunities. From among the six of us, I used to get the chance to play with the club and travel with them. They would choose me every time. Physically, I was much bigger and that was probably why I was getting the chance. But I saw that my friends were disappointed because they were not getting the chance to show the kinds of skills they had. I asked my friends how they felt and shared that I was not happy about this and about travelling alone. I said, "Let's start a team and let's train others, so we can build our own team." It was one of many signs of leadership from Vishnu, to think of others beyond himself and bring others along with him to new opportunities and experiences.

> ### ℹ INFORMATION BOX 21A: MALNUTRITION AND STUNTED GROWTH
>
> About 30% of children under the age of five in India remain clinically malnourished; most women suffer from anaemia (Sengupta, 2016). According to 2014 government figures, 30% of Indian children under the age of five are clinically underweight. It is nevertheless a vast improvement from 2006, which found a child malnutrition rate of nearly 43% (ibid).
>
> Onis and Branca (2016) point out that childhood stunting is a reliable indicator of a child's well-being and a reflection of social inequalities. According to a WHO study in 2013, stunting is the most common form of malnutrition in children, with about 161 million children (worldwide) falling below norms of degree of growth (De Onis M & Branca F., 2016). Despite a global understanding of definition and measurement, stunted linear growth goes unnoticed in communities where short stature is normalised and is not perceived as a healthcare condition (De Onis M & Branca F., 2016). Linear growth failure serves as a marker for disorders associated with reduced cognitive function, an elevated risk of chronic diseases in adulthood and even morbidity (De Onis M & Branca F., 2016).
>
> According to National Nutrition Monitoring Bureau of India, even 50% of healthy-looking children have multiple vitamins and mineral deficiencies (Singh, 2004).

Contd...

This deficiency, also referred as "hidden hunger", can be attributed to unhealthy eating habits and preferences, and may compromise the physical growth and mental development potential of the child. The first three years of life are critical as children are more vulnerable to hazards of malnutrition and undernutrition (Singh, 2004). It is difficult to meet the complete requirements of micronutrients just from the dietary sources, hence, most pre-school children need nutritional supplements for optimal physical growth and mental development (Singh, 2004).

Sources:

De Onis, M., & Branca, F. (2016). Childhood stunting: a global perspective. *Maternal & child nutrition, 12,* 12-26.

Sengupta, S. (2016). *The end of karma: Hope and fury among India's young.* W. W. Norton & Compan

Singh, M. (2004). Role of micronutrients for physical growth and mental development. *The Indian journal of paediatrics, 71*(1), 59-62.

Forming the Dream Rugby Club

Thus, Vishnu and his friends decided to form their own club, recruiting 20 more young people to join them. Starting to build their own team in 2011, the six friends and former participants of the Dream a Dream rugby programme named their new club the "Dream Rugby Club". They were able to recruit 26 young people, around their age, to start training with them. They prepared their fellow club mates for six months, and then took them from Karnataka to participate in a national-level Under-19 tournament that was held in Jharkhand. Vishnu led the team as captain and Dream a Dream, seeing their initiative and enthusiasm, encouraged and supported them by buying kits for them and sponsoring their travel and tournament entry expenses. The team ranked fifth out of 24 teams that participated. They felt that it was significant that they had participated in the tournament and that they had tried. As the best performer on the team, Vishnu was shortlisted as one of only 30 (out of more than 250 players who participated in the tournament) selected for the Under-19 Indian Rugby National Camp. He was the only one who got selected from his state, Karnataka. Vishnu was delighted and proud of this achievement, but he ultimately could not attend the camp as they required a passport to participate, and he could not get the passport in time.

However, Rugby provided Vishnu with the opportunity to travel around India and provided the participants the opportunity to learn life skills such as teamwork. The team that Vishnu and his friends, Ranjith, Nandish, Shaik, Harish, and Manja, created filled the gap that had opened when Dream a Dream stopped offering the rugby programme. They started to ask for and gain support from their local communities. For example, they got coaches who would coach them for free and were delighted to offer the same experience to others. One of the coaches, associated with Rugby Karnataka, also raised money for them by biking and asking people to donate per kilometre he biked. He raised over Rs. 2,00,000 ($2,600 USD), which he gave to Dream to Dream. He asked that it be earmarked for spending on the group of six people leading the Dream Rugby Club, to spend on their careers and to continue their passion. The team used the additional funds to purchase proper safety gear and kits and bought food to bolster their nutrition for playing such a physically taxing sport. As the new club attended many rugby tournaments, including national tournaments, they found that their club members were physically smaller in size than players from other clubs, likely because of their adverse backgrounds that gave them little opportunity when they were growing up to get proper nutrition. However, the Dream Rugby Club members found sponsors who supplied them with additional nutrition, such as Venkatesh, a senior at the high school, who provided refreshment to young people who attended the Change through Rugby camp. Dream a Dream were also supportive of this endeavour, even when the rugby club members' parents were not supportive, saying the sport was too dangerous.

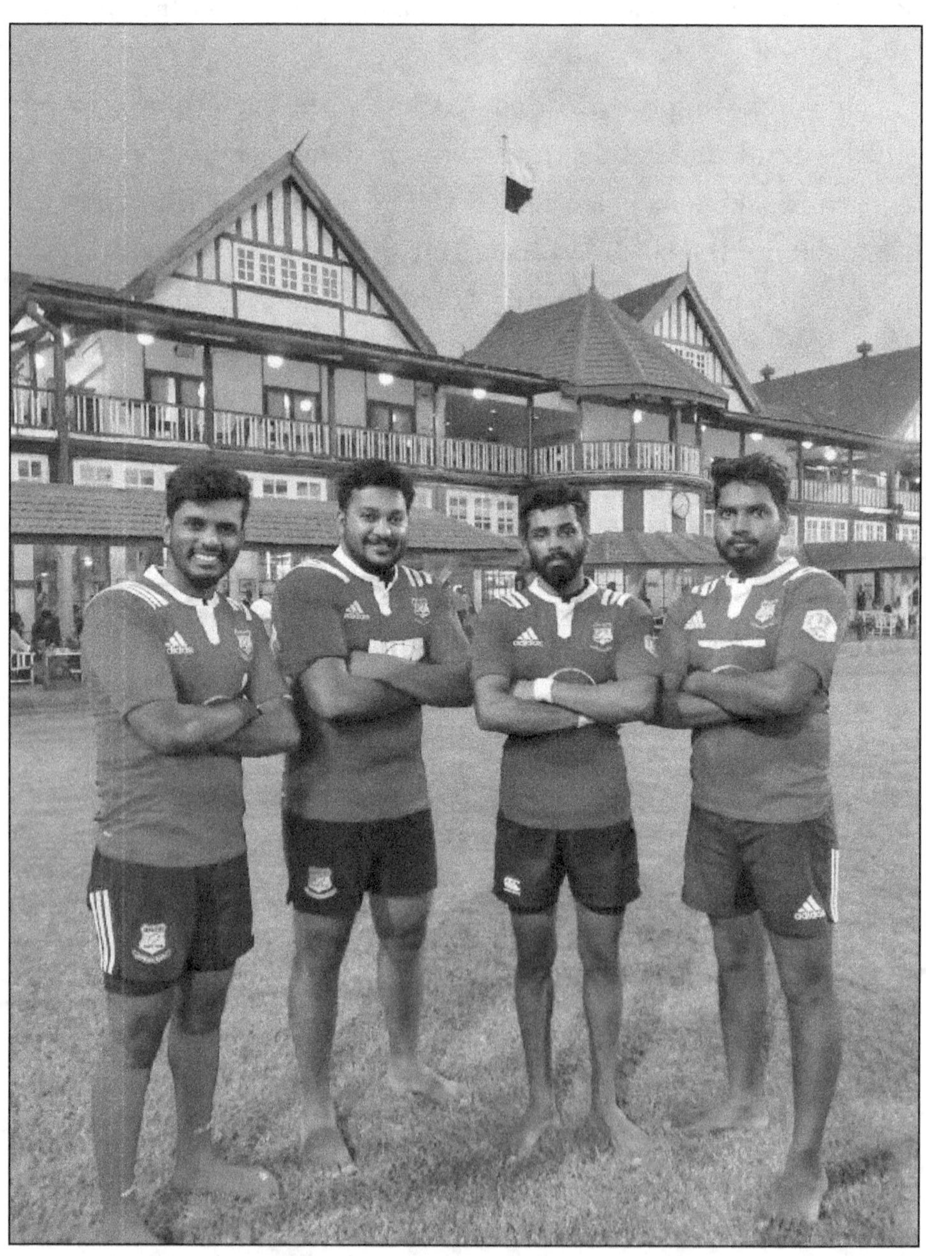

[Vishnu, second from the left, during the Senior National Rugby tournament in Mumbai, 2018]

While some of the club members dropped out because the sport was physically demanding and they suffered injuries, the team began to add more people. As they began to win trophies in tournaments, they brought them to the Dream a Dream office to celebrate with the staff after each win. They would dedicate the trophies to Dream a Dream, in gratitude for empowering them to pursue sports and lead healthier, happier, and more fulfilled lives.

Beyond Rugby: Learning from Dream a Dream to Help His Family

While he was working with his friends to get Dream Rugby Club off the ground, in June 2013, Vishnu joined Dream a Dream as a part-time Football After School Life Skills Programme facilitator, following the encouragement from his friends Ranjith, Pallavi, and Nandish who were already working as facilitators for Dream a Dream. It was his first job interview ever, and he got the job.

The timing was fortunate as his family was going through challenging financial issues, and he needed a part-time job to help his family while he was studying science (electronics and communications) at Oxford Polytechnic College in Bangalore. Neither of Vishnu's parents were working due to health issues such as having blurry vision and physical weakness associated with diabetes. His sister was getting married, and they needed money for the wedding. Also, his parents had borrowed quite a bit of money from what turned out to be loan sharks to fund a business they wished to start. When the business ended up not working out, his parents had transitioned to garment and lathe work, engaging in challenging, physical work. But the amount of money they had borrowed and owed to loan sharks continued to increase as the interest rates were exorbitantly high. The debt continued to pile up. His parents decided to return to their home in Kerala, while Vishnu stayed and began to pay the loan sharks with whatever money he could earn while studying.

Although getting a part-time job at Dream a Dream was a good opportunity for Vishnu, he also felt terribly burdened as a 19-year-old, juggling his second-year pre-university classes with a part-time job and handling the finances for his family. He had taken on the financial stress of managing their enormous debt and arranging for his sister's wedding.

> ### INFORMATION BOX 21B: HIGH INTEREST RATES AND LOAN SHARKS
>
> There is no defined rule for who can engage in moneylending. Anyone with surplus money and authority can be involved in the moneylending business. These moneylenders could be private companies, chit funds, shopkeepers, police, teachers, film financiers, and many others with high surplus incomes. Tirunelveli district in Tamil Nadu is amongst the worst affected region for illegal moneylending (Praveen & Silambarasan, 2020). The usurers have opened branches in major cities such as Bengaluru, Hyderabad, Mumbai, Pune, Chennai, Coimbatore, Madurai, and Andaman and Nicobar Islands. The primary objective of these usurers is to make money out of greed.
>
> As per the World Bank report, in 2012, while there were 35 and 23 banks per 100,000 people in the United States and Hong Kong, respectively, India had only 11. Additionally, the number of people served by one bank branch in India has reduced to about 10,000 in 2014 from over 15,000 in 2006 (Praveen & Silambarasan, 2020). The reasons given above along with the bribes demanded by a few bank officials, motivates those in need to turn to moneylenders. Money is available instantly from these lenders at the convenience of a person's doorsteps. Loan sharks rarely have documentation, security, or guarantee requirements and do not ask for history of borrowing. This reduces the cumbersome processes involved with the banks. Moneylenders hire henchmen to intimidate people to collect back the lent amount. Moneylenders are amongst the largest mafia in Uttar Pradesh, the second largest state of India. Due to non-availability of state-owned banks and government-recognised non-banking financial corporations, the people are generally trapped with these moneylenders. Loan sharks then charge exorbitantly high interest rates which range from 75 to 350% each month, to capitalize on the situation. Private moneylending has even seen an increase of

28% in 2017, in the drought affected, but highly developed state of Maharashtra (Praveen & Silambarasan, 2020).

Chakrabarti and Ravi (2011) also shed light on the microfinance industry and microfinance institutions (MFIs), alternative sources of finance to the moneylenders. Widely considered in government and development circles as a promising solution to reduce poverty and promote financial inclusion, it also emerged as a major profit centre activity in India. According to the Finance ministry's statistics in 2010–11, the overall microcredit outstanding in India was about 6.7 billion USD with about 30 million beneficiaries. However, the interest rate usually exceeds 25%, and increasing recovery pressure due to a reduction in recovery rate had led to a number of farmers committing suicides in a few states. This has transformed the image of MFIs from that of saviours to that of unsympathetic lenders.

Sources:

Chakrabarti, R., & Ravi, S. (2011). At the crossroads: Microfinance in India. *Money & Finance, Forthcoming.*

Praveen, P. J., & Silambarasan, M. (2020). A Look into the Dark Pages of Usury by Ravenous Loan Sharks in India-A Review on Media Reports. *International Journal of Social Science, 9*(1), 25-30.

Learning from Young People with Backgrounds of Adversity

Added to that stress was the disappointment of missing one of the big opportunities he had been waiting for all his life. In 2015, when he was 21 years old, he was selected to try out for the Indian Army services rugby team but missed the opportunity because he did not own a phone. By the time he found out, the try-outs were taking place in Pune in two days, and he was in Bangalore, 800 kilometres away. One of the recruiters from the Army's rugby team had reached out to try to contact him through a friend who had a phone. The friend, however, did not get the message to Vishnu in time for him to prepare a medical certificate and a police certificate to enter the Army rugby team try-out camp; he also did not have the money to travel to Pune on such short notice. Vishnu could not attend the camp. He knew he could not have another opportunity because he was about to turn 22 on the first day of camp, which was the upper age limit for recruitment into the team

However, at the same time, Vishnu felt that he had found his passion of working for young people and decided to continue work with Dream a Dream. It was during this immensely stressful time, that he volunteered with one of Dream a Dream's outdoor adventure camps. His experience was memorable, if not life changing. He went to camp with a mixture of young people from different backgrounds — 59 youth from the Career Connect Centre and 15 young people who came from nearby shelter homes. While most of the young people from the Centre had parents who had the means to support them through university, none of the young people from shelter homes had that kind of built-in family support. When the camp was divided into smaller groups of three adult volunteers and six young camp participants, Vishnu got the opportunity to share his story with the group during an activity called the River of Life, on the second day of the four-day camp.

The River of Life is an activity in which participants tell the story of their lives until that point using the form of a river as a metaphor. Rocks in rivers represent obstacles or struggles, for example, and they share about both memorably good periods as well as memorably negative incidents in their lives.

Vishnu shared his story first, speaking openly about the pressures he faced at home with finances, his parents' illnesses, and additional demands put on by his sister's marriage, and his desire to do well academically while helping everyone around him. He was feeling frustrated by his situation at the time, and he shared those feelings openly and honestly.

Then, one of the young people from the shelter home shared her story. She shared how both of her parents had passed away, and that her father had beaten her mother to death. It was the first thing she shared and the first thing she said she remembers in her life. Her grandmother took care of her after her mother's murder, and then later, the grandmother dropped her off at the shelter home, where she lived. She said that she had been very happy since the day she entered the shelter home, because she had other girls to be friends with. But she shared that she still felt the emptiness from not having a father and mother who were caring for her.

Then another child from the Career Connect programme shared her story, mostly about the opportunities she had received, and how she got a bicycle for her birthday. That kind of sharing went around the circle for over an hour. It gave Vishnu plenty of time to reflect. He found himself thinking, "So, I have everything, but I am still complaining about my parents and my situation. Meanwhile, these children are younger than I am, but they are surviving and fighting for their future." He found himself thinking that he was in the right place, and that he wanted to continue to work with these kinds of young people and support them in their efforts towards creating better lives for themselves.

It was then that he changed his life goal from becoming an Indian Naval officer to becoming someone who works for children. He committed to continuing to work for Dream a Dream. After five years of working at Dream a Dream as a staff member and entering his sixth year, he reflects, "I am very happy to be surrounded by lots of friends and positive people." While he started out as a football facilitator for the After School Life Skills Programmes, he worked in various capacities within Dream a Dream during those five years. He worked as an anchor in the Teacher Development Programme and oversaw the training of 2,000 teachers responsible for 50,000 children in Karnataka every year. He moved up through the organisation quickly, working in a variety of capacities, including piloting a teacher professional induction programme in other Indian states, while also managing 11 to 15 experiential camps per year, like the one that was so life-changing for him.

> **INFORMATION BOX 21C: HOW TO POWERFULLY CAPTURE THE UPS AND DOWNS OF LIFE WITH THE RIVER OF LIFE ACTIVITY**
>
> River of Life is an activity that Dream a Dream adapted from Partners for Youth Empowerment (PYE), an organisation that runs youth camps and trains facilitators to work effectively with youth (https://www.partnersforyouth.org/about/).
>
> The activity allows participants to explore their stories deeply and tell it on their own terms. It is an art-based activity that involves participants drawing key incidents of their lives using the metaphor of a flowing river, choosing to compare events to bridges, flowerbeds, boulders, animals, or anything else that might be in their chosen river ecosystem.
>
> After they complete their drawing, participants share their stories using the drawing of the river with a partner or a group of people. In turn, each person listens intently and non-judgmentally to the stories of others as well. The metaphor of the river allows participants to share as much or as little as they feel comfortable sharing.
>
> The River of Life activity helps participants to begin building or deepen self-awareness, depending on their existing comfort with their own story. Sharing and listening to others' stories can lead to acceptance and building a calm confidence in the community as well as in themselves.

What Vishnu Learnt from Dream a Dream

Vishnu is still friends with the people he met at school when he came from Kerala to Bangalore in the third standard, as many of them are colleagues at Dream a Dream. "Friends" is the first thing he mentions when asked what he feels he has gained from Dream a Dream. He says, "Those friendships are very important to me." He also believes Dream a Dream also taught him not to give up and to ask for help. He remembers that he did not like to ask for help from others, but he has since learnt that it is good to ask for help if help is needed.

He also gained mentors at Dream a Dream, like Vishal, who validated him during tough times. He remembers not knowing what to do when confronted with challenging situations. Now, he handles challenges calmly and can solve problems confidently. He follows through on decisions he has made. He did not believe he could grow professionally as much as he has done over the years with Dream a Dream. He remembers raising his hand and taking on new opportunities whenever they came up and receiving help whenever he could to learn.

His parents now listen to him and respect his maturity, as they also saw how he was able to solve family problems, including their financial situation. By taking on extra jobs, arranging the amount of money to be repaid to each person, and coming up with a schedule of payment, he was able to settle most of their family's debt. He was also able to receive back from the bank the deed to the house that they had kept as collateral now that he was able to pay back the debt. Even though his family is still dependent on him, he is happy to have resolved what had seemed to be an insurmountable amount of family debt, settling it in under four years.

Influencing His Family with What He Learnt from Dream a Dream's Transition to Suchetha Bhat as CEO

Vishnu was also able to influence his family in other ways. He notes, "Sometimes, there is some imbalance in the family where the father is the head of the family and the mother only listens to the father. But I value them equally, and I tell them that every time. Whenever I decide something, I ask for permission from both of them. I treat my sister the same." This valuing of gender equality was something he had gained through his time at Dream a Dream. In their sports programmes, including rugby, Dream a Dream strives for a 50:50 gender balance, and they have worked to create and maintain that kind of culture from the beginning. In the programme itself, the staff taught participants about the value of gender equality and the power of men and women working together. The programme participants did not just hear about gender equality as a slogan but experienced it as they worked together in teams. Vishnu reflects, "We saw how gender equality works by playing together."

In 2018, when Vishal handed over the position of CEO to his partner, Suchetha Bhat, who had also been the COO of Dream a Dream and who had successfully shepherded the organisation through a crisis moment in 2012 and 2013, Vishal gathered the entire Dream a Dream staff. He reminded them that part of the mission of Dream a Dream is to be role models in society and to live out their values with integrity. "In other words, what we say we have to do in the world, we have to do in our organisation," Vishnu remembers Vishal saying. Vishal stressed the many contributions that women can make and said that the world needs to give more leadership opportunities to women as a pathway to changing the world.

Suchetha had joined the organisation in 2007 as a volunteer, as she was earning a master's degree in psychology while working at IBM in software sales. Her parents, like many of the parents of the Dream a Dream participants, had urged her to become an engineer or a doctor or pursue another high-status profession, and had not encouraged her to explore her interests. But while volunteering with Dream a Dream, she found that it helped her to use her interest in psychology, creativity, organisational behaviour, and facilitation among others. She joined as a staff member in 2010, overseeing the curriculum and partnerships, including the structuring of the After School Life Skills Programme and bringing in external experts, such as Grassroots Soccer and PYE, to do so. The Board had given the mandate to scale what Dream a Dream was doing, and the standardisation of the curriculum was a first step.

Meanwhile, the stress of founding a new social entrepreneurial organisation had taken a toll on Vishal, who had worked an enormous number of hours for years, in a climate of uncertainty, pressure, and stress. Most of the decisions had been centralised to him, and with the staff feeling that there was an increased discrepancy between what the organisation espoused and what it practised, about half of the staff resigned in March of 2011.

Suchetha led a group of 8–10 from among the remaining staff members who volunteered to think through the task of reimagining and changing human resource practices and organisational culture, with the help of an external human resources expert and facilitator. For two years, they committed to better align the organisation with what they were asking of the programme participants, centring policies and practices on the belief that every staff member wants to and can create positive change. The product was a document called the People Philosophy that described radical and deeply value-driven human resource management practices.

They felt they needed an organisation where "everyone leads" if they were to grow and scale their practices. It began with establishing an organisational culture that treated everyone as though they were capable adults, if not leaders, able to determine what is best for the organisation and themselves. Accountability, trust, and dignity became core values. Performance management became reflection-based, with the celebration of the individual journeys of people. It centred on staff members determining, with supportive feedback from others, on how and in which areas they wanted to grow. Salaries became more transparent and systemized, with less dependence on Vishal or any one person making individual calls, and decisions, in general, became more decentralised. Vishal was not part of the group that developed the document, and instead, took the time he needed to take care of himself. Even as it dialled down organisational growth during this process of reflection and recalibration, the process of human resources and organisational reorientation and curriculum standardisation also led them to envision supporting teachers to adapt many of the practices and philosophy that Dream a Dream had found helpful in working with young people from vulnerable backgrounds.

They knew that a robust curriculum, while helpful, was not the key to their success. Rather, "it was the caring relationship between adults and children that needed to be the lever for scale," Suchetha recalls as a key insight from a strategic review process. When children have access to caring and compassionate adults, then transformative changes can happen, in the lives of children, in the adults, in schools, and in communities, creating a strong ecosystem for children. With this insight, in 2013, they began the Teacher Development Programme, which became another linchpin in their overall strategic plan to scale up.

Suchetha, in playing a critical role in all these processes that impacted both organisational culture and organisational impact, became more confident. With these new levers for success, including partnerships with state education ministries starting in 2016, from serving 3,000 children with 25 staff members, Dream a Dream grew to serving more than 3 million children with just 110 staff in 2019, multiplying their reach 1,000 times, but only quadrupling the number on their staff.

By 2013, Suchetha had become the COO of the organisation. As she focused on nurturing and systemising a mission-driven workplace environment in which everyone works together to bring everyone along, she began to realise and articulate a different kind of leadership that was more facilitative and feminine, focused on empathy, care, and trust. She formally trained to become a facilitator with PYE and considers facilitation to be one of her best strengths. Her own art practice that she began after encountering PYE led her to practice listening more to her intuition, making connections, and building patterns. Her reflections about how patriarchy, gender, and systemic biases had played out in her personal and professional lives led her to become a more intentional leader.

The People Philosophy explicitly states that each Dream a Dream staff member be responsible for determining when she or he is ready for the next level of responsibility. She began the conversation with Vishal about becoming CEO in 2015. Vishal had been ready for years for someone to take over the role as he focused more on advocacy to a global audience, and they approached the board about the transition. Moreover, he saw first-hand how Suchetha's strengths complemented his, in ways that benefitted the staff and organisation. The founder/hero/Vishal-focused culture had helped the organisation establish and grow to a certain point, but for it to grow and expand, it needed a more horizontal, distributed, facilitative leadership model, and Suchetha was a natural successor. Suchetha and Vishal were married by that time, and the board took a year and a half to thoughtfully make sure that conflicts of interest were limited as Suchetha took over. When Vishnu heard Vishal speak the words, "In other words, what we say we have to do in the world, we have to do in our organisation," Vishal had meant each word and had lived it.

Vishnu reflects that Dream a Dream was Vishal's "child" for 19 years, as he built it from the beginning, and that it must not have been easy to give up the position of CEO. "It's not easy to give something up, to leave something," Vishnu thought. "It was kind of shocking to me because it is not possible for most people to give up power when, usually, decision-making is done by men" in society. With these kinds of thoughts running around in his head, Vishnu did not congratulate Suchetha while everyone else on staff did.

Vishal was Vishnu's informal and formal mentor through the Eisenhower fellowship, and he noticed that Vishnu had not approached Suchetha. After a couple of days, Vishal went to Vishnu and asked why he didn't congratulate Suchetha. No one else had seen him not congratulate her, but Vishal had. Vishnu told him what was on his mind and said that he would go to Suchetha and congratulate her. But first, Vishnu said that he would like to congratulate him for making this decision.

Thinking through Vishal's reasoning for his decisions, Vishnu aimed to change his own behaviour. When he went to his parents about a decision, he made it a point to ask his mother to share her opinions. When he felt that his mother was making the better decision, Vishnu worked to have his father understand and realise that he needed to listen to his wife and include her in his decision-making process. Vishnu reflects, "Before, in my family, all the major decisions were taken by my father, but now, my mother and father both sit together and decide. I'm happy to see this change happening in my home."

Vishnu has also helped his sister to see her son differently. He reflects, "I try to make my sister and her husband understand that each child is unique, and that the child will find his/her/their way. We just have to create space for young people and young adults and take care of them. We have to let them decide because they know what to choose."

Helping His Friends with What He Learnt from Dream a Dream

Vishnu also says that his friends and the young people he works with continue to inspire and encourage him. For example, Rakesh was one graduate of the Career Connect Centre who had been coming to Dream a Dream's experiential camp for the past two years. Vishnu saw his potential as a leader and began to mentor him, sharing about himself and listening to Rakesh's story. Rakesh also wanted to become a facilitator for Dream a Dream so he applied for an opening but did not get selected. But Rakesh did not lose hope and kept trying. Rakesh was also curious about rugby and wanted to try playing. He started to volunteer with Vishnu for the community rugby team, and Vishnu eventually gave him the opportunity to facilitate the rugby programme. As Vishnu, Rakesh, and others were applying to receive a national training certificate in rugby, Rakesh's father passed away. Vishnu did not expect him to come back to the training programme as Rakesh's father's village is far away from Bangalore, but Rakesh came back, finding time to train and participate despite the challenges. Vishnu recalls saying to himself, "That guy, he comes barefoot sometimes, but he doesn't come late." Rakesh ended up being selected along with Vishnu for the state rugby team.

Vishnu found the mentoring training that he received from Dream a Dream helpful as he guides and mentors other young people like Rakesh. He remembers one moment when he was checking on one of his friends who had posted on her WhatsApp status, "God, I'm done here; please call me and take me away." He remembers laughing at the status and joking with her casually as a friend. After the mentoring training, however, he realised that his friend might have been going through a tough situation, facing challenges. He apologised to her, and she then shared with him what she was actually going through. He saw how powerful and effective knowing about how to interact sensitively with other people might be, so he made sure to learn as much as he could about mentoring.

He found this kind of training helpful, as one of his friends, Harish, went through some difficult times. Harish was one of the first among their group of friends to get married. He was happy for the first six months of marriage, but then started to struggle, with stress from moneylenders and from his family. Harish began to drink, and Vishnu, recognising that Harish was struggling, took time to listen to him. Harish, however, suddenly quit Dream a Dream, even though he was earning a good salary and he was happy with his job. Everyone was shocked, and even more so, when Harish fell into spending time with a group of local men and continued to drink too much. Vishnu continued to meet with Harish and was a friend to him, as Harish went through the difficult decisions of trying a new business, calling loan vendors, and taking on new jobs as a delivery person to try to earn enough money to repay the loan sharks.

Eventually, Harish also started to coach and facilitate rugby sessions with Vishnu's budding new organisation. When Harish's brother Sahned got into trouble at school in the eighth standard, instead of blaming his brother, Harish understood that the teachers were not treating nor understanding Sahned well. To the school administrators, it seemed that Sahned enjoyed playing sports more than studying and when they called his home to discuss it with his parents, they found that no one answered and concluded that he came from an unsupportive family. In fact, their mother worked to support them as they did not have a father. The school decided to expel Sahned. While the rest of the family was pushing Sahned to go to work, Harish stood up for his brother. He confirmed with his brother that Sahned wanted to study. He found out that it was the unkind treatment from Sahned's teachers, who did not allow him to both study and play sports, that discouraged him.

After brainstorming with Vishnu and other Dream a Dream staff to find a solution, Harish advocated that his brother go to a youth hostel that was 300 km away but was near a government school that had a rugby programme that Sahned enjoyed. Because they were from the slums, where not many young people go on to receive university education, and because Sahned was only in the eighth standard, his family resisted sending him so far away. But Sahned left and has now successfully continued his education. Vishnu was happy to find Harish finding happiness with his family again and not worrying about what he does not have. Vishnu recalls, "The mentoring training helped me to maintain this kind of relationship. I could help my friend from becoming too sad and self-indulgent. I could help him by just being there and understand what he was going through."

Helping the Community with What He Learnt from Dream a Dream

These kinds of helping, empathising, and mentoring behaviours were not necessarily modelled to Vishnu when he was in school. His principal pushed him away from rugby, but Vishnu found his way back into rugby. Vishnu eventually had the opportunity to represent India in the International Team Camp. In 2018, the club won the Division Two tournament and the South Indian Sevens Tournament. Dream Rugby Club members are still playing rugby, and they plan on launching a non-profit focused on teaching rugby to young people in 2020.

Vishnu says, "every expectation, I pushed against," if he felt that it was not the best for him nor what he wanted to do. He says that through Dream a Dream, he learnt how to follow through on the decisions he made once he made them thoughtfully. He says that young people need those kinds of skills and "the ability to follow their own path. They might be scared; they might be pushed into things that they may not want to do. But if they know what they want, they need to learn to pursue and stay with what they want." Vishnu also reflects that before Dream a Dream, he was more focused on what he could get from a situation, but now, he finds himself asking, "What can I give back?"

He recalls with a smile, "Toward the end of each experiential camp, I get blessings from the children who come; I'm only 25 years old but the children tell me that I took care of them like a father — they felt very happy and felt very safe." Vishnu says that those kinds of affirmations keep him encouraged to continue working even during challenging times.

From July to October of 2019, Vishnu took a three-month sabbatical from Dream a Dream to volunteer at Rugby Karnataka.

While all 24 states in India have associations for rugby, Karnataka's team is not as active. Vishnu volunteered to raise awareness throughout Karnataka and encouraged over 1,800 children from all over the state to take part in rugby. He started a "Change through Rugby" initiative, supported by Rugby Karnataka, the official state rugby union in Karnataka, that provided equipment and invited children, especially from adverse backgrounds, to participate. It is a 10-day camp for 15 to 40 young people; there, they learn to play rugby and learn life skills. Five young people took the initiative and are now running the camp, which continues to be supported by Rugby Karnataka.

Through Change the Game, the organisation that Vishnu co-founded in 2020, more than 80 young people are playing rugby every week. Everyone on the staff of the team has obtained Level One Certificate for rugby, which certifies them to coach at the state and national levels. They trained the state women's team, and 13 out of 14 girls who were selected for the state team came from their club. Vishnu believes that schools are ready to give rugby a chance, and their club is working to change the mindset that rugby is a dangerous sport. While they had started with four or five volunteers, now fifteen 18- to 24-year-olds are facilitating the programme for 10- to 24-year-olds. Vishnu is receiving guidance from Vishal and others at Dream a Dream to start the NGO and plan to offer rugby to students in the fifth standard and onwards, including university. Some young women in their programme have already received rugby scholarships to universities. Vishnu is working to add more schools to expand their two programmes, one for young people who are 13 to 15 years old in the fifth to eighth standards, and another for young people who are 16 to 18 years old and in pre-university education.

In Hinduism, Vishnu is the god of goodness and preservation. He protects the universe from being destroyed and keeps it going. The Bhagavad Gita 4.7–8 includes the following passage about Vishnu:

"Whenever righteousness wanes and unrighteousness increases, I send myself forth. For the protection of the good and for the destruction of evil, and for the establishment of righteousness, I come into being age after age."

It seems that at age 25, Vishnu is continuing to learn to live up to his namesake.

Afterward

It is the beginning of 2022, and the world is just recovering from the loss, devastation and trauma of a global pandemic while other challenges continue to affect us in ways big and small. The war in Ukraine, the unrelenting climate crisis, the rise of fascism, the increasing hatred towards certain communities of people from a different race, class, caste, gender, and sexual orientation and the havoc that misinformation and fake news is playing with our lives. Amidst all this, inequities are rising at an alarming rate in the world.

We check in on some of the young people profiled in this book and how they are doing, three years after Connie's initial interview with them in 2019.

Prasanna and Sukanya are proud parents now and are conscious about what values and experiences they want to share with their child. Sukanya works part time at a school while bringing up their girl. Prasanna continues to pursue his second graduate degree in Law. With colleges being closed for over two years, his dream has been delayed, but he hopes to be a qualified lawyer by 2024. Sukanya and he are thriving.

Revanna got married in late 2021 to a colleague from Dream a Dream. It was not an easy decision, and he faced much discrimination from the community as he belongs to a lower caste and does not have parents nor family members. He and his partner stood their ground, however, and are taking their first steps to build a new life together.

Vijay Bhasker had a difficult two years. The ice-cream parlour where he worked as a manager had been closed for most part of the pandemic and his salary was reduced to half. However, he held onto hope and still maintains his positive attitude.

Sneha got married a year ago and managed to negotiate with her in-laws and family to ensure that she continues to build her career, even after her marriage, something many young women do not do. Now, she is proud to be a language teacher in a higher primary school while also expecting her first child.

Ayesha is working at Accenture as part of the Human Resources and Onboarding team and makes time to volunteer. She has been volunteering closely with A Aa E Ee, a youth-led NGO in Bangalore, aiming to bring holistic development to children from challenging backgrounds through need-based, value-based, and skill-based education.

Afreen is working with Dream a Dream as a facilitator. During the pandemic, when there was much learning loss, she ensured that no child from her community was losing out on opportunities to continue to learn. She acted as an educator to her siblings and other children in her community and ensured they had the resources to continue their education.

Bharath was promoted at work and is now a proud assistant manager at Swiggy Instamart, a leading grocery delivery service in India.

Ranjith decided to go into business together with Vishnu and another friend in 2019 and started a food venture called Shawarma Adda. It was a brilliant idea at the time, and their business was picking up when the pandemic brought their dreams to an abrupt halt. They finally had to close down the business, after struggling to keep it afloat. Ranjith continues to work at Dream a Dream and has learnt a new skill during the pandemic. He became a tattoo artist. He has also been one of the many pillars of Dream a Dream's COVID-19 relief efforts in the past two years.

Pavithra spearheaded Dream a Dream's COVID-19 relief efforts during the past two years while bringing up her new-born during an overwhelming global crisis. Being the sole breadwinner for her and her extended family during the pandemic, she also ensured that her family stayed afloat through this crisis, both financially and emotionally. She continues to be a force to be reckoned with.

Shiva is struggling. He lost his job due to a mistake he made and is learning to live with the consequences of the choices he made. His next job too did not last as he continues to grapple with a fragile family environment with mounting debts.

Rashmi completed her engineering at The Oxford College of Engineering in Bangalore. She is the only child in her family who has completed higher education. Her younger sister and family supported and helped to make her dream come true. She is now working at an information technology firm.

Rajeshwari has grown in the sector as a makeup artist and beauty specialist. She manages a beauty parlour. During the pandemic, she volunteered with the local municipal ward and ensured that relief efforts by the government were reaching those most impacted by the pandemic.

Shahid, while running a technology start-up, also founded a non-profit organisation called Haadi with his college friends to serve those with finarcial and other needs. They began by serving food to the homeless and unsheltered. They have expanded to work with students in schools and colleges and guiding them in achieving their career aspirations.

Kashvi gave birth to a beautiful baby boy. She is now working as a guest teacher in a lower primary government school.

Pallavi got married and is absolutely thrilled with this new development in her life. She continues to be a committed worker in her community, solving complex challenges while building an ecosystem of supporters that include local community members, politicians, philanthropists, and others. She is also supporting her siblings to make positive life choices.

Naavya works at a clinical research firm as a data analyst and feels stable with her career and life choices.

Manjunath, who is working as a freelance trainer, facilitator, and consultant, has had a difficult two years since most freelance assignments were difficult to obtain during the pandemic. Life continues to throw googlies at him, and he continues to field them with courage and ease. He is learning new life skills and used this time to build new professional skills. He continues to run his Football Club; they recently got their licence, which means they are a registered team that can participate in professional tournaments. The boys in the club all come from adversity and continue to practise with little equipment. But they have stayed committed.

Manja continues to thrive at Dream a Dream and has steadily supported his family. The stability has given him the confidence to plan to marry his childhood sweetheart next year and enter a new, exciting phase of his life.

Vishnu, in addition to trying to start a business with Ranjith and another friend in 2019, got married to his childhood sweetheart and moved on from Dream a Dream. After struggling to find a role he liked, he found a job with another non-profit that teaches entrepreneurship to young people. He continues to grapple with complex conflicts within his family and continues to respond with the same resilience, patience, compassion, and grace that has become second nature to him.

Even today, these young people are teaching the staff at Dream a Dream. All of them continue to face a multitude of challenges in their personal and professional lives, but they are all thriving in ways that only they can define. This gladdens and encourages the hearts of those who have supported them over the years.

However, the story of Dream a Dream is not just the story of helping thousands of young people thrive. It is also the story of those that we lost along the way and the systems, gaps, and failures associated with them.

Dream a Dream's continuing work includes the story of Manoj, the young 14-year-old who was failed by an uncaring family, an uncaring school system, an uncaring neighbourhood and an uncaring justice system. He died in a road accident when trying to steal a bike that he did not know how to ride. He took to stealing so that he and his little sister could have food to eat.

To date, Manoj's story reminds us that it is not only up to young people like Manoj to overcome adversity and thrive, but it is also the responsibility of parents, neighbourhoods, school systems, policymakers and each of us to create the conditions to help the Manojs of the world to heal before they learn to thrive.

It is the story of Shridhar who learnt to thrive but was pushed back by an uncompromising world that did not create the safe spaces he needed to talk about his inner turmoil. He died by suicide at the young age of 28.

It is the story of young women we have lost to suicide, and women who were forced into early marriages and suffered domestic abuse in a highly patriarchal society. It is the story of the young men and women we have lost to a world that has shut opportunities for education, livelihoods, and thriving for them because of their race, religion, gender, caste, class, or standing in society.

Hence, our work at Dream a Dream and beyond is hardly done.

What remains true even after 20 years of this work is that the onus of 'improvement' continues to be on the young person, who is often living in systems mired in inequity and discrimination. Imagine a Muslim child from a low-income background, living in a predominantly Hindu-populated community. He attends a middle-class Hindu-majority school where he is constantly subjected to religious slurs. Eventually, because of the bullying, he becomes subdued and quiet. If our interventions tell him that he needs to 'become confident' or 'take leadership' without acknowledging and/or changing his lived reality outside of Dream a Dream that continues to exclude and marginalise him, what impact would they have on him other than further eroding his self-worth, making him feel as though everything is his fault, and that he should try harder in an impossible system and culture?

Therefore, as important as our work has been, we know that it cannot bring about change in isolation. The entire education and social systems need to tackle the structural inequities and systemic barriers arising out of race, caste, class, religion, social status, and gender among other factors that continue to push young people back. To really move towards inclusivity, we will need a change in the mindsets of all the people involved, including in the mindsets of educators, school leaders, parents, and community members. We need to co-construct our society and systems with young people.

According to a recent article by Dream a Dream CEO Suchetha Bhat[78], creating a better future for every child requires us to take an intersectional lens centred on some of the following questions:

1) How can education and employment ecosystems work to stop the perpetuation of systemic barriers that continue to haunt young people in India based on their social identities?

2) How should life skills programmes help young people unpack the ways in which their intersecting identities contribute to increased risk for discrimination and oppression within education and other spaces?

3) How do we recognise and shift our own biases and privileges as parents, teachers, educators, facilitators, school leaders, community members, business leaders, social entrepreneurs, and policymakers, and our own intersecting social identities and their impact on young people in our classrooms and communities?

It is important then that we (adults) share the accountability for thriving with youth. A good first step would be to acknowledge and understand our own intersecting identities as facilitators, teachers, administrators, education leaders, and anyone working in the education ecosystem. For instance, if I am a teacher from an upper

---

[78] Pillai, V., & Bhat, S. (2022, April 6). *Social-emotional learning in India: The importance of intersectionality*. India Development Review. https://idronline.org/features/education/social-emotional-learning-sel-in-india-needs-an-intersectional-lens/

caste, socio-economically privileged household, it is imperative I understand how this privilege plays out in a classroom of largely lower caste students. I might not have the same lived experience, the same language, the same cultural and religious festivals as my students. My stories and context might not align with those of my students. Becoming aware of our own privileges and how these privileges exacerbate discrimination can also aid in building a sense of how social identities function in the lives of children who are often relegated to the margins of our consideration.

An example of this caste-based exclusion is an effort made to address prejudices associated with some Indian last names. Dr. Praveen Kumar, former principal secretary at the Telangana Social Welfare Residential Educational Institutions Society (TSWREIS), brought about many reforms in the TSWREIS schools. But his most significant contribution to developing children's self-confidence was offering all the children a new surname — SWAERO — to help them overcome the systemic discrimination they face when their last names reveal their caste identity. The results over the years tell their own story as thousands of students today proudly add SWAERO to their last name and are thriving in previously unachievable spaces.

The privileges of many of us in positions of power and influence, arising out of being a member of the upper caste/class, especially when exercised without empathy, can blind us into making quick judgements about the characters and motivations of other people. Our privilege in that sense is not visible to us, and we assume it to be the way of the world. For example, a teacher regularly punishes a child for being late to class, quickly judging her as "lazy" and "irresponsible," until he realised that before she came to school, this child needed to get all her siblings ready, do the laundry, and make food for the family. She also did not have a clock at home and never knew the time. As we see in this case, the privileged notion of punctuality being the only indicator of responsibility is deeply flawed and blind to the realities of many of our children. These are the kinds of mindsets that we seek to uncover and address in Dream a Dream's work with educators and other facilitators of learning.

Secondly, when a young woman from a lower caste goes for a job interview and the interviewer is an upper caste employer who had grown up with prejudices and biases against people from the lower caste and opposite gender, it is unlikely that this young woman would get a job, unless the employer has consciously worked to be aware of and break from his biases.

For all the above challenges and blind spots that come from our privilege, developing an intersectional lens is important because only then will we build an equity-centred approach that helps affirm young people's lived experiences and not perpetuate the same discrimination that leads to their marginalisation in the first place. We, as supporters of young people, need to work with young people to create the conditions, environments, and narratives that will help every child learn to thrive, irrespective of their background and identity. That would be the true success of all our work. Being curious and humble and open to our young people would enable us to understand and support them better. This is one of the reasons why Dream a Dream listens to the young people and shifts our practices when needed.

Today, Dream a Dream is reinventing itself from an organisation that has for the past two decades focused on the empowerment of young people through a creative life skills approach to also working to remove the systemic barriers and inherent inequities that prevent young people from thriving. We start with ourselves, and we do this with love, care, dignity, and empathy for young people and adults alike. We believe that at the core of all the stories of thriving in the book is the dream of a world that is driven by love, care, togetherness, harmony, respect, and dignity for all.

Vishal Talreja
April 2022

Acknowledgements

As the research and stories documented in this book show, the quality of our relationships is key to our thriving. Thriving, learning, and growing are communal endeavours, best done in the context of caring and supportive relationships in which we share our strengths and challenges with others. Writing a book is also a communal effort, and I am grateful to everyone who came alongside me in this endeavour.

First, I would like to thank the young people in the book who trusted me with their stories. They chose to be authentic and vulnerable in their sharing, and this book would not be possible without them. This is why they are named as co-authors. As I shared with the Dream a Dream staff, I came away from this research and writing experience thinking that what Dream a Dream has built is not just a life skills programme but a leadership development programme. The future of India is bright because of young people like those who are featured in this book — generous, inclusive, and brave.

I would also like to thank Vishal who invited me to write this book. He trusted me to tell the story of his life's work into which he has invested his heart and soul. I wrote the words on the page, but he first co-created the stories that are in this book through his work with young people, through the choices he made, and with his life. This is why he is named as a co-author. Vishal's unfettered commitment to young people that I saw again and again when our paths crossed over the years in Beijing, Boston, Delhi, Dubai, Killarney, Lisbon, Lyon, Paris, Seoul, Vancouver, Washington D.C., and other places, largely influenced my decision to take on this project. He remained patient, encouraging, and supportive throughout the project. Vishal is an exemplary leader in working with young people, and his spirit infuses this book.

I would also like to thank the members of the Dream a Dream team who supported the birth of this book across its three-year journey. This is why they are named as co-authors. This list includes Suchetha Bhat, Dream a Dream's CEO, who supported the idea of this book and provided valuable insights along the way. Aiswarya Yadalam, Anjali Paul, Tashi Mitra, Kanthi Krishnamurthy, Pavithra KL, Revanna Marilinga, and others welcomed me warmly and helped organise my visit to Dream a Dream in 2019 and the interviews with young people. Revanna in particular, shepherded me throughout Bangalore to visit schools and community spaces to observe Dream a Dream's programmes and to interview young people; he guided me on an excursion to Bengaluru's flower markets in the darkness before dawn and to a park and a temple that young people loved, to see a bit of the broader context of the city; he shared his insights with me along the way. Aishwarya and Revanna also assisted with translations and arrangements for the interviews; they also transcribed the interviews. Aiswarya, Khushboo Kumari, Vikram G. N., Suchitha Balasubramaniam, Sheetal L. P., and Varsha Pillai supported the research around the book, including writing some of the India- and Dream a Dream-specific data and content for the information boxes. Prasanna H. took many of the photographs for the book and helped to source the rest; Manisha Raghunath created the webpage for this book. Varsha and Vikram helped to find the publisher for the book. Vikram drove the overall project management during the final year that helped bring this book to fruition. I would also like to thank Notion Press and their team for the final copyedits and formatting.

The insights from Dream a Dream's staff and partners are woven throughout the book, and where possible, I identify and give credit to them. The stories of young people are possible because of the body of work developed by Dream a Dream and their key partners over the past two decades. As I write in the chapters, people like Dr. Shashi Rao, Dr. Fiona Pearson, Dr. David Kennedy, Charlie Murphy, Peggy Taylor, and Nadia Chaney helped to develop key programmes to become what they are. Without their selfless, voluntary contributions of time, professional expertise, and decades of experience, Dream a Dream would not be where it is today.

In the same vein, there have been a host of board members, advisors, supporters, funders, donors, partners, mentors, and well-wishers who have walked this journey with Dream a Dream, given invaluable insight, and helped the organisation impact millions of young people. This book is a testimony of their unwavering support and commitment to support young people growing up in adversity.

The final year of editing this book through its final drafts coincided with the first year of my Foster America Fellowship, where I was able to observe the work of social workers and other staff at San Mateo County Human Services Agency and elsewhere in the United States. Social workers' task to prevent and interrupt generational and historical trauma is complex, challenging, and often unacknowledged and underappreciated. I am grateful to

San Mateo County Children and Family Services staff, community partners, and Director John Fong for hosting me during my fellowship. It was also a tremendous privilege and honour to work with the young people of San Mateo County during my fellowship. Many thanks to Foster America staff, faculty, and its broader network, including Executive Director Marie Zemler Wu, Director of Learning and Leadership Shannon Scott, and members of my cohort for creating an environment where I felt cared for.

Dream a Dream supported me during the first two months of writing the book so that I could devote my full time to the work, but the rest of the book was written on nights, early mornings, and weekends; it truly was a labour of love.

As I wrote about the importance of supportive relationships in the book, I thought of Andi, Becca, and Laidy, who not only encouraged me throughout this project but also were among the two dozen supporters who made my own journey as a foster parent possible. My lived experience as a resource parent to a child involved in the American foster care system was an important lens with which I could temper and digest what I was hearing in the interviews and what I was reading in research literature for this book. I had worked closely with social worker Lauren from the Massachusetts Department of Children and Families when I was a foster parent, and I owe an enormous debt of gratitude to her and her supervisor for never saying "no" to any of the requests I made on behalf of my foster child, whether it was to enrol him in music, cooking, sports, or arts classes or activities that enabled him to maintain his ties to his older brothers and his friends; they were truly my partners. I remain grateful to them and to Jeanne, Michael, Trevor, Ryan, Annie, Brian, Jon, Dan, Eduardo, Nelly, George, Ian, Carolyn, Tori, Chris, Steve, Grace, Leah, Dan, Jooe,

Victor, Roger, Claire, Dorothy, Meghan, Annalaura, Cliff, Michaiah, Barbara, Grace, Robert, and Yong Yeow, among others. As the director of the Global Education Innovation Initiative, Professor Fernando Reimers supported my journey as a single foster parent even as we built the Initiative. Professor Nancy Koehn encouraged me to write about my experiences as a foster parent, and this book may come the closest to it.

As a fourth-generation educator, I am grateful to my parents and my extended family. As I wrote about Dream a Dream's scholarship programme, I thought of my grandfather, Jung Ki Bae, who, as one of the country's first CEO's, established and administered in the late 1950s, one of the largest scholarship programmes in South Korea; in a country emerging from the chaos of war and division, he envisioned a better future for its children and established a financial aid programme to support middle school students in their studies from high school to college. He was my first and biggest supporter; this book and my life's work with young people are but a paying forward of the love he invested in me.

Connie K. Chung, EdD
California
Easter 2022